Researching Mobile Learning

Giasemi Vavoula / Norbert Pachler /
Agnes Kukulska-Hulme (eds)

RESEARCHING MOBILE LEARNING

Frameworks, tools and research designs

PETER LANG

Oxford • Bern • Berlin • Bruxelles • Frankfurt am Main • New York • Wien

Bibliographic information published by Die Deutsche Bibliothek
Die Deutsche Bibliothek lists this publication in the Deutsche Nationalbibliografie;
detailed bibliographic data is available on the Internet at <http://dnb.ddb.de>.

A catalogue record for this book is available from The British Library.

Library of Congress Cataloging-in-Publication Data:

Vavoula, Giasemi, 1970-
  Researching mobile learning : frameworks, tools, and research designs
/ Giasemi Vavoula, Norbert Pachler, and Agnes Kukulska-Hulme.
    p. cm.
  Includes bibliographical references and index.
  ISBN 978-3-03911-832-8 (alk. paper)
  1. Mobile communication systems in education--Research. I. Pachler,
Norbert. II. Kukulska-Hulme, Agnes, 1959- III. Title.
  LB1044.84.V38 2009
  371.33--dc22
                          2009003109

Cover design: Mette Bundgaard, Peter Lang Ltd
ISBN 978-3-03911-832-8

© Peter Lang AG, International Academic Publishers, Bern 2009
Hochfeldstrasse 32, Postfach 746, CH-3000 Bern 9, Switzerland
info@peterlang.com, www.peterlang.com, www.peterlang.net

Printed in Germany

Contents

Foreword

DIANA LAURILLARD

The feature of "mobility" can seem a curious way to delineate a field of research on learning. It is a field defined entirely by one particular feature of a digital technology that marks it out from other technologies: the fact of its mobility. A mobile technology typically embodies digital capabilities already familiar to us, and yet the simple fact of its mobility has generated a new research field, now reified in books, journals, conferences, and an entry in Wikipedia.

To understand the importance of a new digital technology, and to appreciate why it might have a particular role to play, it can sometimes be valuable to relocate our thinking in the familiarity of the equivalent old technologies. The use of "mobile learning" – learning that is supported across contexts and life transitions – is what learners have always done, using the conventional technologies of books, pencils and notebooks. Why should it be worth investigating now? The familiarity of these technologies renders mobile learning unsurprising and unproblematic. However, the parallel is not with the way we value them now, but with the impact they had then, on their initial introduction into the world of education. Historically, the impact of the printed book was powerful – no longer the hand-crafted treasure chained to the library desk, it became an object of personal ownership. The impact of paper as a technology available to everyone, not just an elite, was critical to the rise of literacy as it supported the individual in the crafting and recording of their own thoughts. The erasable pencil was an early form of word processor. As we think through the implications of these early forms of mobile technology, and what life would have been like without them, we begin to sense the importance of the feature of "mobility".

Given that learners have had mobile learning for so long it is surprising, then, not that it should be worthy of research now, but that it should *not* have been *until* now. Digital technologies often have the effect of acting as a catalyst to a new awareness of the role a technology plays in teaching and learning. Although "mobile learning" is the current epithet for the digital form of a very old learning technology, it is a peculiarity of digital technologies that they combine several equivalents of old technologies: a mobile phone integrates the book, paper, pencil, camera, video camera, radio, computer, and, by the way, telephone (and by the time this book comes out, probably a few other technologies as well). Perhaps it is this powerful combination that triggers the opportunity to reflect on the implications for how we learn.

The idea of "mobile learning" has always been linked to "informal learning" and that holds throughout this book. The reason for this is rooted in the capabilities of mobile technologies in their earliest forms – they offered personal ownership of codified knowledge, user-generated ideas, and user-constructed contexts. They support learning that is personal and contextualised, and controlled by the learner. The researchers in this volume have identified these features as being critical in the modern form of mobile learning. The learning that occurs does so under very different conditions from the formal learning context of education. There is no curriculum, or teacher, or formal feedback, or goals, or assessment – but there are learner goals, feedback from their actions in the world and from the people they interact with, a curriculum formed by their own responsibilities, roles, interests and opportunities. Here the learner is in control, if anyone is, and constructs their own learning environment, selecting from and negotiating within their local context to define their own goals, forms of practice, feedback, adaptation, collaboration, and reflection. This is the value of informal learning. It occurs in many contexts, often alongside formal learning, in the workplace, in the community, and in the home. Part of the value of mobile technologies is the support they offer for all those aspects of informal learning.

The same applies to formal learning, where the value of mobile technologies is to offer digitally-facilitated site-specific support for the learner. Here, unlike informal learning, the learning goals and learning context are likely to be influenced by the teacher, but the very flexibility of the technology can inspire the teacher to relax this and allow the learner to negotiate their own.

This book is built from the experience of researchers who have recognised this new area of learning as being significant, but have also discovered the difficult challenges it presents. Mobile learning blurs the division between formal and informal learning. And informal learning itself has no clear boundaries. Precisely because it is under learner control it is not clear how to evaluate it, either in terms of the learner goal, or the role of the teacher, or who counts as the teacher, or what the learner learns, or how, or why .... The circumstances of the learning are much more varied, and less manipulable than in formal educational contexts. Informal learning is more like "peer learning", or "practitioner learning", in contrast to learning from an expert. It is similar to the difference between tacit practitioner knowledge and explicit expert knowledge. However, just as practitioner knowledge and learning is valued in the workplace, and understood within knowledge management as playing an important part in the innovation an organisation is capable of, informal learning can play an important part alongside formal learning in education and work-based learning. The research reported here is testimony to the value of the interdependence between the two.

With no clear boundaries, how is it possible to do rigorous research on mobile learning? These researchers anchor their research findings in the careful analysis of the particular that can be abstracted to the general, enabling others to learn from that work and apply it to their own context. Their work is objective, disinterested, aimed at codifying and disseminating, making the implicit explicit. On this strong foundation future research on mobile learning will make good progress.

Contributors

CLAIRE BRADLEY is a Research Fellow at the Learning Technology Research Institute at London Metropolitan University. She has a Masters degree in Interactive Multimedia from The Royal College of Art. For the past 12 years she has worked on a number of UK and European research projects involved in eLearning, online communities, multimedia and in the general application and evaluation of digital technologies in teaching and learning. Her recent work focuses on mobile learning. She has co-authored a number of journal articles and papers in these areas.

JOHN COOK is Professor of Technology Enhanced Learning at the Learning Technology Research Institute, London Metropolitan University. He has a cross-university role of E-Learning Project Leader. In addition, he has published widely in the area of Technology Enhanced Learning, having a specific interest in five related areas: informal learning, mobile learning, appropriation, user generated contexts and ICT Leadership and Innovation. For more details see http://homepages.north.londonmet.ac.uk/~cookj/

CHRISTINE DEARNLEY is Senior Lecturer and University Learning and Teaching Fellow at the University of Bradford, UK. Christine has a keen interest and a comprehensive research portfolio in learning and assessment for health and social care practitioners. Her early work was applied to open and distance learning and this led to her current interest in the potential of eLearning and more recently mobile learning, in helping students learn how to learn. She has published widely on the components of independent learning and the implications for students, tutors and the NHS; Independent learning and its relationship with personal and professional development and Learning technologies as a means to supporting independent learning.

JOCELYN DODD is Director of the Research Centre for Museums and Galleries (RCMG), at the Department of Museum Studies, University of Leicester, UK. Her research interests are learning in museums and the social role of Museums and Galleries and how they can challenge inequality. The research of RCMG informs the museums and galleries sector impacting on policy and practice. Jocelyn has worked on a number of learning impact studies in the museums sector. She was a member of the team that developed the Generic Learning Outcomes, now widely used in cultural organizations to report on learning impact. Jocelyn's research interests are informed by her considerable museum experience, particularly at Nottingham Museums and Galleries where she worked in museum learning, community engagement and management, and as a museum consultant.

STEVE GODWIN is a Research Fellow on OpenLearn and is based at the Institute of Educational Technology at The Open University. He has been researching interactive education and eLearning since the year 2000. Previous projects have included "Interactive Education: teaching and learning in the information age" based at the University of Bristol and "The Impact of Interaction and Integration in Computer Mediated Higher Education" based at The Open University. Prior to this Steve spent several years as a lecturer in FE and HE in Birmingham. Other research interests include Mathematics Education.

MARK VAN 'T HOOFT, PhD, is a researcher and technology specialist for Kent State University's Research Center for Educational Technology, and a founding member and current chair of the Special Interest Group for Handheld Computing (SIGHC) for the International Society for Technology in Education (ISTE). His current research focus is on ubiquitous computing and the use of mobile technology in K-12 education, especially in the social studies. He has been researching mobile learning since 2001, has been involved in several mobile projects at local and national levels, and has published and presented widely on mobile learning subjects. Prior to his work at RCET, Mark was a middle school and high school social studies and language arts teacher in Austin, TX. He holds a Drs. degree in American Studies from the Catholic University of Nijmegen, the Netherlands, an MA in History from Southwest Texas State, and a PhD with a dual major in Curriculum and Instruction, and Evaluation and Measurement from Kent State University.

PHILLIP KENT is a researcher at the London Knowledge Lab, Institute of Education, University of London. His main research interests are in designing for learning with mathematical technologies, and the use of mathematics in workplaces. Research projects have investigated the mathematical work of engineers in professional practice, and mathematics in manufacturing and financial services. The latter work is the subject of a forthcoming major book, *Improving Mathematical Learning in the Workplace*.

KRISTIN KNIPFER is working as research associate at the Knowledge Media Research Center in Tuebingen, Germany, within the context of the project "Learning in Museums – The Role of Media for the Recontextualisation of Objects". In her PhD project she examined the potential of discussion terminals as scaffold for critical thinking and reflective judgement about contemporary socio-scientific issues. She is currently involved in a field study using mobile eyetracking as data gathering method for researching mobile learning at a history museum. Her general research interests centre on Cognitive, Educational and Media Psychology, Museum Learning, Science Communication/Public Opinion Research, and Critical Thinking/Reflective Judgment.

MARK A.M. KRAMER is a nomadic research fellow and doctoral candidate at The ICT&S Center for Advanced Studies and Research at the University of Salzburg. His research is helping to determine and shape the future of individual and collective learning by examining the affects of applying mobile, pervasive and ubiquitous technologies and services on individual and collaborative learning experiences and contexts. Mark is widely known as an early adopter, informed critic and participatory observer of all things mobile and spends a great portion of his time travelling and conducting real-world research while sharing his observations and engaging in extreme-mobile learning scenarios.

AGNES KUKULSKA-HULME is Professor of Learning Technology and Communication in The UK Open University's Institute of Educational Technology. She has been researching mobile learning since 2001 and has led several research projects investigating mobile learning innovation at The Open University and across the UK. Her research is conducted with adult learners, often in the context of distance education. She has published widely on learner-driven innovation, mobile usability, issues of staff development, and the evolution and future of mobile assisted language learning. Agnes's original discipline background is in foreign language teaching and translation, and from this linguistic perspective she has a long standing research interest in effective communication supported by technology.

ANTHONY LELLIOTT is a Senior Lecturer and Head of the Division of Mathematics and Science Education in the School of Education at the University of the Witwatersrand, Johannesburg. He leads a research strand in the Marang Centre for Maths and Science Education entitled Science Awareness, Informal Learning and Schools, and is currently researching the role of teachers during school visits to museums and science centres in South Africa. In addition to informal learning and science awareness he carries out research into astronomy education, a focus of his doctoral work. He supervises teaches a range of courses and supervises postgraduate students at the university.

D.W. LIVINGSTONE is Canada Research Chair in Lifelong Learning and Work at the University of Toronto, Head of the Centre for the Study of Education and Work at OISE/UT, professor in the Department of Sociology and Equity Studies at OISE/UT, and Director of the SSHRC-funded national research network on "The Changing Nature of Work and Lifelong Learning" (see www.wallnetwork.ca). His recent books include: *Working and Learning in the Information Age* (Ottawa: Canadian Policy Research Networks, 2002), *Hidden Knowledge: Organized Labour in the Information Age* (Garamond Press and Rowman and Littlefield, 2004) (with P. Sawchuk), *The Education-Jobs Gap: Underemployment or Economic Democracy* (Garamond Press and Percheron Press, 2004, second edition), *International Handbook of Educational Policy* (Springer, 2005) (edited with N. Bascia, A. Cumming, A. Datnow and K. Leithwood), *The Future of Lifelong Learning and Work: Critical Perspectives* (Sense Publishers, 2008) (edited with K. Mirchandani and P. Sawchuk) and *Education and Jobs: Exploring the Gaps* (University of Toronto Press, 2009).

JANE MAGILL is Director of the Robert Clark Centre for Technological Education and Deputy Director of the STEM Education centre at the University of Glasgow. She is involved in teaching and research in electrical engineering and more recently in STEM education, and is a lecturer in a degree programme for future technology teachers. Jane has history of work in computer aided learning and assessment since 1988 which is currently demonstrated by projects in the use of PDAs by undergraduate students for portable learning and in the use of social networks to support transformational change. This work has uncovered some exciting new factors affecting use of technology and its perceptions. Jane has a strong interest in inter-disciplinary education and public engagement particularly using technologies (such as interactive voting) for increasing interactivity and engagement. She is currently leading projects linking art and music with science and technology. Within Glasgow University Jane is leading teams to establish undergraduate public engagement projects and a postgraduate multidisciplinary public engagement team (Glasgow PETs).

EVA MAYR is a research associate at the Research Center KnowComm, Danube University Krems, Austria. Her research interests focus on informal learning and learning with new media from the perspective of Cognitive and Media Psychology. From 2005 to 2008 she was associated researcher in the project "Learning in Museums – The Role of Media for the Recontextualisation of Objects" at the Knowledge Media Research Center in Tuebingen, Germany. In her dissertation she conducted research on collaborative learning with mobile devices in science exhibitions using – amongst other methods – mobile eye-tracking.

PATRICK MCANDREW is Senior Lecturer in The Open University's Institute of Educational Technology. He has led a range of research projects addressing how materials and environments can support learning through the use of learning design and the provision of tools for learners. He was responsible for the final evaluation stages within the European MOBILearn project that reviewed models for mobile learning and developed and demonstrated a flexible task based environment. He is currently the Research and Evaluation Director of OpenLearn, a major initiative supported by The William and Flora Hewlett Foundation to provide open content for free education.

DAISY MWANZA-SIMWAMI is an RCUK Academic Fellow in Networked, Distributed and Mobile Learning at The Open University's Institute of Educational Technology, UK. Her work is currently focused on investigating the design and use of Networked, Distributed and Mobile Technologies to support learning. Her research interests include: e-learning, web-based learning, mobile learning, open learn, collaborative learning, systems design and evaluation, content management and metadata abstraction. Daisy has published widely in these areas since 1996 (see selected publications at http://iet-staff.open.ac.uk/d.mwanza/Publications.cfm). She also supervises PhD topics in these areas. Currently, Daisy is co-supervising a PhD on the research topic of "Digital Technologies and Communities of Practices". Daisy also lectures on the Masters in Online and Distance Education's (MAODE) H809 course on Practice Based Research in Educational Technology. Daisy's educational background is in the multi-disciplinary field of Human-Computer Interaction (HCI). Within HCI, her research centers on *Methods* for informing Systems Design and Evaluation. Daisy primarily uses Activity Theory to conceptualise human practices and interpret acquired insights as part of the Systems Design and Evaluation processes. Daisy is the author of the Activity-Oriented Design Method (AODM) for HCI Research and Practice which was conceptualised as part of her PhD thesis.

MARTIN OLIVER is a Reader at the London Knowledge Lab, Institute of Education. He is also an editor of the journal Learning, Media and Technology. His research focuses on the use of technology in Higher Education.

NORBERT PACHLER is Reader in Education and Co-Director of the Centre for Excellence in Work-based Learning for Education Professionals at the Institute of Education, University of London. Apart from the application of new technologies in teaching and learning, his research interests include teacher education and development and all aspects of foreign language teaching and learning. He has published widely and supervises in these fields. Since 2007 he is the convenor of the London Mobile Learning Group (http://www.londonmobilelearning.net) which brings together an international, interdisciplinary group of researchers from the fields of cultural studies, sociology, semiotics, pedagogy and educational technology. The group is working on a theoretical and conceptual framework for mobile learning around the notion of cultural ecology. The analytical engagement with mobile learning of the group takes the shape of a conceptual model in which educational uses of mobile technologies are viewed in ecological terms as part of a cultural and pedagogical context in transformation. He has (co)organised a number of research symposia in the field of mobile learning and in 2007 has edited, as part of WLE Centre's Occasional Papers Series, a book on "Mobile learning: towards a research agenda" available at http://www.wlecentre.ac.uk/cms/files/occasionalpapers/mobilelearning_pachler2007.pdf.

PALMYRE PIERROUX is Postdoc at InterMedia, University of Oslo, Norway. She has a background in Environmental Design and Art History, and received her PhD in the learning sciences with a dissertation titled *Meaning, Learning, and Art in Museums*. She has participated as member of the Kaleidoscope NoE, in the Mobile Learning SIG and in MUSTEL (Museums and Technology Enhanced Learning). She also participates in Making National Museums (NaMU), a Marie Curie Series of Events. At InterMedia, Pierroux is currently leading *Gidder* (Groups in Digital Dialogues), a three-year project funded by the University of Oslo, which researches how social software and mobile phones may be designed for knowledge production in art museums.

CRISTINA ROS I SOLÉ is Principal Research Fellow in Language Pedagogy at the SOAS-UCL Languages of the Wider World Centre of Excellence in Teaching and Learning, where she leads a project on the use of mobile technology for language learning in a number of languages. Previous to this she was involved in several projects researching Computer Assisted Language Learning at the University of Strathclyde and Hull. She was the co-founder of the distance language Spanish Programme at the Open University where she chaired the design of several multimedia courses and an on-line Spanish language course. More recently she has collaborated in a number of research projects with the Open University of Catalonia, Spain, and the Institute of Education, University of London, UK. Her research publications are in the areas of language learning and subjectivity, the teaching of lesser taught languages, and computer mediated language learning.

SCOTT ROY completed PhD studies in 1994 at the University of Glasgow, then worked in a number of areas, including the design and construction of parallel processing machines, and the Monte Carlo simulation of Si:SiGe HMOS devices and InGaAs HEMTs for VLSI and RF applications. He is presently a Reader in the Department of Electronics and Electrical Engineering at the University of Glasgow, and a member of the Device Modelling and Microelectronics Systems Groups. He has published over 150 papers in the fields of device transport, Monte Carlo simulation, device scaling, bio-nanotechnology, and the development of practical compact models and circuit simulation techniques for nanoscale devices subject to variability. He is an investigator on grants from SEMATECH, EU FP7, Fujitsu, and the EPSRC. As part of his interest in the improved teaching of Engineering subjects in tertiary education he has been instrumental in the introduction of formative assessment through handheld electronic organisers into a number of classes within the faculties of Education and Engineering at the University of Glasgow.

ANDREIA INAMORATO DOS SANTOS is a Research Fellow in the OpenLearn team based at the Institute of Educational Technology, The Open University. Her current research includes the field of cross-cultural issues and sustainability in open educational resource provision. She has carried out research into online teaching and learning, drawing on Discourse Analysis as a theoretical framework. Previously, Andreia worked as a lecturer of English literature at universities in São Paulo, Brazil, and researched in the field of applied linguistics.

MIKE SHARPLES is Professor of Learning Sciences and Director of the Learning Sciences Research Institute at the University of Nottingham. He has an international reputation for research in mobile learning and the design of learning technologies. He inaugurated the mLearn conference series and is President of the International Association for Mobile Learning. As Deputy Scientific Manager of the Kaleidoscope Network of Excellence in Technology Enhanced Learning he coordinated a network of 1100 researchers across 90 European research centres. His current projects include PI: Personal Inquiry, a collaboration with the Open University, UK, to develop 21st century science learning between formal and informal settings, a national survey of social networked learning at home and school, and research on curriculum and pedagogy to inform the UK Government's Harnessing Technology Strategy. Recent projects include MyArtSpace for mobile learning in museums and the L-Mo project with Sharp Laboratories of Europe to develop handheld technologies for language learning. He is author of 160 publications in the areas of interactive systems design, artificial intelligence and educational technology.

DANIEL SPIKOL is a PhD student in Computer Science with an orientation in Informatics at the school of Mathematics and Systems Engineering, at Växjö University (VXU), Sweden. His current research interests include the design of mobile learning environments that explore novel modes of collaboration. He is presently involved in a number of European and National projects exploring how mobile and wireless technologies can be used to support new ways of learning and how these technologies can support groups of learners when they, collectively, share their understanding in these learning environments. Previously he has worked for the Interactive Institute, in Sweden and the LEGO group in Denmark.

JOHN TRAXLER is Reader in Mobile Technology for e-Learning and a Director of the Learning Lab at the University of Wolverhampton. John has co-written a guide to mobile learning in developing countries and is co-editor of the definitive book on mobile learning: Kukulska-Hulme, A. and Traxler, J. (2005) *Mobile Learning: A Handbook for Educators and Trainers*, Routledge. He was invited to present at the South African national science festival, SciFest, at Rhodes University, and at the Microsoft Mobile Learning Summit in Seattle. He publishes regularly evaluating and embedding mobile learning, and is interested in the profound consequences of universal mobile devices on our societies. He is jointly responsible for national workshops on implementing mobile learning for UK universities and has delivered similar workshops to university staff in Germany, Kenya, South Africa, Canada and India. In the UK he works with JISC, LSN, BECTA and other national bodies on various aspects of mobile learning. He is one of the Founding Directors of the International Association for Mobile Learning, the Associate Editor of the International Journal of Mobile and Blended Learning and Conference Chair of mLearn2008 in Ironbridge Shropshire.

JON TRINDER is a part-time PhD student in the Robert Clark Centre for Technological Education at the University of Glasgow. His work has been investigating the use of mobile devices for Computer Aided Assessment and the analysis of device usage logs. Jon's background in is electronics and software engineering and network technology. His first involvement with education and PDAs was providing software for the Cornell University Mobile Mann Library project in 2000. Jon has a specific interest in user interface design and authors custom and shareware applications for www.ninelocks.com. He also works in the department of Electrical and Electronic Engineering at Glasgow University. Jon founded the pda-edu@jiscmail.ac.uk mailing list in 2002 to provide a meeting place for anyone interested in using PDA's in education to exchange information and advice.

GIASEMI VAVOULA is an RCUK Academic Fellow in Learning and Visitor Studies at the Department of Museum Studies, University of Leicester, UK. She has a background in Computer Science (BSc) and

Human-Centred Computer Systems (MSc), while her doctoral research at the University of Birmingham, UK, focused on the design of personal lifelong learning organisers. She has been researching and publishing in the area of mobile learning since 1998, while working on a number of projects including KLeOS (PhD project), MOBIlearn (EU), MELISA (EU), and Myartspace (Department for Culture Media and Sport, UK). Her research interests presently focus on technology-enhanced museum learning; tools and methods for mobile and informal learning research; and the impact of personal and cultural context on learning in informal settings. She is currently involved in the design of two distance-learning Masters Programmes on "Digital Heritage" and "Learning and Visitor Studies in Museums and Galleries", and shares responsibility for a campus-based special option course on "Digital Media and Curatorship".

ESRA WALI is on leave from the University of Bahrain where she is a Graduate Assistant at the department of Educational Technology. Currently, she is a full-time PhD candidate at the London Knowledge Lab at the Institute of Education, University of London. Her PhD focuses on conceptualising "mobile learning" by exploring students' routine learning activities in multiple contexts. Her research also investigates the relationship between context and learning activities. Esra holds a BSc degree in Computer Science from the University of Bahrain (2001) and an MSc degree in Information Systems from the University of Surrey (2004).

STUART WALKER is a Disability Advisor at the University of Bradford UK, with a specific responsibility for Assistive Technology. He supports Disabled Students and staff and aims to enable them via technology. A self confessed techie, Stuart has a keen interest in all areas of technology. He has both aided and led in winning research grants to explore Mobile Technologies and Speech Recognition Systems / Software. He continues to explore both areas and is also researching applications of Open Source Operating systems, principally Linux Distro's eg: Ubuntu, Fedora, SuSE etc., for eLearning, student engagement and accessibility. Stuart is currently in the process of completing an MRes and PhD in the area of Speech recognition and writing styles.

DANIEL WESSEL is a research associate at the Knowledge Media Research Center in Tuebingen, Germany, within the context of the project "Learning in Museums – The Role of Media for the Recontextualisation of Objects". He is currently working on his PhD on interest, knowledge exchange, and mobile devices in museums. His research interests focus on mobile learning, museum learning, critical thinking, and mobile eye tracking.

NIALL WINTERS is a RCUK Academic Fellow at the London Knowledge Lab, Institute of Education, University of London. His main research interests are: (i) the interdisciplinary design and development of technology enhanced learning (TEL) environments, with a particular focus on emerging technologies and (ii) ICT for development (ICT4D). He is currently Principal Investigator on the CoMo project, a Co-Investigator on the MiGen project and the ReMath project, where he directs the development of MoPiX. He collaborates with the VeSeL and Planet projects. He leads the LKL's research on the OLPC initiative and in 2006, co-directed the Learning patterns project. Niall holds a PhD in Computer Science (2002) from the University of Dublin, Trinity College and a BSc (D.Hons) in Computer Science and Experimental Physics (1997) from the National University of Ireland, Maynooth. His PhD addressed how to store and search large datasets of images. The primary application was vision-based mobile robot navigation. Niall has held visiting research positions with the Everyday Learning Group at Media Lab Europe in Dublin, and the Computer Vision Lab at Instituto Superior Tecnico in Lisbon.

Figures

Tables

PART I

Introduction

1. Research Methods in Mobile and Informal Learning: Some Issues

NORBERT PACHLER

Overview

This introductory chapter aims to set the scene for the discussion of research methods in mobile and informal learning in this book. It argues that, in order to be able to fully understand the intricacies of the issues attendant to mobile and informal learning, an interdisciplinary approach and methodological diversity are desirable, if not necessary. It posits that as a field, mobile and informal learning research needs to be guided by a common set of underpinning research purposes, in the same way they exist in other disciplines, with which aims, research questions, data collection / research methods and frames for analysis of individual studies articulate. One intention behind the current volume is indeed to contribute to the delineation of such an overarching set of purposes. This chapter provides a brief overview of some considerations concerning definitional bases for mobile learning and goes on to discuss what issues emerge from them for mobile learning research.

1. Mobile and informal learning as interdisciplinary phenomena

Mobile learning is maturing as an academic discipline. Informal learning, by comparison, already is a relatively mature field of enquiry, not least because of the sustained contributions by academics like Michael Eraut or David Livingstone over the years. I argue here that, due to the affinity of much of mobile learning with informal learning, the former can benefit considerably from an exploration of the insights gained in the latter.

The process of its maturation is, among other things, evidenced through the growing number of scholars working on aspects of mobile learning, the increase in studies carried out and reported at conferences or in journals, as well as the emergence of various theoretical and conceptual frameworks attempting to explain the complex processes and issues governing the field. As a result, the research methods required to provide an empirically sound underpinning are gradually coming into focus.

Although learning across contexts, which, it is argued here, can be seen to be a key characteristic of mobile learning, is not a new phenomenon, researching such learning in relation to the role of new mobile digital devices exposes methodological complexities that need to be addressed. Adding to this complexity is the interdisciplinary (or multi-disciplinary) approach required, including various subfields of education, computing sciences, and cultural and media studies, each with their own research traditions.

2. The need for delineating a set of overarching research purposes for the field

Invariably, any discussion about appropriate research methods requires consideration of the specific aims, objectives and research questions relating to individual research projects. Kjeldskov and Graham (2003) delineate the following research purposes in the context of human-computer interaction (HCI) research:

> *Understanding* is the purpose of research focusing on finding the meaning of studied phenomena through e.g. frameworks or theories developed from collected data.

> *Engineering* is defined as the purpose of research focused towards developing new systems or parts of systems such as e.g. an interaction technique for mobile phones.

Re-engineering describes the purpose of research focusing on improving existing systems by redeveloping them such as e.g. adapting a web browser to a small display.

Evaluating is the purpose of research assessing or validating products, theories or methods e.g. the usability of a specific mobile device design or a theory of interaction.

Describing finally refers to research focusing on defining desirable properties of products e.g. a mobile system.

In order to establish mobile learning as a recognised field of inquiry, it is argued here that researchers also need to be guided in their work by a set of overarching research purposes to which their specific enquiries align. For the field of mobile learning no such explicit frame exists as yet to guide the choice of research methods and the tools for data analysis. By bringing together a number of chapters focussing on possible research methods and frameworks as well as aspects of research design and their underpinning rationales, one aim of this book, therefore, is to contribute to the development of a typology of purposes and attendant methods of data collection and analysis for the field of mobile and informal learning. The example above from the field of HCI research on the one hand serves to evidence that such frames exist in other disciplines and, on the other, it might provide pointers for what a set of overarching purposes might look like for the field of mobile learning research.

3.   What do we mean by mobile learning?

Being able to delineate appropriate approaches to mobile learning research requires clarity about what is meant by mobile learning. In order to be able to put forward a working definition for mobile learning as well as to become sensitised to the particularities of mobile and informal learning environments as research foci, a brief consideration of the characteristics, potential and constraints of mobile devices and their consequences on the learning practice seems advisable.

Mobile digital tools, with their small size, ubiquity and functional convergence, enable new possibilities for learning. Due to the range of connectivity functions, among other things, they offer mobile devices foreground the socio-cultural dimension of learning in that they enable users to communicate readily with other users. At the same time, they potentially impact on the cognitive dimension of learning, for example by providing new means of lessening the cognitive load for learners associated with not having to commit information to memory in order to have it readily available at any given moment ("always on"). The ability to store digital data locally and access it instantaneously on a portable device, or to access remote data through the internet, frees the learner from the constraints of place that are inherent in data access through libraries or desktop computers.

However, the diversity of technological tools, and their very short "shelf life" add unwelcome complexity for the user as well as the researcher. For learners it means having to familiarise themselves frequently with the functionality of new devices. For researchers it is not unusual to witness a particular model being replaced in the course of a research project, which makes longitudinal studies difficult; it also makes it near to impossible to replicate a study with the same hardware.

What is also significant is the change in locus of control, with more and more high specification mobile devices being owned by users, rather than their employers, education providers, local libraries, or internet café proprietors. This can be seen to be beneficial for the learner: among other things, a sense of ownership and the ability to personalise, and appropriate them according to individual needs can result in an increased willingness to utilise mobile devices for learning. Coupled with decreasing costs of data storage and mobile data access, this means that powerful personal digital tools are increasingly available to users independently of location. For the researcher, on the other hand, it means less control over the research context and increased complexity, for example in terms of controlling variables.

The communicative potential of mobile devices can be seen as an important prerequisite for learning, enabling users to engage in interactions with themselves, with others and with their environments (see e.g. Kirschner, 2006, p. 15 or Sharples et al., 2007). Thereby, activity with, and supported by mobile devices has the potential to meet the conditions required for effective learning to take place, particularly if learning is viewed as a process of cognitive and social development in which social interaction is mediated by cultural tools, such as language and technology (Cook, Pachler and Bradley, 2008); and if informal learning is viewed as an activity which is inherent in, and natural to our everyday life worlds, an activity which goes on constantly and which tends to be individualised and contextualised:

> It is our own individual way of making sense (meaning) of life's experiences and using that for dealing with new experiences. ... like breathing, it is the (mental) process of drawing into ourselves the natural and human environment in which we live ... and using it to build up (develop) ourselves. (Rogers, 2006, p. 4)

Sharples, Taylor and Vavoula (2007, p. 225) view mobile learning as "the processes of coming to know through conversations across multiple contexts among people and personal interactive technologies". Importantly, such a definition privileges cognitive and social aspects over technical considerations as well as over perspectives that foreground content provision and transmission. Instead, the emphasis rightly is on contexts, context generation and context crossing. It is argued here that mobile devices, their characteristics and potential for learning, enable the user to re-interpret their everyday life contexts as potential resources for learning. Learning is viewed as semiotic work and meaning making in which users develop, with the aid of mobile devices, new cultural practices with and through which they learn and strengthen their resources for meaning making whilst interacting with the world (Kress and Pachler, 2007, p. 22). We view the purposeful alignment and effective integration of social and cultural practices attendant to learning with portable, multifunctional devices with high degrees of connectivity with and into formal education to be one of the key challenges for the early 21st century. By implication these questions are also of great significance for educational research, which needs to develop appropriate methods for capturing, describing, analysing and understanding them.

Sefton-Green (2004) argues that, in order to be able to understand how and what children learn, one has to look at their normal day-to-day activities, in particular those mediated by technologies such as computers, mobile phones and games. He also posits that all of us learn all the time and that that learning is dependent on tasks and surroundings, and questions whether the term "informal" refers to the "how", "where" or "what" of learning, or to the relationship between the activity and what counts and is valued as knowledge. From a research perspective this, for him, poses the question of mapping "where, and with what resources, children are learning with technologies outside school" (p. 9). And then, of course, there is the question of what they are learning, what role the technology plays in their learning and how learning relates to the established canon, for example what is enshrined in, and promoted through the school curriculum. Mobile technologies invariably will become more and more integral to, and important for the informal learning of children. And, as today's children grow up and become tomorrow's adults, they will take with them these dispositions around informal and mobile learning into the workplace (in work-related and work-located learning situations) as well as into any lifelong learning they engage in.

In the first half 2008 the UK government carried out a consultation on informal adult learning for the 21st century (see DIUS, 2008). The theme of personalisation is prominent and the consultation paper stresses the importance of learner choice and agency. Importantly, the role of new technologies in making new ways of learning possible is given high prominence. In relation to technology, the interconnectedness between different media and technology-mediated experiences, such as TV programs or films, related online offers and software applications or games, live events, sharing related information with others in specific groups, merchandising etc. is particularly noted and how they link to informal learning. The consultation paper also recognises that "ever-expanding" learning opportunities are possible inter alia through the availability of hand-held devices and digitally augmented reality (pp. 26 and 28). The conceptualisation of informal adult learning adopted by governments, together with the role of ICT within them, is of great significance in contextual terms for research into informal and mobile learning and emerging agendas.

4. Developing appropriate methods for mobile learning research: Options and considerations

Just like traditional educational research, mobile learning research, particularly if it focuses on learning as opposed to on technology, has to be concerned with questions of "educational arrangements", i.e. what organisational systems and structures best promote learning, and psychological development, i.e. of mental processes and behaviours in and across various spheres of human activity (see Martin, 2004, p. S72). Mobile learning research with a focus on informal dimensions of learning will, among other things, be concerned with the social and cultural contexts activities are located in, and characterised by as well as the contexts and social and cultural practices created by them. Research foregrounding the technological dimension will be less interested in educational benefit and fields of application and more in aspects such as usability, design, connectivity, interoperability, information processing, data handling and exchange to name but a few. The distributed and informal nature of (the location of) learning with and around mobile devices, and the diverse range of tools used to mediate it, makes questions around educational arrangements and psychological development somewhat harder to answer compared with traditional, formal settings and, therefore, pose a particular challenge for researchers. Martin (2004, p. S73) argues that there is an important correlation between situated cultural practices and cognitive operations with people using different cognitive operations according to place or the problems in hand. With mobile and informal learning taking place in a wide range of sometimes unpredictable and, from a research perspective, often uncontrollable set of contexts, it becomes very difficult to seek to measure mobile learning thus conceived.

Developing appropriate methods for mobile learning research does not necessarily mean having to develop an entirely new suite of methods of data collection and analysis. Instead, it is advisable to build on, and refine existing good practice in order to identify methods that are fit for purpose and adhere to established attributes such as those outlined by Traxler and Kukulska-Hulme (2005):

- rigorous, meaning that conclusions must be trustworthy and transferable
- efficient, in terms of cost, effort, time
- ethical, specifically in relation to the nuances of evolving forms of provision
- proportionate, that is, not more ponderous, onerous or time-consuming than the learning experience or the delivery and implementation of the pilots themselves
- appropriate to the specific learning technologies, to the learners and to the ethos of the project concerned – ideally *built in*, not *bolted on*
- consistent with the teaching and learning philosophy and conceptions of teaching and learning of all the participants
- authentic, in accessing what learners (and perhaps teachers and other stakeholders) *really* mean, *really* feel, and sensitive to the learners' personalities within those media
- aligned to the chosen medium and technology of learning
- consistent across:
    - ◊ different groups or cohorts of learners in order to provide generality
    - ◊ time, that is, the evaluation is reliably repeatable
    - ◊ whatever varied devices and technologies are used.

It also means examining and exploiting the merits of qualitative and quantitative methods taking, where appropriate, a mixed-methods approach. Qualitative methods, for example, can be useful in contexts where self-reporting and retrospection are required to gain access to singular events, such as users reflecting post hoc on the ways in which they used their mobile phones during an educational visit to document their learning experiences; while quantitative methods, for example, can provide useful external perspectives and measure cumulative effects, such as how patterns of use compare across different user groups, sites for learning or projects. As with all other educational research, the chosen data collection methods need to account for the complexity of the phenomena to be explored, and the criteria underpinning data analysis need to be grounded in appropriate conceptual and theoretical frameworks.

Inherent in the use of technological tools, such as mobile devices, is the ability to record and store data generated through the use of such tools, for example usage data, which, in turn, can be used for research purposes. However, as contributions to this volume show, the collection and analysis of such data is not unproblematic, for example in terms of intrusion of privacy, and can lead to a significant distortion of user behaviour.

As with any other social research, there exist not only challenges in relation to data collection, but also in terms of its analysis. One key question pertains to what units of analysis to use. Martin (2004, p. S76) delineates the following: features of participant structures, discourse and argumentation form, physical behaviours and patterns of tool use. There are doubtless many others depending on the research questions framing an empirical enquiry, the research design, the context, the (number of) people involved and their interrelationship and participation structures, the tools being researched, and the duration of the project.

From a research methods perspective, the definitional basis for mobile learning delineated above, with its focus on both cognitive and social aspects, requires researchers to look to a combination of psychological and sociological approaches as well as to take into full account relevant contextual factors in order to achieve a good understanding of mobile learning. Much can be learned from tried-and-tested research methods from across the positivist and phenomenological spectrum but adaptations and modifications are often necessary not least because of the multiplicity of contexts within which mobile learning takes place. For one, many of the practices with and around mobile devices take place in a private or semi-public sphere not characterised by traditional power-relationships between the actors involved and which, therefore, pose entirely new challenges in relation to research ethics. How, for example, can informed consent be gained in such situations? The practices are also personal, intimately bound up with the individuals concerned as well as the formation and reforma-tion of their identity and their relationship with members of their peer group. They are, therefore, qualitatively quite often of a different order to those taking place in the context of well established scripts of make-belief and suspension of disbelief in more formal learning situations such as question-and-answer routines around imagined situations in classrooms (see e.g. Stald, 2008).

Also, the issue of learning contexts is rather more difficult compared with traditional educational research. Sharples, Milrad, Arnedillo-Sánchez and Vavoula (2008) delineate a multi-dimensional view of mobility across physical, conceptual and social space. Add to that the likelihood of learn-ing taking place not just within, but also across these different contexts. And, of course, there is Dourish's (2004, p. 5) notion of context as a rep-resentational problem:

> First, rather than considering context to be information, [the alternative view of context] instead argues that *contextuality is a relational property* that holds between objects or activities. It is not simply the case that something is or is not context; rather, it may or may not be contextually relevant to some particular activity.
>
> Second, rather than considering that context can be delineated and defined in advance, the alternative view argues that *the scope of contextual features is defined dynamically*.
>
> Third, rather than considering that context is stable, it instead argues that context is particular to each occasion of activity or action. *Context is an occasioned property*, relevant to particular settings, particular instances of action, and particular parties to that action.
>
> Fourth, rather than taking context and content to be two separable entities, it instead argues that *context arises from the activity*. Context isn't just "there," but is actively produced, maintained and enacted in the course of the activity at hand.

In short, Dourish proposes a view of context not as representational but as interactional, i.e. "something that people do", which, in turn, poses considerable methodological challenges for researchers and requires sophisticated research methodologies. Contextuality, as Dourish puts it, is something that "comes about only when it is mutually recognized by the parties to some interaction, drawing on their everyday, cultural, common-sense understandings of the nature of the social world" (2004, p. 6), and by implication it cannot be researched adequately from a positivist or an individual cognitive perspective but requires a phenomenological and socio-cultural approach. Phenomenology, in Dourish's terms, "turns analytic attention away from the idea of a stable external world which is unproblematically recognized by all, and towards the idea that the world, as we perceive it, is essentially a consensus of interpretation" (2004, p. 3). This requires studies that provide rich descriptions of situated practice, while studies that try to measure the impact of certain interventions should at best be treated with caution. Mutual recognition becomes even more difficult in distributed social contexts, and in a world where technology is increasingly embedded in the physical world, and therefore largely invisible. In traditional educational settings, which involve technological tools usually confined to fixed locations, it is easier to isolate and control the many variables involved and to operate a control group for comparison. How, for example, can representativeness of samples and context be ensured? Or, how can user behaviour best be tracked?

A study by Isomursu, Kuutti and Väinämö (2004) points the way to some possible innovations in approaches to data collection. In order to overcome the impracticalities, and intrusiveness of following their subjects around, the authors developed a method by which they asked their users to be co-researchers and to gather data by filming short video clips of each other using their mobile phones. As Berth (2005) points out in her commentary on this method, in this way the researchers are likely to get access to higher quality data as "users who knew each other would be much more open and expressive about their experiences with the medium than if they had been followed by a researcher". Such approaches can be seen to raise some important questions, for example in relation to the significance and authenticity of the data obtained: do the subjects' decisions about what to, and what not to record tally with those of the researchers? Or, to what extent are the experience clips "scripted" and "staged"? Also, there is the question of what, if any research training the subjects should receive. Or, to what extent does the act of recording intrude in the authenticity of the situations in questions?

In addition to (variants of) ethnographic approaches, Activity Theory has increasingly surfaced in the literature, particularly in the various attempts to delineate a theory of mobile learning as an analytical frame (see e.g. Sharples, Taylor and Vavoula, 2007 and Wali, Winters and Oliver, 2008; for a comprehensive overview and critique, see Pachler, Bachmair, Crook and Kress, forthcoming). The reason for this re-emergence of Activity Theory is simple: it is motivated by the recognition of the complexity of mobile learning, in particular the interplay between location(s), actors, goals, social settings, content, and tools. Activity Theory, put simply, revolves around "activity systems" comprising a subject acting on an object with a view to transforming it using mediating physical or conceptual artefacts. Also, the subject is influenced by the rule of the context, the community and division of labour. It is argued here that Activity Theory can, indeed, be viewed as a useful heuristic for trying to understand the complexities of learning processes in general, and the role of mobile devices within them in particular. However, a conceptualisation of Activity Theory as a heuristic, as is proposed here, implies a certain scepticism concerning its potential as an analytic frame beyond structural analysis. Alas, there is insufficient space in this introductory chapter to discuss this issue in detail.

5.   Preamble to this volume

An engagement with theory building can be seen to constitute as valuable a contribution to the research effort in a field as empirical studies, particularly in the "pioneering days" of a discipline as they can be seen to make an important contribution to the description and understanding of the field (see also Kjeldskov and Graham, 2003). Importantly, therefore, our emphasis on mobile learning research methods in this book is inclusive of theory building and does not come at the expense of it as we are acutely aware of the importance of making explicit ontological and epistemological assumptions as well as explore the relationship between theory and methodology (see also Brannon and Edwards, 2007, p. 2).

Whilst we are fully aware that this volume can represent all but a starting point in the exploration of the complex issues in hand, we very much hope, and believe it offers a sound foundation for members of the discipline to build on and to develop and refine the methodological repertoire for the field of mobile learning. Invariably, the choice of data collection method and research design influences the results of any research. It is, therefore, incumbent upon us, as researchers of mobile learning, and consumers of mobile learning research, to ensure we give the choice of method the attention it deserves and to seek to find and develop the most appropriate ones for each and every study.

References

Berth, M. (2005). Adaptive ethnography: methodologies for the study of mobile learning in youth culture. Paper submitted to *Seeing, Learning, Understanding in the Mobile Age*. Budapest, 28–30 April. Available at http://www.fil.hu/mobil/2005/Berth.pdf [accessed on 1 June 2008]

Brannon, J. and Edwards, R. (2007). 10th Anniversary Editorial. In *International Journal of Social Research Methodology 10(1)*, pp. 1–4

Cook, J., Pachler, N. and Bradley, C. (2008). Bridging the gap? Mobile phones at the interface between informal and formal learning. In *Journal of the Research Centre for Educational Technology 4(1)*. Available at http://www.rcetj.org/files/RCETJ_4_1_learningwhilemobile_cook.pdf [accessed on 1 June 2008]

Department for Innovation, Universities and Skills (DIUS). (2008). *Informal adult learning – shaping the way ahead.* London, available at http://www.adultlearningconsultation.org.uk

Dourish, P. (2004). What we talk about when we talk about context. In *Personal and Ubiquitous Computing 8(1)*, pp. 19–30. Also available at http://www.ics.uci.edu/~jpd/publications/2004/PUC2004-context. pdf [accessed on 1 June 2008]

Isomursu, M., Kuutti, K. and Väinämö, S. (2004). Experience clip: method for user participation and evaluation of mobile concepts. In *Proceedings of the eighth conference on Participatory design: Artful integration: interweaving media, materials and practices* – Volume 1. Ontario, pp. 83–92

Kirschner, P. (2006). (Inter)Dependent learning. Learning is interaction. Inaugural address. Spoken upon the acceptance of the position of Professor of Educational Psychology, Utrecht University, 16 March. Available at http://www.uu.nl/content/OratieKirschner-LearningisInteraction-Geheel-A4-FINAL.pdf [accessed on 1 June 2008]

Kjeldskov, J. and Graham, C. (2003). A review of MobileHCI research methods. In *Lecture Notes in Computer Science: Human-Computer Interaction with Mobile Devices.* 5th International Symposium, Mobile HCI 2003. Berlin, Heidelberg: Springer-Verlag, pp. 317–335. Available at http://www.cs.aau.dk/~jans/courses/is-courses/kjeldskov-graham%20MobileHCI%202003.pdf [accessed on 1 June 2008]

Kress, G. and Pachler, N. (2007). Thinking about the "m" in m-learning. In Pachler, N. (ed.), *Mobile learning: towards a research agenda.* WLE Centre, Institute of Education, London, pp. 7–32. Available at http://www.wlecentre.ac.uk/cms/files/occasionalpapers/mobilelearning_pachler_2007.pdf [accessed on 1 June 2008]

Martin, L. (2004). An emerging research framework for studying informal learning and schools. In *Science Education (88)*, S71-S82. Available at http://www3.interscience.wiley.com/cgi-bin/fulltext/109062573/PDFSTART [accessed on 1 June 2008]

Pachler, N., Bachmair, B., Crook, J. and Kress, G. (forthcoming) *Mobile learning.* New York: Springer

Rogers, A. (2006). Informal learning in lifelong learning. Paper presented at *Informal Learning and Digital Media: Constructions, Contexts and Consequences*. University of Southern Denmark, Odense. Danish Research Centre on Education and Advanced Media Materials (Dream). 21–23 September. Available at http://www.dream.sdu.dk/uploads/files/Alan%20Rogers.pdf [accessed on 1 June 2008]

Sefton-Green, J. (2004). Literature review in informal learning with technology outside school. Report 7. Bristol: Futurelab. Available at http://www.futurelab.org.uk/resources/documents/lit_reviews/Informal_Learning_Review.pdf [accessed on 1 June 2008]

Sharples, M., Milrad, M., Arnedillo-Sánchez, I., Vavoula, G. (2008). Mobile Learning: Small devices, Big Issues. In Balacheff, N., Ludvigsen, S., de Jong, T., Lazonder, A., Barnes, S. and Montandon, L. *Technology Enhanced Learning: Principles and Products*. Kaleidoscope Legacy Book. Berlin: Springer. Available at http://www.lsri.nottingham.ac.uk/msh/Papers/KAL_Legacy_Mobile_Learning_SUBMITTED.pdf [accessed on 1 June 2008]

Sharples, M., Taylor, J. and Vavoula, G. (2007). A theory of learning for the mobile age. In Andrews, R. and Haythornthwaite, C. (eds), *The SAGE Handbook of e-learning research*. London: Sage, pp. 221–247

Stald, G. (2008). Mobile identity: youth, identity, and mobile communication media. In Buckingham, D. (ed), *Youth, identity, and digital media*. Cambridge, MA: MIT Press, pp. 143–164. Available at http://www.mitpressjournals.org/doi/pdf/10.1162/dmal.9780262524834.143 [accessed on 1 June 2008)]

Traxler, J. and Kukulska-Hulme, A. (2005). Evaluating mobile learning: reflections on current practice. Proceedings: *mLearn 2005*, 25–28 October, Cape Town

Wali, E., Winters, N. and Oliver, M. (2008). Maintaining, changing and crossing contexts: an activity theoretic reinterpretation of mobile learning. In *ALT-J 16(1)*, pp. 41–57

2. Methods for Evaluating Mobile Learning

MIKE SHARPLES

Overview

Mobile learning differs from learning in the classroom or on a desktop computer in its support for education across contexts and life transitions. This poses substantial problems for evaluation, if the context is not fixed and if the activity can span formal and informal settings. There may be no fixed point to locate an observer, the learning may spread across locations and times, there may be no prescribed curriculum or lesson plan, the learning activity may involve a variety of personal, institutional and public technologies, it may be interleaved with other activities, and there may be ethical issues concerned with monitoring activity outside the classroom. The chapter indicates issues related to evaluation for usability, effectiveness and satisfaction and illustrates these with case studies of evaluation for three major mobile learning projects. The Mobile Learning Organiser project used diary and interview methods to investigate students' appropriation of mobile technology over a year. The MyArtSpace project developed a multi-level analysis of a service to support learning on school museum visits. The PI project has employed critical incident analysis to reveal breakthroughs and breakdowns in the use of mobile technology for inquiry science learning. It is also addressing the particular ethical problems of collecting data in the home.

1. Introduction

Mobile learning is not simply a variant of e-learning enacted with portable devices, nor an extension of classroom learning into less formal settings. Recent research has focused on how mobile learning creates new contexts for learning through interactions between people, technologies and settings, and on learning within an increasingly mobile society (Sharples, Taylor, and Vavoula, 2007). For example, a young child visiting a science discovery centre may create a favourable context for learning, through interactions with the exhibits, a multimedia guide, conversation with parents, and observations of other visitors. In a mobile society, people are continually creating such opportunities for learning though a combination of conversation on mobile devices, context-based search and retrieval of information, and exploration of real and virtual worlds.

New modes of learning are being designed, including mobile game-based learning (Schwabe and Goth, 2005), learning from interactive location-based guides (Damala and Lecoq, 2005; Naismith, Sharples and Ting, 2005), and ambient learning (Rogers et al., 2004). While these offer opportunities to support personalisation and to connect learning across contexts and life transitions, they also pose problems in evaluating learning processes and outcomes. If mobile learning can occur anywhere, then how can we track and record the learning processes? If the learning is interwoven with other everyday activities, then how can we tell when it occurs? If the learning is self-determined and self-organised, then how can we measure learning outcomes? These are difficult questions, with no simple answers, yet it is essential to address them if we are to provide evidence of the effectiveness of mobile learning.

With a few notable exceptions (see e.g. Valdivia and Nussbaum, 2007) most studies of mobile learning have either provided evaluations in the form of attitude surveys and interviews ("they say they enjoy it"), or observations ("they look as if they are learning") (Traxler and Kukulska-Hulme, 2005). Although surveys, interviews and observations can illuminate the learning process, they do not provide detailed evidence as to the nature and permanence of the learning that has occurred.

2. Issues in evaluating mobile learning

To propose appropriate evaluation methods for mobile learning, we need to understand what distinguishes mobile learning from classroom learning or learning with desktop computers. Below are some distinctive aspects of mobile learning. Not all are definitive, for example informal learning may be carried out with fixed computers, but taken together they indicate the space of learning activities for which evaluation methods need to be applied. A useful framework to map this space is the distinction (adapted from Livingstone, 2001) between whether the learning is initiated by the learner, or externally (e.g. by a teacher or a curriculum) and whether the learning process is managed by the learner or others, see Table 2.1.

	External management	*Learner management*
External initiation	Formal learning	Resource-based learning
Learner initiation	Voluntary learning	Informal learning

Table 2.1: Initiation and management of learning
(adapted from Livingstone, 2001).

2.1 *Mobile learning may be mobile (but not necessarily)*

If we take as a definition of mobile learning "Learning that happens across locations, or that takes advantage of learning opportunities offered by portable technologies."[1] then it may occur either on the move, or in a fixed location such as a classroom where the learners are using portable devices. Existing methods for evaluating curriculum-led learning in the classroom

---

[1]   A definition contributed to the Wikipedia Mobile Learning page by the author, and as yet uncontested (adapted from O'Malley et al., 2005).

(such as assessments of curriculum learning gains and classroom observation studies) can equally be applied to learning with handheld devices, and indeed already are so, since classroom maths learning typically involves the use of pocket calculators. What is novel, is the evaluation of technology-enabled learning on the move, with the learner travelling while learning, or learning that spans locations and times. This is not easy to capture as there may be no fixed point in time or space to locate an observer or a video camera. To complicate matters further, mobile learning may be distributed, involving multiple participants, spread over many locations, some or all on the move.

2.2 Mobile learning may occur in non-formal settings

Many studies of mobile learning have been in non-formal educational settings, such as museums and field trips. Such settings are designed to support activities that may be initiated by parents or schools, but are managed by the learner Thus, we may know what variety of learning opportunities are on offer, but not how the students will engage in the activity, making choices and creating a path through the exhibits and resources. Contrast this with a traditional classroom, where the lesson plan provides an indication of what should be learned, at what time.

2.3 Mobile learning may be extended and interleaved

An appealing aspect of mobile learning is that it can support the learner over a long period of time, for example in learning a foreign language, and that it can be interleaved with other activities, such as taking a plane journey, or being a tourist. A consequence is that it may not be possible to determine when the learning begins and ends, nor when a person is deliberately learning or just enjoying an activity (which itself may lead to unintended learning).

2.4 Mobile learning may involve a variety of personal and institutional technologies

During a typical day a university student may move around the campus engaging with a variety of technologies and resources that can support learning such as desktop computers, personal laptop computer, multimedia lecture rooms, electronic dictionary, MP3 player, mobile phone, and a variety of books and notes. A tourist may learn from a personal phone or MP3 player, an audio guide, a multimedia booth, a printed guidebook and a human guide. To evaluate the effect of one such device, such as a mobile phone, in this melange of technology would either require setting up an artificial experiment (for example, requiring the student to learn everything though the phone) or to try and isolate the specific learning effects of individual devices.

2.5 Mobile learning presents particular ethical problems

Although it may be technically possible to monitor learning activities outside a formal setting such as a classroom, for example by logging all use of students' laptop computers or setting up cameras in museums or tourist sites, there may be ethical objections to doing so. These include getting permission from all participants to be monitored for research purposes and allowing participants the right to choose when to be monitored. This is particularly sensitive when the participants are children, or the learning is part of an assessed curriculum, since those involved may feel coerced into participating. An evaluation must address both the specific aspects of ethical research and broader issues of the rights of children, at different ages, to escape from continual monitoring and to be free to play and explore without continual pressure to learn.

3. What do you want to know?

It may be obvious, but nevertheless needs to be stated, that the appropriate method of evaluation depends on what the evaluators want to know. Choice of method also depends on who needs to know the results and how they will be used. Evaluation as part of education research will be concerned with understanding how fundamental processes of learning can be mediated, enhanced and transformed. Evaluation to inform design will focus on intervention and enhancement, examining how a combination of technologies and activities can best be developed to address problems and provide new learning opportunities. Evaluation for policy makers needs to provide evidence of learning gains or changes, either through comparison with existing approaches, or by showing how mobile learning can create radically new opportunities, such as linking people in real and virtual worlds. A useful way to approach the evaluation, for any stakeholder, is to address usability (will it work?), effectiveness (is it enhancing learning?) and satisfaction (is it liked?).

3.1   Usability

If the aim is to improve the technology, then there are well-established methods of usability testing in the lab, such as heuristic evaluation (Molich and Nielsen, 1990), that have been successfully transferred to mobile devices. Evaluating usability in the field is more difficult, but the technology itself can assist. The software may be programmed to log user interactions and their times, to show a timeline of user activity or to replay the interactions. One important point is that the technology may not be able to log its own breakdowns, nor what happens when it is deliberately switched off by the user, but it can show when these start and end. A more innovative possibility is to use the inbuilt multimedia capabilities in devices such as mobile phones and laptop computers to audio record and photograph activities, continually, or at timed intervals, or random intervals, or when initiated by the user. For examples of the use of the mobile technology itself to gather evaluation data see also Wali et al., Hooft, and Trinder et al. in this volume.

3.2 Effectiveness

The effectiveness of mobile learning depends on the educational aims and context. What is useful for school or college learning may have little relevance to the learner's informal learning. Conversely, what a person learns outside the classroom may not match the immediate aims of the curriculum, though it may be valuable in supporting aspects of lifelong learning such as carrying out independent research or engaging in social interaction. Thus, any assessment of the effects of mobile learning must be related to the context of the activity and its intended aims. Is the aim to learn a topic, to develop specific skills, or to support incidental and lifelong learning? Is it initiated and managed by the learner, or externally?

3.3 Satisfaction

Satisfaction with mobile learning is superficially the easiest to assess, through attitude surveys or interviews with learners, so it is no surprise that many research papers report these as the main or only method of evaluation. Typically, a paper will present a mean response of, say, 3.8 on a 5 point Likert scale to the question "Did you enjoy the experience?" as if this were evidence of unusual satisfaction, or even of productive learning. It is neither. Almost all results of attitude to novel technology lie within the range of 3.5 to 4.5, on a 5 point scale for satisfaction, regardless of technology or context. More specific questions, such as "Was the technology easy to use?" merely provoke further questions, such as "By comparison to what?"; "For what tasks?". A more refined method of assessing satisfaction is through product reaction cards. The Microsoft Desirability toolkit (Benedek and Miner, 2002) includes 118 cards with words such as "confusing", "flexible", "organised", "time-consuming" that can be used to assess reaction to a technology or to an experience. Typically, people are asked to select the cards that best relate to their experience and these could form the basis of an interview (e.g. "What did you find confusing about your experience?").

4. Case studies

The remainder of the chapter offers three case studies in evaluation of mobile learning. The projects have been chosen because they present particular difficulties, in assessing learning over time, or in different contexts, or because of ethical issues. The evaluation methods are not intended as definitive solutions, but in the spirit of object lessons to be examined critically, to gain insight into the successes and limitations of particular evaluation methods. The aim here is not to report results of the projects, but rather to describe the methods of evaluation and to indicate how successful these were in assessing learning processes and outcomes and in revealing usability, effectiveness and satisfaction.

4.1 Mobile Learning Organiser

The student learning organiser project (Corlett, Sharples, Bull, and Chan, 2005) was an early attempt to provide university students with a personal device to support their learning over a long period of time. The motivation for the project was that many business people carry personal organisers offering a set of tools – calendar, contacts list, email, to do list, etc – to manage their working lives. These are designed to support office work rather than learning, so is there a value in developing an analogous "Mobile Learning Organiser" to assist university students in managing their studies?

Seventeen students on an MSc course were loaned iPAQ Pocket PC devices, with wireless LAN connection but no phone, for one academic year. The devices were equipped with a custom-designed Mobile Learning Organiser that included a Time Manager (for viewing course timetables and lecture slots), a Course Manager (to browse and view teaching material), a Communications Manager (for email and instant messaging when in wireless range) and a Concept Mapper. In addition to these tools, the students could access the full range of Pocket PC software (including calendar, email, instant messaging and files through the normal Pocket PC interface) and were also encouraged to personalise the devices by downloading any media and applications they wished.

Thus, the context of the study was that the students could engage in a variety of activities with the devices, including ones not directly related to learning such as downloading music, in any location within and outside the university, over a period of a year. Given this range and duration, and evaluators' interest in understanding the process of technology adoption and patterns of use, we adopted a mixed-methods approach to evaluation.

The students were asked to complete questionnaires at 1, 4, 16 and 40 weeks after they were issued with the devices. They were asked to indicate the frequency of use of the device ("many times a day", "at least once a day", "at least twice a week", "less that twice a week") and to rate each provided tool as "very useful", "useful", "possibly useful", "probably not useful", "not useful" or "don't know". They were also asked to name the tools that made the greatest impact on their learning, personal organisation and entertainment. The freeform answers were collected under generic headings. The questionnaires were successful in revealing changes in use over the year. For example, ratings for the timetable tool increased over the year (59% of the students rated it as "useful" or "very useful" after 4 weeks, 64% after 16 weeks, and 84% after 10 months), the instant messaging tool increased in popularity at the end (59%, 50% and 71%) and the perceived value of the course materials decreased over time (59%, 43%, 41%). The concept mapper was least successful, declining from 14% at the start to none indicating it as being useful by the end of the trial.

Taken alone these figures are intriguing, but not particularly revealing. Each survey, however, was followed by a focus group meeting with all the students, to discuss the meaning of the results and also to raise other issues and problems. These meetings helped in interpreting the raw results. For example, one reason for the decline in usefulness of the course materials was that later in the course students were engaged in project work rather than structured learning. They also illuminated general and specific usability problems. Thus, battery life was a major factor in the decision of some students to abandon their devices, in particular when some students left them behind over the Christmas vacation and the battery discharged losing their data.

The students were also asked to complete written logbooks of their daily activities with the PDA devices, including the location, duration and type of activity. The logbooks revealed patterns and frequency of use across locations during the first six weeks of the project. These provided some unexpected interactions between location and activity, for example:

- Although email was synchronised to the device and so could be accessed anywhere, students only tended to use this when in an area covered by the campus wireless network.

- Participants used the calendar and timetabling in every location as they had need. So for some students, the PDA became a replacement for traditional diaries.

- Some students reported regularly reading course materials, offline web content and e-books when at home or in their dormitories, even though they all had access to a desktop computer at home.

A final survey was administered at the end of the project. The questions addressed specific issues that had arisen from the earlier surveys and focus groups. Students were asked to rate statements on five-point Likert scale from "Strongly Agree" to "Strongly Disagree". The responses were then weighted from 2 to -2. The sum of weighed responses from each question was then used to measure overall agreement/disagreement. Only four mean responses were in the range +/- 0.5 to 2.0:

Having to use the iPAQ hindered my learning	- 0.7
I found battery life a significant problem	+ 1.1
I felt uncomfortable using the iPAQ because I didn't know how to use it	- 0.8
The advantages of having an iPAQ outweighed the drawbacks of taking part in the trial (attending meetings, doing questionnaires etc.)	+ 0.6

Table 2.2: Survey questions for which the responses were in the range +/- 0.5 to 2.0.*
* Minus figures indicate a disagreement with the proposition.

The evaluation methods were designed to be interpreted as a whole, to reveal patterns and trends in technology adoption. For a more general discussion of adoption of mobile technology for learning see Waycott (2004). The methods were successful in revealing some clear modes of use. Frequency of use fell over the period, with 60% using the devices less than twice a week by the end of the project compared to 18% at the start, however 22% continued to use the PDA many times a day, a similar percentage to that at the start of the project. The students made considerable use of the calendar and timetabling features as well as the communications tools. Content optimized for the PDA was well used, and there was a request from some students that more resources should be made available in PDA format, including administrative information.

An unexpected result, given the aims of the study, was that there was no conclusive evidence of need for a specifically designed suite of tools in addition to those already included in the device, although the time management tools were well received. Ownership of the technology was shown to be important. Whilst the PDAs are loaned, students are reluctant to invest time and money in personalisation and extension. Universities and other institutions will need to provide students with more assistance in learning through personal technologies, including regular updates of timetables and content. It is difficult to commit much organisational resource for a small scale trial, but as more students bring their own devices into universities, change is now being driven by their demands as consumers.

The evaluation methods could not show what or how the students were learning. That is appropriate given the nature of the project, which was to explore the first use of a new technology (wireless PDA) over a long time period. It was not possible to predict in advance how students would use the devices, or even if they would adopt them at all. Since they interleaved use of PDAs with many other tools then it is not possible to factor out learning gains due to the PDAs. Indeed, the main purpose of providing them with the devices was to assist them in making their studies more organised and efficient, rather than to deliver core content. The results did show that some, but not all, students took the opportunity to organise their studies and to preview material using the PDAs. Most important, it did not suggest the need for a dedicated "Mobile Learning Organiser", but rather for a device with communications facilities, a standard range of office and media tools, and access to learning content.

4.2 *MyArtSpace*

The MyArtSpace project also explored the adoption of novel technology, but in the more structured setting of a museum, to support curriculum learning (Vavoula, Meek, Sharples, Lonsdale, and Rudman, 2006; Sharples, Lonsdale, Meek, Rudman, and Vavoula, 2007; Vavoula, Sharples, Rudman, Lonsdale, and Meek, 2007). The aim of the project was to address a well-recognised problem (Guisasola, Morentin and Zuza, 2005) of lack of connection between a school museum visit and preparation and follow-up in the classroom.

In relation to Table 2.1, the learning was externally initiated, as part of the school curriculum, and it shifted from being externally managed, by a teacher in the classroom to learner managed, by the students in a museum or gallery. The duration was much shorter than the Mobile Learning Organiser project, comprising two classroom lessons and a museum trip. The settings were also more predictable, though the students were free to roam through the museum building. Although more constrained, the project posed a substantial challenge in that the evaluation had to inform the design of the MyArtSpace service and also to indicate benefits and problems for the learners, the schools and the museums.

MyArtSpace was a year-long project, funded by the Department of Culture Media and Sport to support structured inquiry learning between school classrooms and museums or galleries. Using the MyArtSpace service, children aged 11–15 can create their own interpretations of museum objects through descriptions, images and sounds, which they can share and present back in the classroom. Before the visit, the teacher in the classroom sets an open-ended question which the students should answer by gathering and selecting evidence from the museum visit. On arrival at the museum, students are given multimedia mobile phones which they can use to "collect" exhibits (by typing a two-letter code shown next to museum exhibits which triggers a multimedia presentation on the phone), take photos, record sounds, or write text comments. This content is transmitted automatically by the phone to their personal online collection. Back at school, the students can view their collected content on a web browser, organize it into personal galleries, share and present their findings in the classroom and then show the presentations to friends and family. Some 3000 children used the service at two museums and a gallery over the period of the project.

The evaluation team was fortunate in being involved throughout the project, from beginning to end. It was contracted to inform the design of the MyArtSpace service, which was being developed by a separate multimedia company, as well as to assess its educational value. To address this broad remit, we adopted a Lifecycle evaluation approach (Meek, 2006) that matches the evaluation method to the phase in the development lifecycle, providing outcomes that can feed forward to guide the next stages of development and deployment and also feed back to assist the design of new versions of the software.

The early stages of evaluation included stakeholder meetings with teachers, museum education staff and the software developers, to establish the goals and requirements of the service. These meetings proposed requirements (112 in total) that the stakeholders were asked to rate using the MoSCoW technique from Dynamic Systems Development Method (Stapleton, 2003) to indicate that, for each requirement:

- *Must*: must have this
- *Should*: should have this if at all possible
- *Could*: could have this if it does not affect anything else
- *Would*: will not have this time, but would like to have in the future

Successive prototypes, starting with "paper" designs, were given heuristic evaluations (Molich and Nielsen, 1990) whereby usability experts identified and rated usability problems. The prototypes were also assessed as to how they met each requirement. From the start, the evaluation covered the entire service, including teacher and museum support and training, so

the teacher and museum guidelines, teacher information packs and training sessions were also assessed.

As the project moved from design and implementation to deployment,
a series of studies were planned to assess the usability, effectiveness, and
satisfaction of MyArtSpace. The team developed a three-level approach
to evaluation.

- *Micro level*: examined the individual activities that MyArtSpace
  enabled students to perform, such as making notes, recording audio,
  viewing the collection online, and producing presentations of the
  visit.

- *Meso level*: examined the learning experience as a whole, exploring
  whether the classroom-museum-classroom continuity worked.

- *Macro level*: examined the impact of MyArtSpace on educational
  practice for school museum visits.

For each level, the evaluation covered three stages, to explore the relationship between expectations and reality:

- *Stage 1*: what was supposed to happen, based on pre-interviews with
  stakeholders and documentation including the teachers' pack.

- *Stage 2*: what actually happened, based on observer logs, focus
  groups, and post-analysis of video diaries.

- *Stage 3*: the gaps between findings from stages 1 and 2, based on
  reflective interviews with stakeholders and critical incident analysis
  of the findings from stages 1 and 2.

Taken together, the levels and stages provide a framework to evaluate
usability (does the service do what was intended?), effectiveness (did the
service support learning as expected, or were there unexpected benefits or
problems?), and satisfaction (did the stakeholders find the service unexpect-
edly enjoyable or unpleasant?), with results that could be passed to systems
designers, educators and policy makers. The specific evaluation methods

included: one-to-one interviews with teachers; focus group interviews with students; video observations of a pre-visit lesson, museum visits and post visit lesson; attitude surveys; and telephone or email interviews with other stakeholders.

As a very brief summary of the results, at the micro level the system worked well, with the phones offering a familiar platform and the two letter code providing an easy way to activate multimedia in context. The transmission of data took place unobtrusively after each use of the photo, audio or note tool. The teachers indicated that their students engaged more with the exhibits than in previous visits and had the chance to do meaningful follow-up work.

At the meso level, a significant educational issue was that some students found difficulty in identifying, back in the classroom, pictures and sounds they had recorded. The time-ordered list of activities and objects they had collected provided some cues, but there is a difficult trade-off between structuring the material during the visit to make it easier to manage (for example by limiting the number of items that can be collected) and stifling creativity and engagement.

A significant issue emerged at the macro level. Although the system was a technical and educational success, there are significant barriers to wider deployment of a system like MyArtSpace. Many museums already provide audio guides and staff may be reluctant to spend time maintaining yet more technology. There is also the issue of who pays for the phone data charges: schools, museums, or students and their parents? The MyArtSpace service is now being marketed commercially as OOKL (www.ookl.org. uk) and has been adopted by some major UK museums and galleries that have the resources to support the service, with the company renting phone handsets to the venues with the software pre-installed. Wider adoption may depend on the next generation of mobile technology, when people carry converged phone/camera/media player devices that can easily capture everyday sights and sounds to a personal weblog (see also Pierroux in this volume). Then, the opportunity for schools will be to exploit these personal devices for learning between the classroom and settings outside school including field trips and museum visits.

4.3 Personal Inquiry

The Personal Inquiry (PI) project (http://www.pi-project.ac.uk/) has some similarities to MyArtSpace in that it connects learning in formal and informal settings, but there is a greater emphasis on providing a generic toolkit to support inquiry learning, starting in the classroom and then continued in a variety of settings including the school grounds, the city, homes, and science centres.

The project is a three-year collaboration between the University of Nottingham and the Open University, UK, to help young people aged 11–14 to understand themselves and their world through a scientific process of active inquiry across formal and informal settings. The children will use handheld and classroom computers to gather and assess evidence, conduct experiments and engage in informed debate. Their activities will be based around topic themes – Myself, My Environment, My Community – that engage young learners in investigating their health, diet and fitness, their immediate environment and their wider surroundings. These topics are key elements of the new 21st century science curriculum (Millar and Osborne, 1998) that requires children to reason about the natural sciences as a complex system and to explore how people relate to the physical world.

The technology will be in the form of an inquiry learning toolkit running on small touch screen computer-phones, with integral cameras and keyboards, plus connected data probes, to enable learners to investigate personally-relevant questions outside the classroom, by gathering and communicating evidence. The toolkit will be designed to support scripted inquiry learning, where scripts are software structures, like dynamic lesson plans, that generate teacher and learner interfaces. These will orchestrate the learners through an inquiry learning process providing a sequence of activities, collaborators, software tools and hardware devices, while allowing the teacher to monitor and guide student activity. The children and their teachers will be able to monitor their learning activity, and to visualise, share, discuss and present the results, through a review tool accessible through a standard web browser running on a desktop or portable computer in the home or school. Teachers will also have a script authoring tool to create and modify the scripts, to support the learning of specific curriculum topics.

A challenge for evaluation is that the project needs to demonstrate the benefits, if any, of the general approach of scripted inquiry learning supported by mobile technology. The proposition is that the integrated system (mobile technology, inquiry methods, and learning between formal and informal settings) will provide the learning benefits, rather than any individual component. Thus, the learning benefits of each part cannot be tested separately, and the entire system is so different from traditional classroom teaching that there is little value to carrying out a comparative study of learning outcomes. Instead of assessing how children might learn better through scripted inquiry learning, the initial aim will be to assess how they learn differently. For the initial school trials we have adopted a critical incident study as one method of evaluation.

Over a two-week period of five science lessons, 30 students aged 14, planned a scientific investigation to explore the relation between heart rate and fitness (lesson 1) which they first explored in the relatively controlled environment of the classroom (lesson 2), then extended through a more active engagement with the inquiry process in the leisure centre (lesson 3), and concluded the work in the school library as they analysed the results (lesson 4) and created presentations (lesson 5). All the teaching sessions were videotaped with three cameras: one fixed camera giving an overview of the lesson and two others to record closer views on the classroom or group activity. Radio microphones were used to provide good sound quality.

A critical incident analysis of the videotapes identified specific learning breakthroughs and breakdowns (Sharples, 1993). Breakthroughs are observable critical incidents which appear to be initiating productive new forms of learning or important conceptual change. Breakdowns are observable critical incidents where a learner is struggling with the technology, is asking for help, or appears to be labouring under a clear misunderstanding. They may either be predictable (e.g. the intervention may be aimed at producing conceptual change) or unpredicted (e.g. a child uses the technology in novel ways, or makes an unforeseen connection or conceptual leap).

The critical incident analysis was conducted as follows: the videotapes were separately viewed by three researchers to identify obvious and informative breakdowns or breakthroughs (for example, where there is some activity and discussion on the video to indicate causes or solutions to the problem, or that suggest the nature of the learning); the identified critical incidents were then compared to reach an agreed set of incidents that might inform design; and a videotape of the selected incidents was also played to a focus group of students, to elicit their interpretation of the events.

As a result of this process we identified eight incidents (four break-downs, three breakthroughs and one incident that could be interpreted as both a breakthrough and a breakdown). An example of a breakthrough was the teacher herself wearing a monitor, continually generating a graph of her heart-rate on the class display which she referred to during the lesson. An example of both a breakthrough and a breakdown came in the fitness centre where the children were able to view and discuss their data as it emerged, successfully creating a micro-site for learning, but the software did not indicate on the graph where a fitness exercise started and ended.

The PI project is still continuing, with further trials planned to connect learning in the classroom, homes and city centres. These will present new problems in evaluation, in particular the practical and ethical problems of conducting evaluations in a home. We are developing ethical guidelines to cover this type of mobile learning evaluation, including: ensuring that the children are fully informed about how their learning activities outside the classroom may be monitored, allowing children to decide where and when to collect data, and ensuring that material captured and created by the children will be subject to normal standards of copyright and fair use, so that inappropriate material will be deleted and the authors of the teach-ing materials and field data retain copyright and moral rights of authorship over their material.

5.   Summary

Evaluation of mobile learning poses particular challenges not only because it introduces novel technologies and modes of learning, but also because it can spread across many contexts and over long periods of time. It is generally not possible to control factors to an extent that would make a comparative study appropriate. However, it may be worth attempting such a study when there is a well-defined learning activity and a comparative less-expensive technology, for example on a field trip to compare learning supported by PDAs with a similar trip using paper worksheets and children's own phone cameras.

To meet the challenges, researchers are developing distinctive methods of evaluation that are sensitive to time and context. A first step in planning a mobile learning evaluation is to determine whether it is concerned with technology development, or appropriation, or the implications of new or existing mobile technology for learning. Technology development can be guided and evaluated by a variety of human-computer interaction methods, though attention will need to be paid to how the technology performs in realistic settings, such as outdoor sunshine. Technology appropriation was discussed in the Mobile Learning Organiser section, with methods that include diary-interview and periodic surveys. These can reveal changing patterns of use and interest, but not the processes and outcomes of learning. Waycott (2004) presents a valuable framework for analysing the appropriation of mobile technologies for learning, derived from case studies.

In evaluating learning with mobile technology it may be useful to start with Table 2.1 to determine whether the learning is initiated and managed by the learner, or others. Mobile learning that is self-initiated and managed (for example, long-term language learning, or learning on vacation) is unlikely to be predicable either in content or context. Capturing evidence of the learning may be difficult, particularly if it spans multiple technologies. Vavoula has developed a successful method to study informal mobile learning based on structured diaries kept by learners, followed up by interviews (Vavoula, 2005). This is a labour-intensive process but it has revealed contexts and conditions of mobile learning. Another possibility is to phone or text the learner at pre-agreed intervals to ask about current or recent learning activities.

For learning that is either externally initiated or managed, the contexts and topics are more likely to be pre-determined, so there are likely to be opportunities to examine teaching materials and settings in advance and plan where and how to observe the learning. Data capture methods include videotaped observations of individuals or groups (preferably wearing radio microphones for good sound quality), log files of human-computer interactions, and observer notes. Analysis of the data can include critical incident methods (including interviews with participants to discuss replays of the incidents), interaction or discourse analyses, and analysis of log data (possibly synchronised to videotapes) to reveal changing patterns of interaction, for example as the learner alternates between engagement in a learning activity and reflection on findings.

Lastly, learning that is both externally initiated and structured (for example, use of handheld technologies in a classroom) can be evaluated through a variety of methods, including those above, as well as learning outcome measures and comparative studies.

Evaluation of mobile learning is not intrinsically different to other forms of learning, in that we want to understand the individual and collective processes of coming to know and the resulting changes in knowledge, skill and experience. This chapter has suggested some ways in which those processes can be observed and analysed across contexts and long time periods.

Acknowledgements

The Mobile Learning Organiser was a project of the Educational Technology Research Group, Electronic, Electrical and Computer Engineering, University of Birmingham. Susan Bull, Tony Chan and Dan Corlett contributed to the project and its results.

Peter Lonsdale, Julia Meek, Paul Rudman and Giasemi Vavoula contributed to the evaluation of MyArtSpace. The project was funded by the Department for Culture, Media through Culture Online. The MyArtSpace was designed and developed by The Sea (http://www.the-sea.com) and is now marketed as OOKL (www.ookl.org.uk). We thank the students, teachers, and museum educators who took part in our trials.

The Personal Inquiry project acknowledges support from the Economic and Social Research Council and the Engineering and Physical Sciences Research Council UK through the Teaching and Learning Research

Programme. The design and evaluation discussed here were carried out by Stamatina Anstopoulou, Steve Benford, Charles Crook, Chris Greenhalgh, Claire O'Malley, Hazel Martin and Michael Wright. We are grateful for the support and engagement of the teacher and children who participated in this study. The project is a collaboration between the University of Nottingham and the Open University, UK.

References

Benedek, J., and Miner, T. (2002). *Measuring desirability: New methods for evaluating desirability in a usability lab setting.* Paper presented at the UPA 2002 Conference, 8–12 July, Orlando, FL

Corlett, D., Sharples, M., Bull, S., and Chan, T. (2005). Evaluation of a mobile learning organiser for university students. *Journal of Computer Assisted Learning*, 21(3), 162–170

Damala, A., and Lecoq, C. (2005). Mobivisit: Nomadic Computing in indoor cultural settings. A field study in the museum of Fine Arts, Lyon. In X. Perrot (ed.), *ICHIM International Cultural Heritage Informatics Meeting*, 21–23 September 2005, Paris, France

Guisasola, J., Morentin, M. and Zuza, K. (2005). School visits to science museums and learning sciences: a complex relationship. *Physics Education*, 40(6), 544–549

Livingstone, D.W. (2001). *Adults' Informal Learning: Definitions, Findings, Gaps and Future Research* (No. Working paper 21). Toronto: NALL (New Approaches to Lifelong Learning)

Meek, J. (2006). *Adopting a Lifecycle Approach to the Evaluation of Computers and Information Technology.* Unpublished PhD Thesis, The University of Birmingham, UK

Millar, R. and Osborne, J. (1998). *Beyond 2000: Science education for the future*: King's College, University of London

Molich, R. and Nielsen, J. (1990). Improving a human-computer dialogue. *Communications of the ACM*, 33(3), 338–348

Naismith, L., Sharples, M., and Ting, J. (2005). *Evaluation of CAERUS: a Context Aware Mobile Guide*. Available at http://www.mlearn.org. za/CD/papers/Naismith.pdf [accessed on 8 May 2008]

O'Malley, C., Vavoula, G., Glew, J.P., Taylor, J., Sharples, M., Lefrere, P., Lonsdale, P., Naismith, L. and Waycott, J. (2005). Guidelines for learning/teaching/tutoring in a mobile environment. MOBILearn project report D4.1. Available at http://www.mobilearn.org/download/ results/public_deliverables/MOBIlearn_D4.1_Final.pdf [accessed on 13 August 2008]

Rogers, Y., Price, S., Fitzpatrick, G., Fleck, R., Harris, E., Smith, H., et al. (2004, 1–3 June). *Ambient wood: designing new forms of digital augmentation for learning outdoors*. Paper presented at the 2004 conference on Interaction design and children: building a community (IDC 2004), Maryland, USA

Schwabe, G., and Goth, C. (2005). Mobile learning with a mobile game: design and motivational effects. *Journal of Computer Assisted Learning*, 21(3), 204–216

Sharples, M. (1993). A Study of Breakdowns and Repairs in a Computer Mediated Communication System. *Interacting with Computers*, 5(1), 61–77

Sharples, M., Taylor, J., and Vavoula, G. (2007). A Theory of Learning for the Mobile Age. In R. Andrews and C. Haythornthwaite (eds), *The Sage Handbook of Elearning Research*. London: Sage, pp. 221–247

Sharples, M., Lonsdale, P., Meek, J., Rudman, P.D., Vavoula, G.N. (2007). An Evaluation of MyArtSpace: a Mobile Learning Service for School Museum Trips. In A. Norman and J. Pearce (eds), *Proceedings of 6th Annual Conference on Mobile Learning, mLearn 2007*, Melbourne. Melbourne: Universitty of Melbourne, pp. 238–244

Stapleton, J. (2003). *DSDM: A Framework for Business-Centered Development*. Boston, MA: Addison-Wesley Longman Publishing Co

Traxler, J., and Kukulska-Hulme, A. (2005). *Evaluating mobile learning: Reflections on current practice*. Paper presented at the mLearn 2005, Cape Town

Valdivia, R., and Nussbaum, M. (2007). Face-to-Face Collaborative Learning in Computer Science Classes. *International Journal of Engineering Education*, 23(3), 434–440

Vavoula, G., Meek, J., Sharples, M., Lonsdale, P., and Rudman, P. (2006). A lifecycle approach to evaluating MyArtSpace. In S. Hsi, Kinshuk, T. Chan and D. Sampson (eds), *Proceedings of the 4th International Workshop of Wireless, Mobile and Ubiquitous Technologies in Education* (WMUTE 2006), 16–17 November, Athens, Greece. IEEE Computer Society, pp. 18–22

Vavoula, G.N. (2005). *D4.4: A Study of Mobile Learning Practices, Report of MOBILearn project*. Available at www.mobilearn.org/download/results/public_deliverables/MOBIlearn_D4.4_Final.pdf [accessed on 8 May 2008]

Vavoula, G., Sharples, M., Rudman, P., Lonsdale, P., Meek, J. (2007). Learning Bridges: a role for mobile technologies in education. *Educational Technology*,Vol. XLVII, No. 3, May–June 2007, pp. 33–37

Waycott, J. (2004). The appropriation of PDAs as learning and workplace tools: an activity theory perspective. Unpublished PhD Thesis, The Open University, Milton Keynes

3. Basic Research on Lifelong Learning: Recent Survey Findings and Reflections on "Capturing"Informal Learning [1]

D.W. LIVINGSTONE

Overview

This chapter summarizes findings from the 1998 and 2004 national surveys of lifelong learning and work, including profiles of and relations between *paid employment and unpaid* (domestic, volunteer) *work* on one hand and *formal* (schooling/further continuing) *education* and *informal* (job/house-work/volunteer work/general interest related) *learning* on the other hand. Features of the hidden informal part of the "iceberg" of adult learning are emphasized, particularly the very weak links between formal education and informal learning. Methodological limitations of both survey and case study empirical research to date on informal learning are noted, with some reference to the ongoing computerization of everyday life. Implications for "tracking" or "capturing" informal learning in mobile contexts are suggested.

---

1   Revised version of keynote address to "Workshop on Research Methods and Mobile Learning: How to Get the Data We Really Want", Institute of Education, University of London, 14 December 2007.

1. Introduction

The basic theme of this chapter is appreciation of the very significant limitations of evaluative assessments when applied to subtle aspects of human life such as informal learning. First, permit me an illustrative joke. Two behavioural researchers were hired to do an assessment of a mobile learning project for a certain open learning institution. They became romantically attracted to one another and started going out together. After they consummated their affair, one turned to the other and said: "That was good for you. How was it for me?"

I want to encourage reflection on the relative merits of enabling versus evaluative approaches for engaging with informal learners in the context of the increasing priority being devoted to "capturing" informal aspects of lifelong learning for credentialing, job rewards or other instrumental objectives.

We can start by recalling that as homo sapiens (Latin for "knowing human") our most distinctive feature is continually relating to our environment by learning—developing language, abstract reasoning and introspection, exchanging ideas and creating complex social structures. A generic definition of learning involves the gaining of knowledge, skill or understanding anytime throughout our lives and anywhere through individual and group processes. Any identification of forms of learning is a somewhat arbitrary exercise. But several basic forms of learning may be roughly distinguished in terms of the primacy of teachers and the organization of the body of knowledge to be learned.[2] These basic forms are formal education, further education courses, informal education and self-directed informal learning. These forms may be defined as follows. Education involves the presence of a teacher, someone presumed to have greater knowledge, and a learner or learners to be instructed by said teacher. When a teacher has the authority to direct designated learners to learn a curriculum taken from a pre-established body of knowledge, the form of learning is *formal*

---

2   For a fuller discussion of these distinctions and review of other relevant surveys, see
     Livingstone (2005).

education or schooling. When learners opt to acquire further knowledge or skill beyond schooling by studying voluntarily with a teacher who assists their self-determined interests by using an organized curriculum, the form of learning is *further education* (also known as "continuing education" or "adult education"). When mentors instruct novices in spontaneous learning situations without sustained reference to an intentionally-organized body of knowledge, such as by guiding them in acquiring job skills or in community development activities, the form of learning is *informal education*. Finally, all other forms of intentional learning in which we engage either individually or collectively without direct reliance on a teacher or mentor and an externally-organized curriculum can be termed *self-directed or collective informal learning*.

Such distinctions continue to be actively debated and also contrasted with more implicit and reactive forms of learning (see Smith, 2000) but for our purposes I will assume: (1) that formal and intentional informal learning are best understood as a continuum with interplay and overlap between different learning activities[3] (Colley, Hodkinson and Malcolm, 2003); (2) that more informal learning activities have tended to be ignored or devalued by authorities and researchers (Livingstone and Sawchuk, 2004); and (3) that methods that necessarily rely on respondents' self-reports can only "scratch the surface" of the iceberg of informal learning by documenting intentional informal education and self-directed learning that respondents recognize as leading to new knowledge (Livingstone, 2005). Incidental informal learning is increasingly recognized as substantial and significant (e.g. Marsick and Watkins, 2001) but studies to date that have attempted to measure more tacit forms of informal learning have been prone to the shortcomings of the earnest behavioural researcher's imputation about his lovers' emotional state!

I have reviewed the origins, findings and limitations of prior research on informal learning in other publications (see Livingstone, 1999, 2008).

---

3   From this perspective the commonly used term "non-formal education" becomes illogical or misleading as it was intended to refer mainly to further education courses. See Colley, Hodkinson and Malcolm (2003) for further discussion.

Basic findings to date are that the incidence of intentional informal learning far exceeds rates of participation in further education courses, is not very closely related to either level of formal education or participation in further education and – unlike participation in further education – does not diminish greatly as one ages.

From this perspective on forms of learning, distance education can be seen as a formal instructional system of either formal education or further education delivered through information technology to students who are not usually physically on site with the instructor. Mobile learning or "mLearning" is related to distance education in that it involves learning across locations aided by information technology. But the distinguishing feature is learning with mobile devices, portable technologies. The scope of mobile learning is therefore expansive both in terms of extending curricular settings beyond traditional classroom sites to museums, outdoor field trips, on-the-job training programs, etc., as well as in aiding informal learning initiated by any learner anywhere using portable information systems, such as handheld dictionaries. Mobile learning therefore can span the spectrum of forms of learning.

2.   WALL Research Network Findings

In this context, I would like to outline some of the results of the research network on the Changing Nature of Work and Lifelong Learning (WALL) conducted in Canada between 2003 and 2007.[4] The WALL network began

4   The research network on The Changing Nature of Work and Lifelong Learning (WALL) was funded by the Social Sciences and Humanities Research Council of Canada (SSHRC) as a Collaborative Research Initiative on the New Economy (Project No. 512-2002-1011). This network is composed of a 2004 national survey and 12 case study projects. I thank the members of the WALL network for assistance with questionnaire design, the Institute for Social Research at York University for administering the survey, David Northrup of ISR for advice on its development, Doug Hart, Milosh Raykov and Antonie Scholtz for conducting the computer-based

with expansive definitions of learning, as indicated above, and of work which included paid employment but also housework and community volunteer work. Most of the findings presented here are drawn from the 2004 WALL national survey of work and learning and compared with the prior national survey we conducted in 1998 (see Livingstone, 1999). The twelve WALL case studies also build on earlier case studies done in the late 1990's with a focus on informal learning. There is a wealth of material on both national surveys and all of these case studies on the network website (www.wallnetwork.ca).

So let me present some of the substantive findings on the incidence of forms of learning. The first point to mention is that we are increasingly highly educated. In the advanced market economies, growing proportions of people are spending more and more of their lives in organized formal schooling and further education. In Canada, for example, we have 60% of the current 25–29 year old cohort completing some form of post secondary education. Over the past generation there has been a rapid upward trajectory in higher education in virtually all of the advanced market economies: more of us are spending more time in organized schooling every year. This is the context for Table 3.1.

analyses, and Rhonda Sussman for text formatting. Further information about WALL, this national survey and the related case studies may be found at the network website: www.wallnetwork.ca. Detailed information on the prior NALL survey may also be found through this site or www.nall.ca.

	Taken adult education past year* (%)		Done Informal learning (%)	
Year	1998	2004	1998	2004
No Diploma	18	23	81	80
HS Diploma	53	48	97	94
College	58	52	97	96
University	70	63	99	96
TOTAL (%)	43	45	92	91

Table 3.1: Formal Educational Attainment by Adult Education Courses
and Informal Learning. Sources: NALL Survey, 1998; WALL Survey, 2004.
* Including current students.

If we look at people with different levels of formal schooling, what else are they doing in terms of learning activities? We have asked them about their further education courses. We find that in 1998, 43% of Canadians were involved in further education course of some sort; in 2004 the rate was 45%. Compare these figures to the 1961 rate of 4%. While Scandinavian countries still lead the world in further education participation levels, many other countries are catching up. More of us are trying to do more formal learning throughout our lives.

If you look at the relationship between the level of schooling and the level of further education course participation, Table 3.1 replicates what all earlier researchers have found in the past: the more schooling you have, the more adult education participation you tend to get. But we should note that there is an upward trend in further education for those who have no diploma. Diminishing numbers of people have no diploma. Those who have dropped out of school are being increasingly made aware of the requirement of educational credentials for jobs and are trying to get further certification, whether to try for decent jobs or for more fulfilling lives.

We have asked people to give us their self-reports on whether or not they do informal learning. As the right hand side of Table 3.1 illustrates, the vast majority of people are engaged in intentional informal learning activities. There is a slight tendency for those with no diploma to indicate that they are less engaged in such intentional informal learning activities, but about 80% of those who did not complete their secondary education actively engage in informal learning activities. This high level is not a trivial finding. Although the instinct of most social scientists is to say that if there is not a lot of variation between groups, then it is not very interesting for us to study, the most interesting finding here is the lack of variation – underlining that, indeed, all homo sapiens engage continually in informal learning which is not only valid but enhancing competencies in a variety of spheres. Our case study research explores these learning processes in unique ways. For example, we have done the first studies of housework and learning. Margaret Eichler's (2005) team has documented an array of forms of quite sophisticated learning that people accomplish through housework. Most of us, particularly women, do housework but the significance of this learning is still very much denigrated, devalued or ignored most of the time by nearly all of us.

Table 3.2 looks at learning by age. The vast majority of people are engaged in lifelong learning activities throughout their lives. What changes is that, once you get past your middle years, there's much less inclination to be engaged in further education courses. Presumable experience is of some benefit to some of us and there are some things we do not need to relearn. Our experiential learning can prepare us to become mentors for other younger, less experienced people in some spheres of life. In any event, as you can see for the 55–64 and over 65 age groups, these people are increasingly engaged in further education courses as well. In fact, we have done studies of older age groups including those over 80 and there is a recent trajectory upward in further education for all older age groups. Again, more of us are doing more formal and further education throughout our lives. But, more significantly, the vast majority of people continue to be actively engaged in informal learning projects into their 80s (Livingstone, 2007). Most people engage in many important substantial informal learning projects throughout their lives and many of these are not related to their formal schooling level or to their further education participation in easily discernible ways.

	Taken Further Education Course in Past Year		Do Any Informal Learning		Avg. Hours Informal Learning / Week*	
	1998	2004	1998	2004	1998	2004
Age	%	%	%	%	Hours	Hours
18–24	67	65	99	95	23	17
25–34	53	55	94	96	17	16
35–44	55	51	97	95	17	13
45–54	46	48	94	94	15	13
55–64	25	34	84	88	12	12
65+	10	15	79	77	12	13
Total	44	45	92	91	16	14
N	1533	8772	1538	8772	1422	7348

Table 3.2: Age by Participation in Further Education and Informal Learning.
Sources: NALL Survey, 1998; WALL Survey, 2004. * Average hours exclude those
reporting no informal learning.

The pervasiveness of informal learning may be self evident in some
respects and I may seem to be belaboring the point. But just look in a little
more detail at a few of the aspects of intentional informal learning in the
following tables. Table 3.3 summarizes the incidence of informal learning
of different topics by the employed labour force in 1998 and 2004. The
pattern in both years is fairly similar. The majority of employed people are
engaged in learning around new general knowledge, new job tasks, new
equipment, computer-based learning, health and safety, and various kinds
of problem solving activities.

	1998	2004
New General Knowledge	71	62
Teamwork, Problem Solving	63	55
New Job Tasks	63	56
Computers	61	55
Health and Safety	55	56
New Equipment	52	58
Employment Conditions	43	43
Organisational or Managerial Skills	38	42

Table 3.3: Topics of Job-related Informal Learning, Employed Labour Force
Participating in Informal Learning, 1998–2004.
Sources: NALL Survey, 1998; WALL Survey, 2004.

Table 3.4 summarizes the main learning topics for those engaged in
housework, virtually all of us. The highest frequency of intentional informal
learning is reported in the areas of home renovation and gardening which
typically require deliberate planning, as well as cooking which permits
considerable creativity.

	1998	2004
Home Renovations & Gardening	60	48
Cooking	57	50
Home Maintenance	51	45
Home Budgeting	43	37
Child- or Eldercare	42	32
Cleaning	39	43

Table 3.4: Housework-Related Informal Learning Topics,
Eligible Participants,* 1998–2004. Sources: NALL Survey, 1998; WALL Survey, 2004.
*Only those performing housework were asked questions about related informal
learning.

Table 3.5 summarizes informal learning associated with volunteer work. I hasten to point out that the majority of people are not actively engaged in organized volunteer activities. The current participation rate in volunteer organizations in Canada is around 45% (Hall, Lasby, Gumulka and Tryon, 2006). The main sorts of significant learning that volunteers recognize is related to interpersonal and communication skills they develop in working with other members and organization clients, as well as knowledge about the social issues their organizations address.

	1998	2004
Interpersonal Skills	62	56
Communication Skills	58	59
Social Issues	51	44
Managerial Skills	43	36

Table 3.5: Volunteer Work-Related Informal Learning Topics, Eligible Participants,* 1998–2004. Sources: NALL Survey, 1998; WALL Survey, 2004. *Only those who reported doing some volunteer work were asked questions about topics.

So, in terms of paid and unpaid work-related activities, these are the sorts of topics that adults readily recognize in terms of significant informal learning occurring in their own lives. The particular topics, the frequencies and the achieved competencies may vary substantially between societies and different social groups. But the pervasiveness of intentional work-related informal learning throughout our lives should be established as a reference point for future policy initiatives intended to increase or measure lifelong learning in relation to work.

With regard to general interests not specifically tied to work, Table 3.6 summarizes the most commonly recognized topics (compare Tough, 1979). The issue that is most central to most people is health and well being. If you think about your own life, that's probably the issue you have been most preoccupied with learning about informally throughout the different phases. Finances and leisure/hobby activities also consistently involve the majority, the first out of necessity for economic well-being, the second though genuine free choice.

	1998	2004
Health and Well-Being	74	63
Finances	58	44
Leisure / Hobby	58	53
Social / Personal Skills	55	47
Public and Political Issues	51	48
Computers	50	44
Sports and Recreation	49	43
Cultural Traditions	42	40
Intimate Relationships	41	33
Religion and Spirituality	40	38
Science and Technology	35	32
Language Skills		23

Table 3.6: General Interest Informal Learning Topics, All Respondents, 1998–2004. Sources: NALL Survey, 1998; WALL Survey, 2004.

More generally, particularly in terms of the concern with learning technologies, a growing proportion of the population is actively engaged in using computers in relation to varied informal learning activities. Computerization may be the most prominent trend in our lives. Those of us who are beyond middle age can recall a time when computers were not very involved in everyday life. Today they percolate into virtually every sphere of our existence in some way. According to the WALL survey and other sources, over 80% of Canadians now indicate that they use computers. But, if we contrast the large majority who are using computers with the minority of mostly older people who are not, we find that there is only a slight positive mediating effect of computers on engagement in informal learning. The vast majority of people who are not computer users also actively engage in informal learning.

The WALL network findings lead to the conclusion that we should not reify learning by identifying it with the frequent use of computers or other tools. Nor should we presume that informal learning is always directly mediated by tools. Reflective learning is central to our lives. It's profound, it's often of high quality and relevance. Measures of learning via tools or tests are inevitably limited.

Estimations of prior learning experience that permit people to demonstrate competencies in various fields of knowledge in order to gain recognition or reward in formal education programs or employment can be quite constructive (see Livingstone and Myers, 2007). But measures by open learning centres and other formal educational institutions of the competencies that people have attained in their everyday lives can only appreciate the extent of the learning that people are doing in minimal ways. As with the mobile learning researcher-lovers, I would suggest that some learning is best left to the appreciation of each of the learners themselves.

3. Discussion

3.1 Formal qualifications, informal learning, and employment

The basic results regarding the relationship between formal educational credentials and employment are presented in (Livingstone, 2004; Livingstone et al., 2009). More and more people are getting more and more formal educational credentials and there is a growing phenomenon of underemployment (a.k.a. "underutilization", "overqualification" or "overeducation"); that is to say, growing numbers of people have a greater level of educational qualification than their jobs require. Something of the order of 30% of the current employed workforce has a greater a credential than is required either for entry into their jobs or performance of their jobs. A large array of studies confirm this pattern, including the most recent "UK Skills Survey" (Felstead, Gallie, Green and Zhou, 2007).

What can we do about underemployment? The historical tendency in dealing with economic problems has been to propose educational solutions.

In the post WWII period, it seemed logical – since there was an expanding economy and people had relatively low levels of schooling – to put a greater emphasis on training people for various technical occupations. So we did. The correspondence between economic growth and increasing formal educational participation led people to believe that more education would produce more economic growth. That is not the case now. People are continuing to get more formal education, the economic growth pattern is spotty at best and we have increasing underemployment. The logical solution to that, at least from my standpoint, is to modify the job structure. That means things like democratization of work, more extensive distribution of decision making and technical discretion for people who are in lower level positions, and job enrichment. It means creation of new types of green jobs and the redistribution of work time so the polarization between people who are working too long and people who are not employed at all or not working long enough to meet their needs is modified to some extent. These are all obvious options that have some practical feasibility if there is political will to address underemployment. There is a lot of interest among ordinary people in different workforces/workplaces to move in these directions. But we have not found the political imagination or will to go very far yet.

Arguing for still more emphasis on education in general is not going to resolve the economic problems. The "new economy" is not likely to emerge in a straightforward, generative way from greater educational investment. The solution is not to wind down formal educational institutions nor to diminish efforts to address the educational needs of more marginalized populations (clearly continuing access for those with little schooling and low level literacy is needed so they are not left behind by the "credential society"). But the basic point here is that we have got it wrong in terms of the general solution to our economic problems. The essential solutions are economic reforms, not educational reforms.

Education is a basic right. More flexible educational institutions such as the Open University can respond effectively to a wide diversity of educational needs, including the needs of more marginalized populations for programs that recognize relevant prior experiential learning. For the majority of the population who are now increasingly highly formally educated, there will continue to be areas of specialized need and special interest where specialized courses and information resource bases can facilitate ongoing learning. In a dynamic, advanced market economy, there are always areas of under-supply or over-supply of workers with technical specializations. Some of the shortages, such as skilled trades in Canada, may be chronic. But most skill shortages can be addressed by concerted educational initiatives in fairly short order. Conversely, chronic underemployment of the many who have educational qualifications exceeding their job requirements is an enduring problem that will not be resolved by still more education.

Those with educational qualifications continue to seek more education. School dropouts do not become discouraged informal learners. Learning remains endemic among homo sapiens. Institutional barriers to learning and its recognition should be broken down wherever possible. We need a suppleness in our educational programming to respond to a changing environment and a humility to admit that evaluative efforts to comprehend the depths of knowledge of informal learners will always be a substantially limited project. But we also need wider visions to address economic problems with economic solutions.

We have spent a lot of our energy on trying to find educational solutions to a wide array of economic and social problems. We need to recognize that education cannot do everything. We cannot find secular salvation through education if we are dealing with an economic issue.

3.2 Intentional and non-intentional informal learning

The iceberg of adult learning is largely under the surface. The surveys that we have done, in particular, can only ask people about what they're consciously aware of. There is only a very short time to ask the questions in a telephone survey and people's own self-reports will only address this conscious awareness. So I want to clearly circumscribe that notion and not to presume that what they are telling us with their conscious mind of the moment is reflective of anything close to the totality of the learning in which they are actually involved. There is a great deal of passive learning that all of us do from the early socialization in our lives and a lot of incidental tacit learning that is vital to our continuing lives. So I do not want to suggest that surveys of informal learning are capturing or really reflecting the full extent of the informal learning activities that we do. Learning is in some ways coterminous with our being.

But I think it is important for educators to realize that we face people coming from diverse experiential learning situations, that they are trying to combine our formal curricula with often vast forms of tacit informal knowledge and that we should be prepared to be resource facilitators for people who are coming with different motivations, different agendas, and who will take the material we give them most effectively if they can connect it quite directly with their own problems and their own specific situations, rather than having a standardized curriculum in all cases. Disciplined understanding of bodies of formal knowledge such as language grammars and scientific principles is important as a base for much continuing adult learning. But in our "information age", many people have a systematized, cumulative understanding of the world. In most cases, it's a matter of resource educators respecting this and helping people to continue to enhance their own understanding of the world through their intentional learning efforts.

3.3 Informal learning experiences and employability

Generally, informal learning experiences are being undervalued by employers, and certainly by job advertisements. It's somewhat ironic because, in formal terms, we have a growing situation of underemployment with a surplus of credentialed education in many spheres of work. But at the same time, there is an underappreciation of the informal learning that people are doing. There is a burgeoning literature on workplace learning which recognizes that most of the knowledge that people have acquired to do their jobs is through informal on-the-job training (e.g. Livingstone and Sawchuk, 2004). On-the-job learning from more experienced workers is the pivotal part of job knowledge, in particular, the mentoring that older workers do for younger workers. This becomes a graphic problem when younger workers are laid off, older workers retire, and then there is virtually nobody who retains the real tacit knowledge to keep the workplace moving. In any event, the basic point is that informal knowledge of workers is underestimated, underappreciated by employers, by the labor movement and by workers themselves.

What can be done? Give more attention to the experience that people bring to the job through use of richer portfolio profiles. Various employers do some of this in ad-hoc ways through their interviews and assessment of resumes. Prior learning experience is severely underestimated in job entry processes. Most young people today get some job experience while still in school. Growing numbers are formally involved in co-operative work-study programs. But most of this prior learning remains disconnected from the hiring process for post-school jobs.

It could well be that one consequence of the current research interest in "lifelong learning" is that prior learning assessment and mobile learning assessment initiatives will be used increasingly to measure informal learning activities. You might anticipate that, a decade from now, the mobile learning activities that you are starting to measure and assess could become part of the resumes that people are presenting to employers. One needs to be cautious again about the extent to which you use these kinds of measures as vehicles for differentiation among people either in employment, civil society or life generally.

4. Concluding Remark

These findings based on recent Canadian national surveys may be pertinent to understanding relations between work and learning in most advanced market economies. There is a wealth of additional relevant material on the (www.wallnetwork.ca) website. Readers are encouraged to use this research as a resource as they grapple with the potential and perils of mobile learning. The literature on informal learning, its relation to paid and unpaid work, and the issues regarding its assessment/accreditation may be particularly pertinent as pressures to understand and evaluate informal learning supported by mobile technologies mount.

References

Colley, H., Hodkinson, P. and Malcom, J. (2003). *Informality and formality in learning*. London: Learning and Skills Research Centre

Eichler, M. (2005). The other half (or more) of the story: Unpaid household and care work and lifelong learning. In N. Bascia, A. Cumming, A. Datnow, K. Leithwood and D.W. Livingstone (eds), *International handbook of educational policy* (Vol. 13). Dordrecht: Springer

Felstead, A., Gallie, D., Green, F. and Zhou, Y. (2007). *Skills at Work, 1986 to 2006*. Oxford: ESRC Centre of Skills, Knowledge and Organizational Performance

Hall, M., Lasby, D., Gumulka, G. and Tryon, C. (2006). *Caring Canadians, Involved Canadians: Highlights from the 2004 Canada Survey of Giving, Volunteering and Participating*. Ottawa: Minister of Industry

Livingstone, D.W. (1999). Exploring the icebergs of adult learning: Findings of the first Canadian survey of informal learning practices. *Canadian Journal for the Study of Adult Education*, 13(2), 49–72

Livingstone, D.W. (2004). *The education-jobs gap: Underemployment or economic democracy* (2nd ed.). Aurora, ON: Garamond Press

Livingstone, D.W. (2005). Informal learning: Conceptual distinctions and preliminary findings. In Z. Bekerman, N. Burbules and D. Silberman (eds), *Learning in places: The informal education reader*. Berlin: Peter Lang, pp. 203–228

Livingstone, D.W. (2007). Age, Occupational Class and Lifelong Learning: Findings of a 2004 Canadian Survey of Formal and Informal Learning through the Life Course. Keynote address to "The times they are a-changin': researching transitions in lifelong learning" conference, Centre for Research on Lifelong Learning, University of Stirling, Scotland, 22–24 June 2007

Livingstone, D.W. (2008). Re-exploring the Icebergs of Adult Learning: Comparative Findings of the 1998 and 2004 Canadian Surveys of Formal and Informal Learning Practices. *Canadian Journal for the Study of Adult Education*, 21(2), 1–24

Livingstone, D.W. and contributors. (forthcoming, 2009). *Education and Jobs: Exploring the Gaps*. Toronto: University of Toronto Press

Livingstone, D.W., and Myers, D. (2007). "I might be overqualified": personal perspectives and national survey findings on prior learning assessment and recognition in Canada. *Journal of Adult and Continuing Education*, 13(1), 27–52

Livingstone, D.W., and Sawchuk, P. (2004). *Hidden knowledge: Organized labour in the information age*. Toronto: Garamond Press and Lanham, MA: Rowman and Littlefield

Marsick, V. and Watkins, K. (2001). Informal and incidental learning. *New Directions on Adult and Continuing Education*, 89, 25–34

Smith, M. (2000). Informal learning. Available at www.infed.org [accessed on 28 September 2007]

Tough, A. (1979). *The Adult's Learning Projects: A Fresh Approach to Theory and Practice in Adult Learning*. Toronto: OISE Press

Suggested Readings

Collins, R. (1979). The Credential Society: An Historical Sociology of Education and Stratification. New York: Academic Press

PART II
Frameworks

4. In the Workplace:
Learning as Articulation Work, and Doing Articulation Work to Understand Learning

PHILLIP KENT

Overview

This chapter offers an account of a methodological approach to understanding and developing learning that has been successfully used in a research project on mathematical skills in workplaces. The approach makes use of the concept of articulation work, which is concerned with the processes of coordination and integration by which different social worlds intersect and negotiations take place between them, and the role of "symbolic boundary objects" as mediators for negotiation. Suggestions on the relevance of articulation work for research on informal and mobile learning are made.

1. Introduction: Articulation work

This chapter describes using the concept of articulation work in the development of a methodological framework that was part of a project which investigated mathematical skills in workplaces, and developed novel forms of learning interventions to support employees in developing new skills.

The concept of articulation work was developed by the sociologist Anselm Strauss (1993), to account for the under-valued and often "invisible" forms of work (particularly, for him, the work of women at home and at work) which are nevertheless critical to the completion of tasks in everyday life, or in workplaces (see also Livingstone, this volume). Suchman

(1996) presents the striking example of a legal office in which the attorneys (almost all male) regarded the work of their (almost all female) "document coding" support staff (that is, doing the preparation of the database index of the hundreds or thousands of documents involved in each legal case) as "mindless", yet upon investigation the work was seen to involve many aspects of judgements based upon knowledge and practical experience; moreover, it was judged that the support staff were sufficiently skilled to be capable of doing some of the work done by junior attorneys, but this capability was not recognised by the attorneys. Suchman's example shows a feature which we have also observed, that undeveloped capacities exist amongst "lower-skilled" employees which could be developed or enhanced through appropriate learning of technical skills. In the case considered in my research, these are "techno-mathematical" skills, which conventional workplace training cannot easily address, and the research has pursued methods of developing mathematical software tools to support "technology enhanced" learning and practice in the workplace.

In Strauss' terms (cf. Hampson and Junor, 2005; Suchman, 1996), articulation work is the coordination and integration that must go on such that organisational arrangements between the "social worlds" inhabited by people are established, maintained and revised. Strauss (1993, p. 212) defines a social world in terms of there being a primary *activity* (or more than one); *sites* where the activity occurs; *technology* that is involved; and *organisations* that evolve to further one or more aspects of the world's activity.[1] Here "organisations" refers to both formal organisational structures of, say, a workplace, but also the informal structures that evolve amongst employees to maintain the practice. Such informal structures, perhaps hardly recognised by senior managers, can be very important: in one customer service department that we observed (see Kent et al., 2007) the employees had developed their own "library" of information relating to different types

---

[1]   There are similarities here to the "cultural-historical activity theory" approach (cf. Mwanza-Simwami, this volume), which has been used in our other writings (Kent et al., 2007; Bakker et al., 2006). In order to keep my thread of argument simple, I will not discuss these similarities in this short paper. (Cf. also Fjuk, Nurminen, and Smordal, 1997.)

of customer queries – and they wanted to be entrusted by managers to do more of such information organisation. "Interactional" processes are central to articulation work, including negotiating, compromising and educating. Social worlds intersect along "fluid boundaries" (Strauss, 1993) which are continually negotiated, and I am particularly interested in the technological and mathematical artefacts ("symbolic boundary objects" – see below) through which these boundary negotiations take place.

In the following, I will discuss the different uses made of the articulation work concept as part of an educational research project on mathematical skills in workplaces.[2] (N.B. most of the research had been carried out before use was made of articulation work in analysing it, so what is presented here involves some re-interpretation of research activity – the point is that there we discovered a close fit between the ideas of articulation work and how we had conducted our research.) The aim of this research was to understand the nature of mathematical skills in practice and to identify any "skills gaps", and then to develop learning interventions to support the improvement of employees' skills. If work is interpreted as articulation work, then attempting to extend the capabilities of employees through learning interventions can be seen as an exercise in articulation work in which employees attempt to integrate the results of learning into their existing practices. We used the articulation work concept in three connected ways:

- as an analytical description of how mathematical knowledge and skills become integrated within working practices;

- as a principle for the design of software-based mathematical tools ("technology-enhanced boundary objects") to support learning in workplaces; and

2   Techno-mathematical Literacies in the Workplace project, 2003–2007. See www. lkl.ac.uk/research/technomaths.

- as a methodological principle for conducting workplace research which may probe into the nature of mathematical thinking and learning "in context".

The next three sections consider each of these points in turn.

2. Mathematics in the workplace: Articulation work in financial services

In our research in workplaces, I and my colleagues were interested in the role of mathematical skills in a range of workplace types, one of these being customer service call centres for financial services companies, which were providers of pension and investment or mortgage products direct to customers (Kent, Noss, Guile, Hoyles, and Bakker, 2007; Hoyles et al., in preparation). Articulation work is central to this type of work, since it is all about the employee's ability to articulate between the informational needs of the customer and the IT-based information systems which store and process the customer and product information.

We found that the articulation work of customer services was very often compromised by a lack of mathematical understanding on the part of employees; indeed, their roles had generally been setup not to require such understanding. This is perhaps not surprising, given the shortage of mathematical skills in the (United Kingdom) labour market, and the wage premium employers must pay to obtain them. Thus, among the social worlds within a company which interact around the IT system, there has been an intentional system design on the part of managers and financial-mathematical experts such that the mathematical models and relationships used for the calculations within the IT system have been made to be invisible, except to those expert employees.

Why should this matter for companies? The informational needs and expectations of customers are changing; customers want to know more, and this puts a pressure on customer service employees to explain more, which challenges the mathematical understanding of both employee and customer. An example of lack of understanding that we observed involved pension customers seeking information about the annual pension statement which had been sent to them, which contained a projected value of their pension at the point of retirement (see Figure 4.1). The projection was based on a mathematical calculation (compound interest) that was unknown to the employees; thus they could only provide scripted responses to customer questions (likely not to satisfy the customer), or pass the customer query on to technical departments (an expensive exercise for the company).

Our research involved trying to find means of developing employee understanding of some of the mathematical calculations that featured in the IT systems they worked with. They reported dissatisfaction in that they perceived calculations as "just magic", and we wanted to replace such perceptions with a solid (although necessarily limited) understanding of what was happening. A need for informal learning presented itself: informal in the sense of being unlike (formal) school maths, and drawing on employees' personal experiences and understandings. Any attempt to introduce "school maths" would alienate most employees, and fail to take account of the complexities of the workplace context. The learning was informal, also, in that our time with the employees could only be very short, thus we wanted to offer tools and ideas to the employees which would allow them informally to work on changing their own understanding and practice over an extended period of time.

3. Learning as articulation work: Technology-enhanced boundary objects

The key to the approach we took to mathematical learning was to make use of the "symbolic boundary objects" that form part of practice, that is, the graphs and numerical tables that are the inputs and outputs of the IT systems. Figure 4.1 shows an example of a pension statement that proved problematic for communication between employee and customer.

The pension statement is a regulated document: the rules for the calculations used and the form of wording are prescribed by the national regulator (the UK Financial Services Authority). The pension projection involves two models/calculations, one of which is simple and the other much more complicated. The first calculation is the growth of the policy holders' investment by *compound interest*, at rates of 5, 7 or 9% per annum (like a cash savings account); these provide the numbers in the "at age 60 ..." row. It is pertinent to ask, and customers do, why compound interest should be relevant to a pension, which is equity-based and not a cash investment; the answer is that, looking back 40 to 50 years, the historical performance of equity-based investments has consistently averaged around 7% per annum, though in any short period it can be well below or well above this average. It is also pertinent to ask (and customers do) why the values of 5, 7, and 9% are used, when UK bank interest rates have been around 5% for many years; customers sometimes ask "why didn't my pension grow by 7% last year? Isn't that the average growth?" – a confusion of model and reality which we found service employees could only answer by quoting from standard scripts. It is also not easy to think of pensions as long-term investments, as nearly all investments that we deal with are for considerably shorter periods of time.

The second calculation/model, which converts the lump sum cash value to an annuity (paid out at regular periods for the rest of the life of the customer) is very complex, as it is based on mortality statistics of thousands of previous pension customers; we quickly decided that developing a simplified model of this was impractical in the time we had available to engage with employees. Indeed, the issue of compound interest proved complex enough in itself – a surprising result for us at the time, as we had initially thought the mathematics involved would be too simple. Steen's (2003) observation is relevant: "Mathematics in the workplace makes sophisticated use of elementary mathematics rather than, as in the classroom, elementary use of sophisticated mathematics." This observation about mathematics points to a general characteristic of formal learning, which favours "pure" knowledge (complex ideas, removed from realistic contexts) compared with informal learning (simple ideas, in complex, real contexts).

Statement date: 24 April 2005
Date of birth: 19 April 1961   Pension age: 60

Your fund value at the statement date is: £14,223 , no additional premiums to be paid

Projected benefits at pension age:

	Lower rate (5%)	Mid rate (7%)	Higher rate (9%)
At age 60 your fund would be	£31,000	£41,900	£56,500
This could buy a pension annuity of	£838 pa	£1,970 pa	£3,780 pa
OR			
A tax-free lump sum of	£7,760	£10,500	£14,100
and a pension annuity of	£629 pa	£1,480 pa	£2,840 pa

These are only examples and are not guaranteed – they are not minimum or maximum amounts. What you will get back depends on how your investment grows.

Figure 4.1: A simple example of a pension statement "symbolic boundary object". (Notes: (1) The pension annuity is calculated as a percentage of the "age 60" value, which in reality is adjusted (made higher) to compensate for life expectancy; the basic, non-adjusted percentage shown above is 2.3% less than the annual growth rate. Thus, Lower rate = 5% - 2.3% = 2.7%; (2) Management charges, not included here, will reduce the "age 60" value; (3) The tax-free lump sum is 25% of the "age 60" value; (4) the annuity with lump sum is the percentage of the remaining part (75%) of the "age 60" value.)

Service employees we spoke to knew that a compound interest calculation was used in the pension statement, and some could state what compound interest involves (it pays "interest on interest") but none were able to make a calculation, or could recognise the mathematical formula for it. Many did not distinguish between the fact that compound interest is a simple calculation, but annuity calculations are not – everything was "magic" performed by the IT system. Since the pension projection boundary object was central to employees' practice, we set ourselves the goal of helping employees to understand the overall mathematical structure of the projection, and to develop a detailed understanding of the compound interest model.

	A	B	C	D
4				
5	Year		Interest	Interest
6		Value	Earned	rate
7	0	14,223.00	711.15	5.00
8	1	14,934.15	=B8*D8/100	5.00
9	2	=B8+C8	784.04	5.00
10	3	16,464.90	823.25	5.00
11	4	17,288.15	864.41	5.00
12	5	18,152.55	907.63	5.00
13	6	19,060.18	953.01	5.00
14	7	20,013.19	1,000.66	5.00
15	8	21,013.85	1,050.69	5.00
16	9	22,064.54	1,103.23	5.00
17	10	23,167.77	1,158.39	5.00
18	11	24,326.16	1,216.31	5.00
19	12	25,542.46	1,277.12	5.00
20	13	26,819.59	1,340.98	5.00
21	14	28,160.57	1,408.03	5.00
22	15	29,568.60	1,478.43	5.00
23	16	31,047.03	1,552.35	5.00
24	Annuity	838.27		
25				
26	Lump sum	7761.76		
27	Annuity	628.70		

Figure 4.2: Extract from an Excel spreadsheet for simplified pension projections, for the case of 5% annual interest growth. Cells C8 and B9 show the two formulae in use, which simply repeat down the columns.

As a general principle for our research, we sought to adapt and modify symbolic boundary objects for the specific purposes of learning, incorporating them within software-based mathematical learning tools which we designed. We termed the resulting tools *technology-enhanced boundary objects (TEBOs)*. In this case, an appropriate mathematical software tool to investigate pension projections was a spreadsheet (Microsoft Excel), which is ideal for the construction of tabular data, and it allows users to do algebraic constructions through the use of "point and click" formulae, so that explicit algebraic language may be avoided (but it is there if users wish to look for it), and moreover the spreadsheet will do the work of carrying through the algebraic manipulations and calculations for particular numbers. Thus in dealing with pension statements, we asked employees to re-construct a pension statement such as Figure 4.1 in a spreadsheet, starting with the most simple case and then building in additional details (for example, management charges of various forms). See Figure 4.2.

An additional advantage of the spreadsheet is that it is software which most employees have access to on their own computers, and already use in the most basic fashion for recording or consulting information. Thus we could hope that employees might take on board the ideas we showed them for re-thinking their understanding of mathematics in their routine practices. Ideally, this would be supported by managers, though we encountered hesitancy about simply giving service employees more technical knowledge to deal with customer enquiries, without thinking through the forms of employee judgement that would be entailed, as there is a problem that the more information some customers (the "difficult" ones) would be given, the more they would want to know, and this could easily become unmanageable in the context of a telephone conversation. Though it may appear cynical, the managers' attitude was that some customer engagement would be better closed down than opened up; but giving employees better abilities to make technically-based judgements underlines exactly the issue of extending employees' capacities for articulation work.

4. Research as articulation work

In looking at articulation work inside workplaces, we as researchers are also doing articulation work, as we bring our social world into intersection with the social worlds of the workplace. In some sense, it is obvious that researchers must do this, but I would like to stress how necessary we found it to think of ourselves in this way, adopting the position of co-developers and co-teachers with company trainers and technical experts, rather than as outside educational experts who ("objectively") observe the situation and deliver a learning "solution".

We have also found ourselves as co-learners with learners, as the following example shows. We started our learning sessions for the pensions company with the following short exercise, concerning two hypothetical British tourists visiting the USA:

> Geoff and Susan book themselves a bargain long weekend break in New York City. Going into shops, they find it a bit confusing that all prices are given without "sales tax" added, and then a sales tax of 8% is added when they pay at the till.

> In one electronics shop, they find a special offer of all digital cameras with 15% discount. They decide to buy a camera which has an original (pre-discount) price of $250. At the till, the shop assistant takes 15% discount from the original price and then adds the sales tax.

> Geoff is not happy with this and complains to the manager: he thinks the assistant should add the sales tax first, and then take off 15%, because that way he will get a bigger discount.

> Who is right – Geoff or the manager – and why?

The initial employee reaction we got to the Shopping Trip question was a complete surprise to us: they insisted that only one way could be *legally* correct, an interpretation that simply had not occurred to us in designing the exercise: "the 8% tax has to be on the price paid, so the customer is not right." In *our* reading of the exercise, we looked through the hypothetical context to what mattered *to us*, thinking about the mathematical relationships involved, and understanding Geoff's situation in mathematical terms.[3]

---

3   There is *no difference* in the final price of the camera by one order of calculation or the other. Very few employees were able to answer this correctly, and quite a

In other words, we thought we had fully understood the problem context and knew what the employees needed to learn; in fact, the employees knew something that we needed to learn.

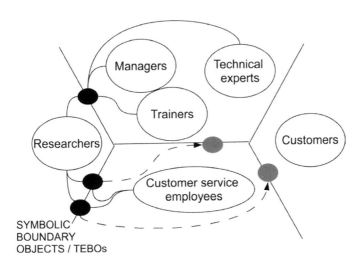

Figure 4.3: Boundary objects at the intersections of social worlds: we depict four zones with boundaries between them; black dots indicate symbolic boundary objects and TEBOs introduced by the researchers, which are used first as research tools for understanding the workplace organisation, then developing prototype learning resources for use in training; the intention is these boundary objects may be adapted into roles within the organisation (i.e. the dotted lines with arrows leading to the boundaries), to support training, practical engagement with customers, and engagement between customer services and technical departments within companies.

---

few mathematically-trained people who should know better likewise got it wrong. The mathematical structure of percentages is that multiplication is commutative (a formal way of saying that the order does not matter). One reason that employees do not ordinarily realise the structure is that when using electronic calculators, as they mainly do, one actually presses "+ 8 %" so that it appears to involve addition/subtraction. The act of devising percentage formulas in a spreadsheet forces attention on the mathematical structure of the "+ 8 %" key presses, and so on.

This shows that the "why" of the context is as crucial as the "what", and that "mathematical experts" should not expect to understand what matters mathematically in the context, without doing the detailed articulation work of negotiation with the social worlds of the context. And I think it is appropriate to call this articulation work, because researching in workplaces really did involve for us a continual negotiation and a very gradual, emergent coming-to-understand of the context. I also suggest that boundary objects (and their developments as TEBOs) are an especially valuable means for articulation work to take place.

5.   Conclusions

In summary, the research described here typically involved looking for workplace situations where there are "intended" boundary objects, through which sharing and communicating about knowledge are intended to happen, but fail to happen because of a lack of knowledge in one or more of the communities involved, or an effective means of mediating the knowledge for all. In such cases, we worked on learning interventions which aimed to introduce new boundary objects (usually technology-enhanced, TEBOs), which: (1) helped us to learn about the nature of the (mathematical) knowledge in the situation, through the process of co-designing with trainers/ managers, and (2) were intended to "repair" the flaws in the situation by introducing new (software-based) forms of mediation for the (mathematical) knowledge.

What I particularly like about this approach is that there is a continuous, coherent flow from initial observation of workplace practice around symbolic boundary objects, to the design of boundary objects which "capture" the mathematical concepts at issue in the practice, testing these through learning interventions, and moving finally towards the sustained use of the tools and ideas in workplace training and practice.

I will conclude with a few points about how the methodology described in this chapter may have wider relevance for research on informal learning (including mobile learning). Vavoula (2007) identifies the following as some of the key problems of researching informal learning (please note I am interpreting these in my own terms, not solely those of the original author):

- Capturing and understanding the context of the informal learning experience and how it interleaves with the learner's life context;

- Research needs to study not only the learning that occurs during a direct learning experience, but what happens afterwards in the subsequent accumulation of experiences;

- The subjects of the learning may not possess the appropriate skills for producing reflective accounts of their experiences (reflective accounts such as learner diaries being a common research device for informal learning);

- Informal learning outcomes are highly personal, and often hard to pinpoint, even for the learners themselves.

From the perspective of articulation work, a learning experience brings about a change in the learner's capacities for articulation work, within a certain context. For the purposes of research, we need to find out at least something about: (1) the prior state of knowledge and understanding of the learner; (2) what happened during the learning experience; (3) what changes occurred to the learner's capabilities/ behaviour after the learning experience.

The problems mentioned above relate to two basic research issues: *visibility of knowledge and learning*, and the *evolution of learning over time*. Boundary objects are a powerful means to increase the visibility of what learners understand and do not understand, and what might be "missing" in learners' understanding, in relation to a context. Things learnt informally are not made explicit in the same way as in formal learning; this is why, for example, learners may not be readily able to describe reflectively what they have learnt during a particular learning experience. By inviting learners to work with a boundary object (to do something, rather than talking/describing), there comes a need for them to *externalise* their knowledge and understanding, making it more visible to themselves (in terms of both prior knowledge and immediate outcomes of a learning experience), and to the observations of researchers (by the way, this principle is far from new – it can be dated back to 1970s work with Logo; Weir (1987) and Noss and Hoyles (1996) explain this principle in terms of how the act of working with (computer) tools opens up "windows" onto learners' thinking that would not otherwise exist). In the case of scientific and technical learning, the use of symbolic boundary objects – for example, the Excel spreadsheet in relation to the pension statement, above – the learners' manipulation of the symbols makes visible to researchers something about their developing processes of thinking, and the micro-details of learning.

Boundary objects may help to understand the evolution of learning over time, by affording researchers the possibility to look for changes in practice over medium-term timescales as evidence of learning – as the learner seeks to integrate boundary objects with their existing practice/ behaviour: that is, we provide TEBOs which extend the capabilities of the employee/learner, and look for the impacts of this on practice/behaviour. This is highly constrained in workplaces by internal and external rules/ regulations; for example, these would forbid the use of a crude spreadsheet model, such as we devised, as part of daily practice of customer service in pensions, as it may lead to incorrect information being offered to customers. However, the constraints on use of TEBOs are much looser in many other informal learning situations.

It is a notorious problem in educational research to engage "research users" and achieve long-term sustainability of learning interventions that begin as developments by research projects. For educational research in the UK, this has become a key issue as research funders, led by the large government research agencies, are placing increasing emphasis on the need for research to make impact on "users" of research beyond the academic confines of education and social science. The articulation work/boundary object approach engages organisations, and individuals within them, in a collaborative (co-designing, co-teaching) way that encourages the organisation to take control of what begins as researcher-led intervention.

Acknowledgements

The research work reported here was part of the "Techno-mathematical Literacies in the Workplace" project, 2003–2007, funded by the ESRC Teaching and Learning Research Programme (www.tlrp.org), Award Number L139-25-0119. The contributions of my project colleagues, Arthur Bakker, Celia Hoyles, and Richard Noss, to the development of the ideas presented in this chapter are gratefully acknowledged.

References

Bakker, A., Hoyles, C., Kent, P., and Noss, R. (2006). Improving work processes by making the invisible visible. *Journal of Education and Work*, 19(4), 343–361

Fjuk, A., Nurminen, M.I., and Smordal, O. (1997). Taking articulation work seriously – an activity theoretical approach. Technical report, Turku Centre for Computer Science, Finland. Available at http://heim.ifi.uio.no/~ftp/publications/others/OSmordal-5.pdf [accessed on 1 August 2008]

Hampson, I. and Junor, A. (2005). Invisible work, invisible skills: Interactive customer service as articulation work. *New Technology, Work and Employment*, 20(2), 166–181

Hoyles, C., Kent, P., Noss, R., and Bakker, A. (in preparation). *Improving Mathematical Learning in the Workplace*. To be published by Routledge–Falmer

Kent, P., Noss, R., Guile, D., Hoyles, C., and Bakker, A. (2007). Characterising the use of mathematical knowledge in boundary crossing situations at work. *Mind, Culture, and Activity* 14(1 and 2), 64–82

Noss, R. and Hoyles, C. (1996). *Windows on Mathematical Meanings: Learning Cultures and Computers*. Dordrecht: Kluwer Academic Publishers

Steen, L.A. (2003). Data, shapes, symbols: Achieving balance in school mathematics. In B. Madison and L.A. Steen (eds), *Quantitative literacy: Why literacy matters for schools and colleges*. Washington, DC: The Mathematical Association of America, pp. 53–74

Strauss, A.L. (1993). *Continual Permutations of Action*. New York: Aldine De Guyter

Suchman, L. (1996). *Supporting articulation work*. In R. Kling (ed.), *Computerization and controversy (2nd edition): Value conflicts and social choices*. Orlando, FL: Academic Press, pp. 407–423

Vavoula, G. (2007). Introduction to the workshop on research methods in informal and mobile learning. In Vavoula, G., Kukulska-Hulme, A., and Pachler, N. (eds), *Proceedings of the WLE Workshop on "Research Methods in Informal and Mobile Learning: How to get the data we really want"*. WLE Centre of Excellence, Institute of Education, London, 14 December 2007. www.milrm.wle.org.uk

Weir, S. (1987). *Cultivating Minds: A Logo Casebook*. New York: Harper and Row

5. "I Don't Really See It": Whither Case-based Approaches to Understanding Off-site and On-campus Mobile Learning?

NORBERT PACHLER, JOHN COOK, CLAIRE BRADLEY

Overview

This chapter reports on the methodological dimension of a qualitative study of the use of high-end mobile phones for off-site and on-campus mobile learning. The aim of the study was to investigate how mobile devices are being integrated by learners in their informal/private "space" and what use they make of mobile devices in formal learning contexts. The main focus of this chapter is on the research methods used in our study. The methodology draws on qualitative and narrative approaches to data collection and analysis focusing in the main on subjective and perceptual aspects of students' personal and study-related experiences in using mobile phones. With reference to relevant literature in the field, we discuss the relative merits of narrative and case-based approaches and seek to demonstrate their appropriacy in the study of mobile learning, with a particular emphasis here on data analysis.

1. Introduction

The use of mobile devices in UK Higher-Education (HE) is an under-explored area. Our related preliminary research (Cook, Bradley, Lance, Smith and Haynes, 2007) took the stance that a productive pedagogical vision is one that views the cultural emergence of innovative educational

practice in terms of what Bakardjieva (2005, p. 34) calls "user appropriation" or "technology-in-use-in-social-situations", and what we are terming
"learner-generated contexts" (Cook, 2007; LGC, 2007). Although the
preliminary study using a survey generated interesting results, we recognised that the analysis had only scratched the surface of the notion of
"appropriation". Therefore, using background data gathered as part of the
preliminary study, three students, who appeared to represent a broad range
of views, were invited to be involved in follow-up interviews. Essentially,
using initial interviews as the basis for their decisions, researchers (second
and third authors of this paper) in the preliminary study formed a view
of which participants were likely to provide a range of perspectives, from
being apparent positive adaptors of technology to sceptics. This chapter
foregrounds issues relating to research methodology. In two other papers
(Cook, Pachler and Bradley, 2008a and 2008b) we offer a detailed analysis
of the findings of this qualitative study and an in-depth discussion of the
notion of appropriation respectively.

The context for this research is UK Higher Education, where students
who were taking an MA module had to complete an assessment which
required them to gather data in the form of video clips and photos from an
off-campus event and give a presentation. They had to work in groups, and
each group had an online "mediaBoard" (developed by Tribal Education)
where they could upload their media files and share ideas about the assessment. Each student was loaned a Nokia N91 phone for a 7-week period
to help with the task, to ensure that they could all capture media, upload
it and communicate with each other (it was free to make calls amongst
themselves). Students already owned a mobile phone as well; we did not
stipulate the modes of communication that the students should use for
group work (i.e. they could use loaned phones, private phones or other
means at their disposal as they wished). They were asked not to make
unreasonable use of the phone to communicate with people outside of
the Vodafone network, but were encouraged to personalise the phones
e.g. to put music on them if they wished. They were of course able to use
their own phones or other devices (e.g. cameras, video cameras) if they
preferred to. They also had to answer certain questions (i.e. fill knowledge
gaps) that were posed by an "events checklist", a didactic intervention in

the form of a mobile learning object pre-installed on their phones. The learning design underpinning the events checklist intended to provide an appropriate mix between guiding learners' experiences of remote informal contexts (visiting a live media event to gather data for the assignment task) and providing formal assessment opportunities (e.g. PowerPoint presentation) for their onsite and off-site learning activities. Furthermore, the wider learning design also provided the opportunity for social construction of knowledge relating to meeting the learning outcomes for the formal assessment task (constructing a marketing plan for the live media event that the group visited) through the shared uploading environment (the proprietary mediaBoard (http://www.m-learning.org/products/mediaboard.htm)), and it included an explicit formal judgment on their attainment of the intended learning outcomes (see Cook et al., 2007 and Laurillard, 2007 for a detailed discussion).

The aim of the study was to investigate how mobile devices are being integrated by learners, in this case female international students in their mid twenties, in their informal/private "space" and what use they make of mobile devices in formal learning contexts. In particular, we were interested in the bases of the appropriation of new mobile communications systems. We expected to find novice users of the smartphones demonstrating agency in relation to discovering the relevance of mobile learning to their own contexts. In an attempt to gain richly textured insights into the ways in which learners integrate mobile devices, in particular mobile phones, into the private spheres of their everyday lives, we experimented with a case-based, narrative approach to data analysis in this study. Our approach was premised on the assumption that, through narrative, deeper messages can be communicated about the complex tapestry of socio-cultural practices around the use of mobile devices.

2. Methodological orientation

The methodology of this study draws on a range of different approaches to qualitative data research focusing in the main on subjective and perceptual aspects of students' personal and study-related experiences in using mobile phones. It can best be described as being "eclectically purposive", drawing loosely on narrative and case-based approaches underpinned loosely by the general principles of grounded theory. By eclectic we mean the process of the deliberate selection of those components to the various approaches to data which appear to best suit the aims and objectives of our study without feeling obliged to adhere slavishly to methods in the way their leading proponents might have prescribed. This we do not see as "selling out" to methodological relativism, rather as ensuring fitness for purpose of the chosen methods in relation to what the study set out to achieve.

Strauss and Corbin (1990) suggest that grounded theory is especially useful for complex subjects or phenomena where little is yet known – as arguably is the case in mobile learning. This is because of the flexibility of the methodology which can cope with complex data and which is characterised by continual cross-referencing between raw data and emergent categories; this allows for grounding of theory in the data, thus uncovering previously unknown issues. We have found grounded techniques useful as a way of guiding our research, where concepts are classified and grouped together under higher order, more abstract formations called categories. It is noteworthy that there is a productive tension between initial theories (e.g. Bakardjieva, 2005) that guide the formation of research questions and the putting of such preconceptions on hold whilst the data is analysed to build, possibly new, concepts out of that data.

Mobile learning is not only a complex and as yet little understood phenomenon, it is characterised by a plethora of often fluid and multi-layered contexts, and takes place across and between different geographical, physical, perceptual, virtual and/or temporal spaces. Moreover, mobile learning crosses traditional boundaries of public and private spaces, is inextricably bound up with learners' life worlds and it is, therefore, often more inconspicuous than traditional manifestations of learning and its attendant artefacts. Furthermore, mobile learning is facilitated and mediated by a range of technological tools with a diverse range of functional attributes and affordances requiring different prerequisites for effective utilisation. These characteristics make mobile learning very difficult to "pin down" empirically and afford (retrospective) metacognitive approaches, such as think-aloud protocols or reflective diaries/blogs, an important role in the research of mobile learning.

In order to gain the necessary insights into the processes governing mobile learning, particularly at the interface between the subjective and personal life worlds and experiences of the learners with the more formal requirements of Higher Education study, we decided to experiment with narrative approaches to research methodology in our study. Greenhalgh, Russel and Swinglehurst (2005, p. 443) rightly remind us of Bruner's (1986) distinction between logico-centric ("science of the concrete") and narrative ("science of the imagination") cognition. They note that conventional research paradigms usually focus on attempts at scientific rather than experiential dimensions of human cognition. With Greenhalgh et al. (2005) we would posit here the potential of narrative as a means of understanding processes of learning.

We consider it important to differentiate between the use of narrative qualitative research methods for data *collection* and data *analysis*. We focus here on the latter. Narrative data collection methods are normally based on eliciting biographical data from subjects and involve minimal interviewer intervention. They also usually involve a number of follow-up interviews to explore responses in more depth (see e.g. Wengraf, 2001). Alternatively, there is naturalistic story gathering through ethnographic approaches. Narrative data analysis we understand as the composition, post hoc, of narrative cases characterised by rich and authentic description on the basis of the qualitative data available from interview transcripts, reflective diaries, blog entries etc. The analysis in our study was characterised by an iterative inductive approach in which the "story" is allowed to emerge through systematic analysis and categorisation of available data in discussion with other researchers to achieve a certain degree of consensual interpretation (see also Greenhalgh, 2006, pp. 78–81).

Whilst acknowledging the potential benefits of narrative methods of data gathering, we deem the use of narrative for data analysis to have a higher level of efficacy. This is not because we view the inherent subjectivity of narrative as a disadvantage – far from it. We see it as an advantage, not least because in the case of this specific study we wanted to gather subjective data about the use genres and process of appropriation of mobile phones for informal learning. Subjectivity relates closely to the inherent pre-requisite of *good* stories: "not to convince by their objective truth but by their emotional impact on the reader" (Greenhalgh et al., 2005, p. 443). However, this "emotional impact" tends to be achieved not only or necessarily by the immediacy of the narrative but through such features as aesthetic appeal, metaphor, and moral order. In other words, narratives and stories[1] need to be carefully crafted and comprise certain building blocks such as chronology, emplotment,[2] trouble and embeddedness (see Greenhalgh et al., 2005, p. 443) in order to be effective. It is our contention here that, with the exception of immediacy, the researcher – for a number of reasons – is often better placed to construct "instructive" narratives, or cases as we prefer to call them, than the subjects themselves. For one, the researcher is not subject to the same constraints of time and is more readily able to "step back". Also, in all probability s/he will be more used to dealing with the metacognitive and stylistic burdens of constructing an instructive narrative. Post hoc "storying" allows for cases to be single or multi-authored, enables a dialogue between different researchers as well as a greater degree of reflexivity. It also allows for cases to be purposed and "repurposed": they can be written and re-written to foreground and background specific issues and themes, which emerged from the analysis:

> "Storying" the case – that is, constructing a chronological emplotted account of the key actions and events – is a way of selecting which data to focus on and which to omit. It is also a way of drawing meaning from different data sources and making causal links between aspects of the case, either tentatively (as hypotheses to be tested in further research) or more firmly as lessons or conclusions (if the links are particularly strong and plausible). (Greenhalgh et al., 2005, p. 446)

---

1   We use these terms interchangeably here.
2   Emplotment is understood here as narrative structuring.

In his chapter "From anecdote to narrative case studies", John Schostak (2006) points out the dangers inherent in researchers trying to account for experience by reminding his readers that "Life is not composed as a narrative"; and, "A narrative kills" (p. 141). Schostak illustrates this by way of one of his own case studies and notes that the profile in his account had become transfixed,

> borrowing its life from the interpretations made of others, haunting intertextually, later writings and readings. ... Yet life goes on ... . In accounting for a life, as in a profile, the little snippets of narrative told in an interview are sewn together to generate a different kind of unity from any that may be perceived by the teller. (p. 141)

With reference to Bourdieu's notion of "symbolic violence" as well as the notion of "the politics of interpretation", Schostak makes the valid point that "Each method like the scrape of a scalpel or the crushing of a hammer sculpts or shatters the data into a shape that fits" (p. 141). The operative word here for us is "each": whichever approach one chooses to adopt as researchers, one invariably encounters challenges that require careful handling. In this chapter, we try to overcome potential problems of interpretation by privileging the voice of individual subjects and emplotting them into a coherent narrative whole.

Schostak also talks about structuring, or more precisely the "structurality of the structuring ... through which data gets to be shaped into quasi-unities for all practical, political and ethical purposes" (p. 142). In particular, he stresses the importance of anecdotes, which he sees as a device to organise content temporally (p. 143) whilst acknowledging that it is not data of scientific procedure (p. 144):

> Thus, it can be argued that far from anecdotes being a weak form of "evidence", they provide – in their formal (logical, structural, relational) and substantive (or content) dimensions – the route into the underlying structures and processes constructed by individuals who occupy particular positions or ranges of positions in intersubjectively maintained networks. (pp. 144–145)

Whilst problematising some of the challenges and inherent dangers of using narratives, Schostak does argue for the collection of anecdotes in order to enable the studying of the "dynamic, multi-dimensional and multi-layered narrative frameworks through which everyday and professional experience and action is organized" (p. 145). He sees anecdotes, the term he uses for narrative elements with specific qualities, as providing the building blocks and structure for cases which, in his view, can offer "a powerful means of establishing the evidence base necessary to inform the development of theory, critique and thus inform judgement, decision making and the implementation of courses of action" (p. 145). However, he warns of mimesis, of falling prey to believing in a seemingly realistic and unproblematic representation of reality characterised by a "mirage of integrity and cohesion" (p. 145). Instead, he argues for what he calls "a poetics of the real" with its function of "suspending assumptions concerning what is and is not real". He sees this poetics of the real operationalised in cases "as sites of multiple views for the construction, elaboration and exploration of experience" (p. 150). Interestingly, he also stresses the importance of hegemony in narrative cases, which describe how power is organised (pp. 152, 158). The final element of narratives Schostak delineates is what he calls "the plays of position, interest and transgression" which describe what actions and decisions are available to individuals (pp. 155–156, 159).

A discussion of narrative methodology also needs to make reference to Lee Shulman's (1996) case-based learning which, whilst rooted in teacher education and development, is of interest in the context of research in mobile learning for the possible structure it affords to document mobile phone use and mobile learning practices, thereby making them less ephemeral and rendering them accessible for analysis and discussion. Shulman (1996) rightly posits that cases "take advantage of the natural power of narrative ways of knowing"(p. 199). Shulman views cases as "ways of parsing experience so that practitioners" – and researchers, we would argue – "can examine and learn from it" and he sees them comprising intention/anticipation, vicissitude/chance, judgement and analysis/reflection (p. 213). Shulman acknowledges that the act of transformation of an experience into a narrative requires and entails selection and conceptualisation but he views this act as being less problematic than Schostak, namely as an "act of theory", i.e. as active engagement in the process of theory building (pp. 208–209). Shulman views case construction and analysis as an important aspect of professional learning and delineates four constitutive processes of case building and professional learning from cases: enactment, narration, connection (or recounting) and abstraction (p. 209). In his view, case-based learning supports all the conditions for "effective, substantive and enduring learning", namely: activity or agency, reflection or meta-cognition, collaboration and the formation of a community (p. 210).

We agree with Greenhalgh et al. (2005, p. 443) who note that narrative research raises epistemological questions about the nature of narrative truth which, in turn, has implications for other key concepts of and issues in research such as rigour, reliability, validity and replicability. We welcome such a debate; indeed, it is our hope that this chapter will foster it in the field of mobile learning research. Epistemological questions particularly come into focus in relation to one specific strength of storying, also noted by Greenhalgh et al. (2005, p. 444), namely its ability to offer insights into "what might have been", through researchers deliberately or unconsciously using some "literary licence" and their imagination by going beyond the data. Greenhalgh et al. (2005, p. 448) delineate a set of questions, which, they posit, can help to inform judgements about when narrative can be classified as research and when not. These include intentionality,[3] adherence to a recognisable, and we would add coherent and appropriate, methodological approach, rigour and transparency, reflexive awareness, identifiability of units of analysis and reference to a recognisable theoretical frame.

---

3   Probably best understood here as the intention to explain how learners engage with the world and come to understand it.

3. Study set-up

The questions that guided our research were:

- What are the learners' personal stories concerning their use of mobile devices?

  ◊ If it is in evidence, where does the learners' fascination with technology come from?

  ◊ What are the affective issues (do they think it is cool, fun, etc)?

  ◊ How would the learners change the technology if they could?

- Could learners see themselves using this mobile learning technology regularly for personal, work-based and/or more formal educational use in the future?

- Was there an appropriation of the technological tools by motivated learners?

In order to answer these research questions, in-depth interviews with three course participants were conducted on the basis of purposive sampling. In preparation for the interviews a set of interview questions was drafted, and agreed, around each of the research questions. These interview questions framed our interests and constituted a semi-structured approach to ensure that each student would, as far as possible, be asked the same questions and that all our research interests would be covered in each interview. Initial questions were focussed on putting the interviewee at ease and asking about their first uses of mobile phones to provide useful background contextual information.

The interviews were conducted on a one-to-one basis by one of the researchers, who was already known to the students from earlier evaluation activities during the study. The researcher was not part of the teaching or assessment team. Each interview was scheduled to last about an hour. It was recorded and transcribed verbatim to preserve the precise language used by the students.

The interview transcripts were analysed qualitatively using an iterative inductive approach to the data whereby themes were allowed to emerge through systematic reading by three coders, the authors of this paper. The themes were then used to categorise the data (see the brief discussion section below for the emergent themes). Throughout the analysis of the data, which took place with a view to composing narrative cases, the researchers were also mindful of the five overlapping stages of narrative analysis delineated by Muller (1999) and referred to by Greenhalgh et al. (2005, p. 444):

- entering the text (reading and preliminary coding to gain familiarity);
- interpreting (finding connections in the data through successive readings and reflection);
- verifying (searching the text and other sources for alternative explanations and confirmatory and disconfirming data);
- representing (writing up an account of what has been learned); and
- illustrating (selecting representative quotes).

Our methodological approach was modelled on Daly, Pachler, Pickering and Bezemer (2006). In common with Daly et al. (2006), we were in an ongoing dialogue about the "principles of meaningful interpretation, or what constitutes a 'good story' in terms of yielding meanings which have value" (p. 5) in the context of the research questions. And, we also attempted to be guided by Greenhalgh's (2006, pp. 9–12) criteria of a good story (quoted here from Daly et al., 2006, p. 5):

- Aesthetic appeal: the narrative is pleasing to hear and recount; it contains an internal harmony
- Coherence: the narrative is clear and makes a logical whole; it contains a "moral order" or sense
- Authenticity: the narrative has credibility, based on the experiences of the listeners/readers

- Reportability: "the 'so what' value" of what is narrated; its significance

- Persuasiveness: the narrative convinces of the teller's own perspective.

In the research reported here, these criteria are not so much seen as characteristic of the learners' narratives (as these were circumscribed by a number of specific interview questions), but rather of the sample cases we constructed out of the interview data.

4. The case of Émilie[4]

Three narrative case studies have been created from the responses given by each of the students in their interview. One of them is reproduced below as an example: all three cases are presented and analysed in detail in Cook, Pachler and Bradley, 2008a.

Émilie is a 23-year-old international student from Belgium who moved to England in order to do her Masters degree. She considers her IT experience and mobile phone ability to be adequate.

Émilie has owned a mobile phone from the age of 18, the first being a hand-me-down from her sister who was given it by her boyfriend. It was a promotional phone which she wanted to change to a "cooler" model to get rid of the logo of a multinational soft drink company that adorned it visibly, despite being very happy with the phone.

Émilie places importance on the device being affordable, easy to handle – "I just want to click on the one button" – "cool" and "nice", without explaining in detail how these adjectives best be defined. Other characteristics she values in a mobile phone are "flatness" and battery life. For Émilie

---

4   Pseudonyms are used instead of student's real names and informed consent was sought from participants.

ease of use is the main criterion that influences her purchase decisions. She professes to problems with working advanced features of mobile phones – "I have difficulties learning new technologies" – and, therefore, doesn't place much importance on them, although she admits to have been tempted into buying her current phone on the lure of it coming with Bluetooth, even if she doesn't (know how to) use it. Functionality, she says, "is nice to have", but she doesn't "have the urge" to actively use the features.

Émilie's main uses of her mobile phone are phoning and texting – an assertion that the quantitative user data from her project phone corroborates (taken from Table of phone usage, not provided here due to space limitations). She describes herself as being "quite old fashioned" in relation to technology and asserts that she "just wants to keep in contact with some people". She also describes herself as a "lagger": "I will first see and hear from other people how new technology is". By way of an example she mentions her adoption of an iPod which she had as a present from her partner and which, she says, she would never have bought for herself as it is too expensive and because she doesn't "really need it". Interestingly, once Émilie had worked out how to use the project phone as an MP3 player, she would do so with delight: "But once I got the hang of it ..., it was really painful to give it back ...". Also, she can see herself use a Personal Digital Assistant (PDA) once she has matured from being a student into a business setting and might need it. She watches fellow train passengers using their PDAs with interest.

Émilie views manuals as a barrier to learning about the functionality of mobile phones: "... when I buy a new phone, I'm really enthusiastic about it. I want to know everything so I start reading the manual and after the first page I'm already like, I don't want to read this anymore". Her description of how she best learns about using the functions of her project phone foregrounds learning by doing and the social dimension of the learning process in that she mentions the sharing of knowledge in a group as being conducive: "... within the group, I said to a friend, tell me now, step by step, how I have to upload that software and stuff like that ...". "But we didn't really sit down and discuss how you could use the phone. It's like more when you're doing stuff. It's like, how do you do this? Do you know that?

Yes. And you learn much quicker in that way than reading it from a book or a manual. In that way we shared some knowledge."

Émilie views mobile phones as essential for herself in particular and adults more generally to keep in contact with friends and family and for making practical, every-day arrangements such as being picked up by her partner from the station – "I can't live without it" – but not necessarily for children and teenagers: "I see sometimes young children of 7 years old already have a mobile, then I ask myself the question why they have that".

The social networking dimension provides a clear motivation for Émilie: "You need it for group work because if you can contact each other because you never know when people are going to ... check their emails so it's always nicer to give them a text or a call." "And then, yes, it's just to keep in contact with each other because we only see each other 8 hours a week with student colleagues so we have to keep in touch with each other, mainly to do group work."

Émilie sees herself immune to peer pressure and not as a fashion victim: "I'm not going to buy things because the other ones have it". However, later in the interview, she does admit that "it's nice to show off".

When asked about using her own mobile for learning purposes, Émilie is quite categorical: "I don't really see the point in using a mobile for learning purposes". "Ok, you can take pictures with your own phone but I don't really see it, having a mobile added to your learning purposes because you already have the internet, you already have the learning platforms specially designed for group work. It's going to be too much media and people are going to get confused ..."; "... it was just so confusing. You had to check that platform every day. You had to check your e-mail every day. Then, oh, yes, your phone is ringing with that information". "The only thing I thought was good for learning purposes is when you send a message on our phone to say, like, class is changed, or check your email. That was nice. I really liked that"; "I can't see us doing that with a mobile, taking notes"; she didn't use the learning content on the mobile phone, but thinks "there is potential in it".

Émilie has a good concept of what informal learning might be but she is not prepared to see mobile phones as making a contribution to it: "No. School side no, I don't use my mobile. If I want to learn something personally, informally, no, I don't use it. I just use it for basic things and that's it. It's not like, if I walk in a forest or something and I spot a nice tree, I'm going to take a picture of it and take it with me back home and look it up on the internet and see what it is. If that's what you mean by informal learning, I'm not going to do that." Curiously, not because she can't conceptualise the role of mobile phones, but "Because I'm not interested in it (informal learning). Maybe if I found things that interest me, maybe I would do it then. What interests me? That's a hard one. Maybe if you have a particular interest in, I don't know, motor shows or something, and you want to learn about it, then maybe why not take pictures. But then again if I went to a motor show I would take my digital camera with me which is more convenient. So, no, personally I wouldn't use my mobile for learning."

5. Discussion and analysis

Three such case studies were generated, but only one is featured in this chapter (all three cases are presented and analysed in detail in Cook, Pachler and Bradley, 2008a). The three students are not necessarily representative of the large mobile phone user base and confined to a small sample of female international students in their mid twenties who, whilst not early adopters, have all been part of the early large wave of mobile phone users. All three participants are well educated and belong to a particular socio-economic stratum, and provide a fascinating tapestry of attitudes to and practices of mobile phone use. Whilst we make no claims that our – necessarily brief – analysis of the rich data here is generalisable more widely, we can see a number of broad categories emerge from the data that constitute variables that impact on existing mobile phone use and conceptualisations of potential uses, namely:

- user biographies;
- technical skills of users and functionality of devices as barriers or facilitators;
- "techno-centricity" of users, and how this relates to conceptualisations of identity;
- attitudes towards learning; and
- user attitudes towards social networks.

Émilie's mobile phone practices in social and learning contexts, for example, appear highly bound up with her attitudes towards technology as well as her conceptualisation of herself as a social being. She has perceptual barriers about informal learning: her fraught relationship with advanced technical functionality coupled with her reluctance to use manuals to acquire new skills sets as well as, even more importantly, her seemingly high affective filter about informal learning conspire against her ability, and willingness, to conceptualise imaginative mobile phone uses and practices, particularly for informal learning.

We leave it to the judgement of our readers to determine the extent to which Émilie's case is cognisant of the wide-ranging methodological considerations discussed above as well as to determine whether it success-fully address Greenhalgh's 2006 criteria of a good story. The experience of constructing cases out of the raw data can add considerable value, for example to the presentation of the interview transcripts, inter alia in rela-tion to the aesthetic appeal of the findings presented, the persuasiveness and coherence of the data for the intended readership.

6. Conclusions and implications

Like Greenhalgh et al. (2005), we are convinced that "storying a case" is a way of selecting which data to focus on and which to omit, thus enabling us to draw out meaning from different data sources; but accept that several cases are needed to gain a broad range of perspectives. The approach is one of constructing a chronological plot of the key actions and events and making causal links between aspects of the case. If constructed with skill, using such building blocks as anecdotes (Schostak, 2006), such stories may communicate effectively the key ingredients of what the authors (i.e. the researchers) of the stories had in mind quite simply because people remember stories! Psychologists have found that the human brain has a natural affinity for narrative construction. People tend to remember facts more accurately if they encounter them in a story rather than in other communicative styles like lists. For example, McAdams (2006) has found that a successful or generative life story (of Americans) is one characterised by overcoming adversity, connections with others, and a belief in the future. These narratives thus guide behaviour in every moment, and frame not only how we see but how we see ourselves in the future. Tapping into these inbuilt stories that frame how we see ourselves and future events may be a way to effectively communicate use genres of mobile learning that cross traditional boundaries of public and private spaces, that are inextricably bound up with learners' life worlds and that are, therefore, often more inconspicuous than traditional manifestations of learning. The very act of taking this deep approach to analysis surfaces many issues surrounding socio-cultural learning that in turn have an impact on our understanding of mobile devices for mobile learning. Stories and myths have always had a power to communicate deeper messages. In recent years Western societies have become very literate in terms of understanding the language and semiotics of stories as told through film and TV. What we are advocating here is nothing less than the researcher as literary writer. Our study, we feel, has demonstrated the *appropriacy* of the use of narrative and case-based approaches to the study of mobile learning.

The cases we were able to construct in this study based on qualitative user data suggest to us that, in order to maximise our insights into the potential of mobile devices for formal and informal learning, there is great benefit in explicitly engaging learners in discussions about possible uses as well as attendant barriers. We hope to have been able to demonstrate in this chapter through the construction of a sample case on the basis of narrative principles that it is possible to gain a better understanding of the socio-cultural practices surrounding the use and appropriation of mobile phones which can inform the design of their pedagogic use across formal and informal learning contexts.

We follow up the analysis of this chapter by developing the broad themes briefly outlined above by a more fine-grained analysis, which seeks to identify sub-categories within the broad themes (see Cook, Pachler and Bradley, 2008a). We do so with reference to sociological concepts, in particular Bourdieu's notion of "habitus" (Lizardo, 2004) and Bakardjieva's (2005) notion of "appropriation".

References

Bakardjieva, M. (2005). *Internet society. The internet in everyday life.* London: Sage Publications

Bruner, J. (1986). *Actual minds, possible words.* Cambridge: Harvard University Press

Cook, J. (2007). *Generating new learning contexts: novel forms of reuse and learning on the move.* Invited talk at ED-MEDIA 2007 – World Conference on Educational Multimedia, Hypermedia and Telecommunications, 25–29 June, Vancouver, Canada

Cook, J., Bradley, C., Lance, J., Smith, C. and Haynes, R. (2007). Generating learning contexts with mobile devices. In Pachler, N. (ed.), *Mobile learning: towards a research agenda.* WLE Occasional Papers in Work-Based Learning 1, London. Available at http://www.wlecentre.ac.uk/cms/files/occasionalpapers/mobilelearning_pachler2007.pdf

Cook, J., Pachler, N. and Bradley, C. (2008a). Bridging the gap? Mobile phones at the interface between informal and formal learning. In *Journal of the Research Centre for Educational Technology. Special Issue on Learning while mobile.* Kent State University. Available at http://www.rcetj.org

Cook, J., Pachler, N. and Bradley, C. (2008b). Towards m-maturity: the nature and role of appropriation in mobile learning. Paper accepted for *mLearn.* Telford, Shropshire, October 2008

Daly, C., Pachler, N., Pickering, J. and Bezemer, J. (2006). *Project Report: A study of e-learners' experiences in the mixed-mode professional degree programme, the Master of Teaching.* WLE Centre, Institute of Education, London. Available at http://www.wlecentre.ac.uk/cms/files/projects/reports/PR_Daly-Pachler-Pickering-Bezemer_2006.pdf

Greenhalgh, T. (2006). *What Seems to be the Trouble? Stories in Illness and Healthcare.* Oxford: Radcliff Publishing

Greenhalgh, T., Russell, J. and Swinglehurst, D. (2005). Narrative methods in quality improvement research. In *Qual Saf Health Care 14*, pp. 443–449

Laurillard, D. (2007). Pedagogical forms of mobile learning: framing research questions. In Pachler, N. (ed.), *Mobile learning: towards a research agenda.* WLE Centre Occasional Papers in Work-based Learning 1. London: Institute of Education, pp. 153–175

LGC (Learner Generated Contexts). *Wiki for the Learner Generated Context Group.* Available at http://learnergeneratedcontexts.pbwiki.com/ [accessed November 2007]

Lizardo, O. (2004). The cognitive origins of Bourdieu's "Habitus". In *Journal for the Theory of Social Behaviour,* 34(4), pp. 376–401

McAdams, D. (2006). *The redemptive self: stories Americans live by.* Oxford: Oxford University Press

Muller J. (1999). Narrative approaches to qualitative research in primary care. In Crabtree, B.F. and Miller, W.L. (eds), *Doing qualitative research.* 2nd ed. London: Sage Publications, pp. 221–238

Schostak, J. (2006). Interviewing and representation in qualitative research. Buckingham: Open University Press

Shulman, L. (1996). Just in case: reflections on learning from experience. In Colbert, J., Desberg, P. and Trimble, K. (eds), *The case for education: contemporary approaches for using case methods.* Boston: Allyn and Bacon, pp. 197–217

Strauss, A. and Corbin, J. (1990). *Basics of qualitative research: grounded theory. Procedures and techniques.* London: Sage

Wengraf, T. (2001). *Qualitative research interviewing: biographic narratives and semi-structured methods.* London: Sage

6. Using Activity-Oriented Design Methods (AODM) to Investigate Mobile Learning

DAISY MWANZA-SIMWAMI

Overview

The past few years have witnessed significant interest and developments in researching mobile learning, with a lot of important contributions being made towards understanding and defining mobile learning (Kukulska-Hulme and Traxler, 2005; Sharples et al., 2007; Wali et al., 2008; Winters, 2007). However, current research efforts are being redirected towards a new agenda to establish appropriate methods for investigating mobile learning, as this book testifies (see also Kjeldskov and Graham, 2003; Hagen et al., 2005; Sharples, 2007). This chapter contributes to this research effort by articulating how to adapt Activity-Oriented Design Methods (AODM – see Mwanza, 2002) for use in mobile learning research.

1.   Mobile learning in perspective

Mobile learning as a research field has accumulated valuable insight to help us understand (a) the nature of learning that takes place, (b) the environments in which learning takes place, and, (c) tools that mediate learning. In this regard, two perspectives appear to dominate the interpretation of the concept of mobile learning: first, those that define mobile learning from the point of view of the *portability* of technological tools or devices used to mediate learning activity; second, those that understand mobile learning from the point of view of the *mobility* of learners whilst using portable devices and wireless technologies to support learning. The first definition of mobile learning is commonly associated with early research in mobile learning that emphasised the personalised nature of mobile learning due to the prominent use of personal digital assistants (PDAs) and other handheld devices to support learning (Waycott and Kukulska-Hulme, 2003; Sharples, 2000). This vision of mobile learning is driven by the assumption that mobile learners are proactive in their ability to learn independently using a range of mobile technologies to initiate, manage and support learning anytime and anywhere (Nabeth et al., 2008; Sharples, this volume). In the meanwhile, the second definition of mobile learning is largely inspired by recognition of the significance of flexibility in the way that learners access and use mobile devices and wireless technologies to support learning in various settings (Caudill, 2007; Luckin et al., 2005; Scanlon et al., 2005; Vavoula and Sharples, 2002; Zurita and Nussbaum, 2004). For example, mobile learners generate content in both physical and digital environments for learning. In digital spheres, mobile learners are able to collaborate with peers through mechanisms such as mobile instant messaging systems (Kadirire, 2007; Parviainen and Parnes, 2003) wikis and mobile blogging. In physical spheres, mobile learners are able to enhance their learning experiences by engaging in direct physical interaction with both real and virtual environments. For example, in the Savanna project (Facer et al., 2004), a combination of simulation games, handheld devices and wearable computers, and wireless networking were used to create a gaming experience that responds to changes in the learner's physical environment. Therefore, this fusion of portability of devices and mobility of learners create new possibilities for mobile learners to enhance their learning experiences through sharing interactive experiences and co-construction of knowledge.

Finally, rapid advancements in the design and integration of mobile devices and networked technologies into day to day activities are creating new perceptions about the exploitation of mobile technologies in teaching and learning. Consequently, there is growing demand for customised, efficient and flexible systems for supporting learning in various settings. However, fulfilling learner demand for customised support requires better understanding of activities, operational contexts and purposes for which mobile devices are deployed to support learning. Therefore, our position with regard to methods for researching mobile learning focuses on evaluating the interaction between the two elements of portability of tools and mobility of learners in relation to the context of use and purpose for using mobile devices to mediate learning. In practice, this entails considering both HCI factors and social-cultural perspectives as important elements to consider when evaluating mobile learning. Whilst HCI factors can be addressed by conducting learner technology interaction studies as traditionally considered in HCI studies (Dix et al., 2003; Preece et al., 1994) and in Mobile HCI research (Kjeldskov and Graham, 2003; Hagen et al., 2005), social-cultural perspectives need to be addressed by evaluating issues relating to learner motives (Jones and Issroff, 2007) and the context of use as explored in social-cultural studies of human activity (Bannon, 1990; Leont'ev, 1978; Mwanza, 2002; Mwanza and Engeström, 2003; Mwanza-Simwami et al., 2009; Scanlon and Issroff, 2005; Taylor et al., 2006; Uden, 2007; Vygotsky, 1978; Wali et al., 2008).

In order to address research issues raised in foregoing discussions, this chapter will consider how Activity-Oriented Design Methods (AODM – see Mwanza, 2002) can be used to investigate mobile learning. The paper begins by describing activity theory, which is the theoretical framework that underpins the development and use of AODM. The section that follows introduces AODM. Key features of AODM methodological tools are outlined. Thereafter, we describe how AODM tools and techniques were applied in various systems design and e-learning projects. Finally, we discuss how AODM tools can be adapted for use in mobile learning research. The paper concludes by reflecting on the benefits of using AODM tools as a method for investigating mobile learning.

2. Activity Theory: An introduction

Activity Theory (AT) is a descriptive framework for understanding human activities as processes that continuously develop and redevelop over a period of time, and as a result of influences from the context in which human activities are carried out (Leont'ev, 1978 and 1981). Therefore, the basic unit of analysis in activity theory is human activities, or "what people do". According to Leont'ev (1978), the concept of activity refers to specific forms of human practices that are socially formed and always involve elements of consciousness. AT is therefore committed to understanding both individual and collective practices from a social-cultural and historical perspective.

Central to theorising in activity theory is the concept of tool mediation, which presents the view that human beings develop and use tools to help them achieve targeted objectives. The concept of "tools" is used here to refer to both physical tools (e.g. PDAs, mobile phones, etc) and conceptual tools such as human language and software applications. Activity theory is focused on establishing the means by which human beings master and use tools in everyday activities from a social, cultural and psychological perspective. This line of thinking is based on the understanding that the tools that human beings use to mediate their activities facilitate the performance of actions at hand whilst at the same time they reveal and transform the individual's mind. For example, through the development and use of conceptual tools, human beings internally transform their own and other people's perceptions of the activity that they are engaged in. At the same time, by developing and using physical tools, human beings externally transform the activity that they are engaged in. Therefore, the idea of studying human activities as developmental processes is crucial for identifying changes and contradictions that exist in an activity. Contradictions serve as the means by which new knowledge about the activity being examined emerges (Engeström, 1987).

Leont'ev (1981) explains that the concept of activity entails a complete system of human practices that has a structure. The structure of human activity can be understood as a dynamic and self-regulating system that is motivated towards the fulfilment of needs or objectives. In the meanwhile, human objectives are achieved by engaging in practical activities that are mediated through both physical and mental actions. In turn, human actions are directed towards the achievement of conscious goals, whilst at the same time, actions are satisfied through specific operations, whose successful execution is dependent on the conditions under which a particular action is performed. For example, a mobile learner wishing to share knowledge with colleagues using a smart phone to support mobile instant messaging will initiate the actions of: establishing the online availability of colleagues, selecting colleagues from the contact list, typing short messages and attaching files to send. However, successful execution of the operation of sending the messages and files will be dependent on whether or not the learner has adequate bandwidth and continuous connection to a wireless network (see Balachandran et al., 2003; Kadirire, 2007). If not, the operation of sending mobile instant messages and files will fail even if the actions leading to the execution of these operations had been successful.

In summary, activity theory seeks to explain the social and cultural embeddedness of human activities by linking them to issues relating to motives of those involved in carrying out activities, and, the nature of the relationships that exist between and among those participating in activity (Leont'ev, 1978). Finally, by emphasising the social and cultural embeddedness of human activities and tool usage behaviour, activity theory recognises the unity of consciousness and activity (see Kaptelinin and Nardi, 2006). Activity theory was developed by Russian psychologists S.L. Rubinstein and A.N. Leont'ev, and, has its roots in the works of Lev Vygotsky – another Russian psychologist of the 1930s (Leont'ev, 1981; Vygotsky, 1981/1930). Vygotsky emphasised the idea that human beings' interaction with objects of the environment is mediated through the use of tools and signs (Vygotsky, 1978). This idea is illustrated in Vygotsky's original model of human activity as shown in Figure 6.1.

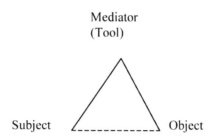

Figure 6.1: An adaptation of Vygotsky's original model of human activity
(Mwanza, 2002, p. 55).

Engeström (1987) developed a model that helps to capture and unify key concepts of activity theory by adding the "rules and regulations", "community" and "division of labour" components to Vygotsky's original model of human activity. The added components together with the "tools" component that was originally introduced by Vygotsky (1978) serve as mediators of a collective activity system. The various components of an activity system are shown in Figure 6.2.

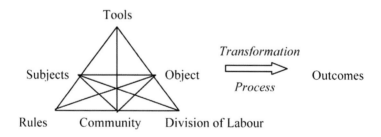

Figure 6.2: The Activity System (Engeström, 1987).

Figure 6.2 shows the various components of Engeström's model of human activity, which is also known as the activity system. The activity system captures the various components of human activity into a unified whole. Participants in an activity are portrayed as *subjects* interacting with *objects*[1] or objectives of an activity in order to achieve desired *outcomes*. In the meanwhile, human interactions with each other and with objects of the environment or context (*community*) in which activity is carried out are mediated through the use of *tools, rules* and *division of labour*. Mediators represent the nature of relationships that exist "within" and "between" participants in an activity in a given community. The activity system reflects both the collaborative and collective nature of human activity through the "subject" and "community" components. When researching mobile learning, this approach to modelling human activity would draw the researcher's attention to issues to consider when evaluating mobile learning, such as, understanding the: (a) inter-relatedness of learning episodes in mobile learning; (b) history of the development and use of mobile devices in the learning activity being investigated; (c) role of tools, rules and regulations, also the division of labour as mediators of learner activities.

This chapter will now introduce Activity-Oriented Design Methods (AODM – Mwanza, 2002) as a research method that can be used to operationalise key concepts of activity theory using the activity system (Figure 6.2) as a model for unifying these concepts.

3. Activity-Oriented Design Methods (AODM)

Activity-Oriented Design Methods (AODM) was developed as an analytical and practical approach for applying key concepts of activity theory to HCI research and practice (Mwanza, 2002). AODM present *four*

---

1   The term "object" should not to be confused with the "object-oriented" concept used in the computing science and programming fields of study. In AT, "object/s" refer to the motivational or purposeful nature of human activity. The motive of human activity is reflected through the "object" or "objective" of that activity. Therefore, AODM introduced a hyphened "object-ive" (see Table 6.1 and Table 6.2) in order to reflect and emphasise the purposeful nature of human activity through the object component of the model of human activity (see Mwanza, 2002, p. 67).

methodological tools designed to support early phases of computer systems design namely: the processes of gathering and analysing systems design requirements, systems evaluation, and, communicating design insight to stakeholders in the design activity. The four methodological tools incorporated in AODM are discussed below.

3.1 AODM Tool 1: Eight-Step-Model

The Eight-Step-Model		
Identify the:		Question to Ask
Step 1	Activity of interest	What sort of activity am I interested in?
Step 2	Object-ive	Why is the activity taking place?
Step 3	Subjects	Who is involved in carrying out this activity?
Step 4	Tools	By what means are the subjects performing this activity?
Step 5	Rules & Regulations	Are there any cultural norms, rules or regulations governing the performance of this activity?
Step 6	Division of labour	Who is responsible for what, when carrying out this activity and how are the roles organised?
Step 7	Community	What is the environment in which this activity is carried out?
Step 8	Outcome	What is the desired Outcome from carrying out this activity?

Table 6.1: AODM's Eight-Step-Model (Mwanza, 2002, p. 128).

Description

The *Eight-Step-Model* (ESM) is used to translate the various components of Engeström's model of human activity (Figure 6.2) in terms of the situation being examined. This entails working through the eight steps shown in Table 6.1 to gather and analyse data that will provide initial information about the activity and the context in which it is carried out.

3.2 AODM Tool 2: Activity Notation

The Activity Notation				
Actors (Doers)	~	Mediator	~	Object-ive (Purpose)
Subjects	~	Tools	~	Object
Subjects	~	Rules	~	Object
Subjects	~	Division of Labour	~	Object
Community	~	Tools	~	Object
Community	~	Rules	~	Object
Community	~	Division of Labour	~	Object

Table 6.2: AODM's Activity Notation (Mwanza, 2002, p. 152).

Description

Table 6.2 presents AODM's *Activity Notation*, which is used to reduce complexity in activity analysis by facilitating the modelling and decomposition of the activity system through the production of sub-activity triangle models (see Figure 6.3). This enables the researcher to conduct a detailed analysis of human activity. The operational procedure of the Activity Notation is enhanced by using *three-operational guidelines* that facilitate:

a. Levelled abstractions during analysis by enabling the decomposition of the main activity system into sub-activity triangles.

b. Reduction of cognitive complexity when analysing an activity system by generating sub-activity triangles to work with. The sub-activity triangles are united through the shared object of the main activity system.

c. The analysis of relationships *within* and *between* the various components of the main activity system so as to identify contradictions.

d. Detailed and more focused analysis by generating research questions based on sub-activity triangles.

Figure 6.3 illustrates how an activity system might be decomposed and modelled into sub-activity triangles through use of the Activity Notation.

3.3   AODM Tool 3: Technique of generating research questions

The Technique of Generating General Research Questions
What Tools do the Subjects use to achieve their Objective and how? What Rules affect the way the Subjects achieve the Objective and how? How does the Division of Labour influence the way the Subjects satisfy their Objective? How do the Tools in use affect the way the Community achieves the Objective? What Rules affect the way the Community satisfies their Objective and how? How does the Division of Labour affect the way the Community achieves the Objective?

Table 6.3: AODM's Technique of Generating General Research Questions (Mwanza, 2002, p. 155).

Description

The *technique of generating research questions* shown in Table 6.3 is used to operationalise sub-activity triangles resulting from the decomposition process so as to support data gathering and analysis from an AT perspective. Six general research questions based on components of the activity system are presented to aid the development of a wide range of both general and more focused research questions. These research questions can be used to analyse user interactions with each other and with tools or technologies being used to mediate activity as shown in Figure 6.3. Questions can also be used to examine the relationships that exist within and between the various components of sub-activity triangles (see Figure 6.3). This technique also facilitates detailed abstraction through decomposition and operationalisation of sub-activity triangles (see Figure 6.3).

3.4 AODM Tool 4: Technique of Mapping Operational Processes

Description

Figure 6.3 presents AODM's technique of *Mapping Operational Processes* (MOP) which is used to interpret and communicate research findings. MOP is a cognitive support tool that makes it easier to understand AODM entities and operational procedures by presenting a visual representation of the transition of the activity analysis from the decomposition of sub-activity triangles to the generation of research questions, and the identification of contradictions or problems in the activity. Contradictions are identified when results of an activity analysis do not match with desired outcomes or when problems emerge whilst the learner is interacting with tools or with other learners participating in that activity. For example, a contradiction is identified when a mobile phone fails to transmit a short message due to poor network connection. Problems may also occur as a result of rules and regulations that restrict or prevent the learner from carrying out a task e.g. mobile learners may not be allowed to take and share digital photos in certain parts of an international airport. MOP works like a concept mapping tool that facilitates understanding of the operational process as well as communicating study findings.

The four AODM methodological tools presented above can be applied systematically or iteratively in a six stage process presented as follows.

Stage 1.   Interpret the situation being examined in terms of activity theory

Stage 2.   Model the situation being examined

Stage 3.   Decompose the situation

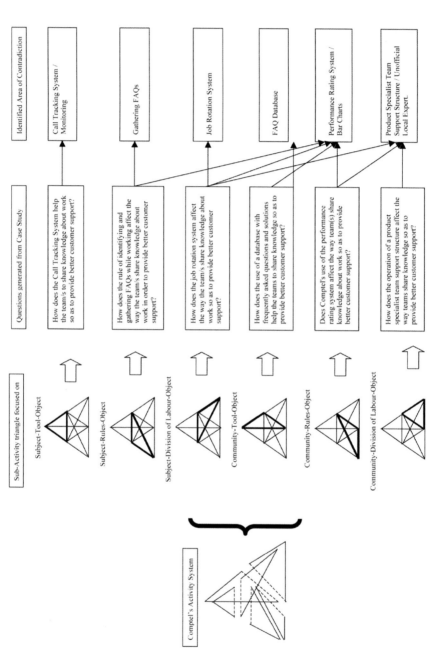

Figure 6.3: AODM's Technique of Mapping AODM Operational Processes (Mwanza, 2002, p. 162).

Stage 4. Generate research questions
Stage 5. Conduct a detailed investigation
Stage 6. Interpret and communicate findings

A detailed explanation of how the four AODM tools can be applied in the six stages outlined here will be presented later when discussing how to "use AODM tools to investigate mobile learning".

4. Previous use of AODM

AODM tools have been successfully used to inform design and investigate practices in several system design and evaluation projects mainly in the field of e-learning. For example, AODM tools were used to support information gathering and data analysis processes in a large e-learning project (i.e. the Lab@Future project[2]) that was funded by the European Union (EU) to design and evaluate new technologies for supporting learning in European high schools (see Courtiat et al., 2004; Baudin et al., 2004; Mwanza and Engeström, 2003). AODM methodological tools were also successfully used to support and enrich metadata abstraction and information management practices in the Lab@Future e-learning project (see Mwanza and Engeström, 2005). AODM tools were used to support systems requirements gathering in another large international e-learning project (i.e. Mobilearn project[3]) that was focused on investigating the design and use

2   The Lab@Future project was a European funded research and development project focused on anticipating future technological support needs for European youth. The project started in May 2002 and ended in April 2005. The author worked on this project as part of the University of Helsinki team. Further details of the project are available at www.labfuture.net/.

3   MOBIlearn was a European-led worldwide research and development project focused on exploring advancements in mobile technologies by amongst other objectives, defining theoretically-supported and empirically-validated models of mobile learning. The project started in July 2002 and ended in December 2004. The author participated

of mobile devices to support mobile learning (see Sharp et al., 2003). More recently, AODM has been taken up in the field of Computer Supported Collaborative Learning (CSCL) where AODM tools were used to develop a comprehensive understanding of practices of collaborative knowledge building among course design teams and their students (see Greenhow and Belbas, 2007). The broad exploitation of AODM tools demonstrates that this method can be flexibly adapted for use in various fields including mobile learning. The chapter will now discuss how AODM can be used to research mobile learning.

5.   Using AODM tools to investigate mobile learning

In order to apply AODM to mobile learning research, we recommend that the investigator begins by familiarising themselves with theoretical concepts of activity theory, as a basic understanding of AT concepts is vital to appreciate the richness of the framework of AT and to appropriately label and interpret components of the activity system. The actual process of applying AODM tools to researching mobile learning would involve working either systematically or iteratively through the six stages of AODM as recommended below.

5.1   Stage 1. Interpret the situation being examined in terms of Activity Theory

Begin by understanding existing practices in the environment or context in which mobile devices are being used to support learning. The initial task would be to interpret the activity triangle model or activity system (Figure 6.2) in terms of the mobile learning activity that you want to investigate. It is therefore important to identify a specific activity of interest

---

in this project as part of the Open University team. Details of the project are available at http://www.mobilearn.org/.

to research within mobile learning. This entails working through the open-ended questions that are incorporated within the Eight-Step-Model (Table 6.1) so as to meaningfully translate the various components of the activity system in terms of activity theory. ESM can be used on its own as an open-ended questionnaire or aide memoire in observational studies. Research outcomes will be in the form of qualitative data such as descriptive narratives of practices of the context of use and tools used to mediate learning. Through this translation process, general information about learner practices, mediators and contextual issues would be gathered.

Example use of AODM's ESM in the Mobilearn project

Within the Mobilearn project's Open University (OU) case study (Sharp et al., 2003), AODM's ESM tool was used to gather information about practices of OU first-aiders. We needed to find out about work patterns of OU first-aiders, e.g. did they move about and outside their normal work environment to attend to first-aid incidents? Step 7 of AODM's ESM enabled us to answer that question. We also needed to find out what activities were carried out by OU first-aiders so that we could narrow down to a single activity of interest that we would target for detailed investigation. Step 1 in ESM enabled us to achieve this. We discovered that OU first-aiders carried out various activities within the remit of rendering first-aid at work. These activities included: attending to personal injuries and accidents at work; attending first-aiders' meetings and training courses to refresh their practical skills e.g. to share experiences and information about how to use new first-aid equipment. We also needed to gather information about tools that first-aiders used when carrying out their activities. ESM's Step 4 enabled us to establish that OU first-aiders used portable devices such as blood pressure monitors and defibrillators when attending to first-aid incidents. First-aiders also used both landline based office telephones and mobile phones to communicate and share experiences about first-aid incidents.

Example use of AODM's ESM in the Lab@Future project

In the Lab@Future project (Baudin et al., 2004, Courtiat et al., 2004, Mwanza and Engeström, 2003, Mwanza and Engeström, 2005), AODM's

ESM was used to gather information about user practices, tool use, context of use, etc., in the various case studies used as part of the systems design requirements capture. Working as part of the University of Helsinki team, we initially gave representatives of the nine partners[4] that were participating in this project a basic introduction to AT. This happened during one of the project meetings. Thereafter, partners were asked to use ESM in observational studies and during interviews with case study participants in order to gather specific information about human activities in those case studies. For example, by working through ESM's Step 7, a case study carried out in Slovenia established that teaching and learning activities in the subject area of environmental awareness were carried out in both the school setting (i.e. scientific laboratories) and in the natural environment through field trips and the "school in the nature" programme (see Mwanza-Simwami et al., 2009; Mwanza and Engeström, 2003; Mwanza and Engeström, 2005). Again by working through ESM's Step 4, we were able to establish that both learners and teachers used portable devices such as cameras to take photos of items of interest during field trips. Students and teachers also used portable devices such as test tubes to collect water samples from lakes to be used when testing for pollution in scientific laboratories.

ESM enables the researcher to gather huge amounts of qualitative data, which in most cases is complex; therefore, other AODM tools are required to support the investigative processes of analysing emerging issues.

5.2   Stage 2. Model the situation being examined

During the second stage of using AODM, information gathered in Stage 1 is used to produce an activity system of the situation being examined. This modelling process makes it possible to interpret and verify the correctness of the information gathered about learner practices in the setting being

---

4   The nine partners involved in the Lab@Future project were drawn from both industry and academia in several European countries. English was the official working language on the project. However, partners had their own country specific official working languages including: French, Greek, German, Finnish and Slovenian.

studied. Modelling also supports the process of communicating information gathered to other stakeholders. However, it is difficult to conduct a critical analysis of learner activities in the activity system generated at this stage because the information gathered is too abstract or general. This is due to the fact that the activity system produced at this stage is complex because it incorporates within it several other processes or sub-activities that together make up the main activity system. To address this situation, a levelled abstraction of this complex activity system is required so as to reveal the various sub-activities and relationships incorporated within the activity system. For example, when investigating mobile learning, the researcher would typically produce an activity triangle model from the information gathered in Step 1 of ESM. If we use the Lab@Future case study of learning about environmental awareness as an example, the resulting triangle would have items such as cameras and test tubes under the "tools" components of the case study's activity system.

5.3 Stage 3. Decompose the activity system

At this stage AODM introduces the *Activity Notation* to decompose the complex activity system that was produced in Stage 2. This decomposition helps to reduce complexity by introducing smaller manageable constitutive units or sub-activity systems to work with. These sub-activity systems are linked together through the shared object or objective of the main activity system. The shared object is that of the main activity system produced in Stage 2 and is common to all components. The activity system produced in Stage 2 is further divided into sub-activity triangles as shown in Figure 6.3.

5.4 Stage 4. Generate research questions

Stage 4 uses the AODM's *technique of generating research questions* (Table 6.3) to produce research questions that are based on sub-activity systems or components resulting from the decomposition in Stage 3. Each research question is therefore directly linked to a particular sub-activity system or component within the main activity system. Generating research questions in this way makes explicit the link between research questions generated and the various components of the main activity system. Research questions generated at this stage can then be used to support further data gathering and analysis. The questions can also be used to support the process of evaluating and validating whether or not learner objectives are being met. Figure 6.3 gives an example illustration of the generation of research questions. As an example, in the Mobilearn project, after gathering, analysing and modelling data (AODM Stages 1 to 3) about practices of OU first-aiders, we wanted to conduct a detailed investigation about tools that first-aiders used to capture and share knowledge whilst on the move attending to first-aid incidents. The combined use of ESM and the Activity Notation enabled us to establish that whilst both office telephones and mobile phones were used to communicate with other first-aiders and stakeholders such as hospital accident and emergency departments when attending to first-aid incidents. In such situations, other portable devices such as cameras would have been useful for capturing images of injuries in order to enrich data shared amongst stakeholders. These devices were not in use at the time of the study.

5.5   Stage 5. Conduct a detailed investigation

At this stage, it is possible to conduct a detailed and more focused investigation that uses the research questions generated in Stage 4. Research questions can be used in interviews, questionnaires, and observations. At this point, it is worth mentioning that AODM does not stipulate how to conduct interviews or observations when using the generated research questions. We considered such an elaborate approach to be too restrictive and not suitable for all purposes. Whilst AODM is focused on providing a well-structured application procedure, the need to be flexible in the method's application mechanism is equally vital.

In addition to this, research questions generated in Stage 4 can also be used as pointers to what to look for when analysing data gathered during the study. During data analysis, the investigator would examine relationships that exist *within* and *between* learners and tools used to mediate learning activity so as to identify contradictions or problems. The aim of this kind of analysis is not to find or predict possible solutions for the identified contradictions, but instead to obtain a comprehensive understanding of the means by which these contradictions develop, from a social-cultural and historical perspective. For example, in the Mobilearn project's OU first-aiders case study, detailed analysis of the relationship between tools and first-aider practices revealed a possible contradiction between first-aiders' use of portable devices such as mobile phones to communicate with others whilst attending to an incident, and the requirement to concentrate on stabilising the victim as part of the first-aid task. Contradictions emerge due to the fact that both tasks require mental concentration and use of hands. Having gathered and analysed data during a detailed investigation, the next step is to interpret and communicate findings.

5.6 Stage 6. Interpret and communicate findings

In the final stage of applying AODM tools, the information obtained in Stage 5 is interpreted and communicated to other stakeholders by re-modelling the activity system of the situation being examined. At this stage, it is also possible to graphically show the mappings between sub-activity systems and research questions generated in Stage 4, and also the identified areas of conflict. This kind of mapping is illustrated in Figure 6.3. The technique of mapping components and operational processes provide a reversible conceptualisation of the various entities and operational processes that exist when using AODM. Using this approach, it is possible to identify and map contradictions onto the sub-activity triangle component in which they exist. The AODM technique of modelling mappings of entities and operational processes helps the investigator to explicitly communicate observed conflicts or problems in the learners' relationships with others and their own use of mobile devices to support learning. Finally, the technique of mapping operational processes directly support the AT notion of capturing the historical development or transition of human activities as part of the investigation. This element of AODM is particularly important for research in mobile learning as it could help to link the relationships between learning episodes (Vavoula and Sharples, 2002) and learner objectives. The idea of capturing the transition of learning activities can also enable the researcher to understand the relationships between various episodes of mobile learning, many of which happen in various settings that include both formal and informal settings (Scanlon et al., 2005).

6. Conclusion

There are currently no universally accepted methods for investigating mobile learning. This chapter has proposed Activity-Oriented Design Methods as a structured and flexible method for investigating mobile learning. AODM presents a theoretically grounded descriptive approach for investigating human activities and tool usage behaviour in the context in which activities are carried out.

Key benefits of using AODM to researching mobile learning include, first, its capability to allow the researcher to investigate the *relationship* between learner *motives* and technology usage behaviour. AODM methodological tools facilitate a holistic approach to investigating *mediators* of human activities by studying tools in use, rules and regulations, and division of labour, whilst linking observations to targeted goals and desired outcomes. Second, AODM can be used to investigate the inter-connectedness of learning episodes in mobile learning through its support for levelled abstractions and decomposition of learner activity models. This approach also helps to capture the developmental transition of learner behaviour and the analysis of contradictions that exist in learner activities.

Weaknesses and shortfalls of AODM include, first, the requirement for users to familiarise themselves with basic theoretical concepts of activity theory (Mwanza, 2002; Greenhow and Belbas, 2007). Methodological tools presented in AODM attempt to closely interpret key concepts of activity theory so as to capture the richness of this framework in their operational structure. However, this AT orientation can discourage some researchers. Nevertheless, as pointed out by Greenhow and Belbas, (2007), the benefits of being able to characterise the messiness of real world practices in a way that is valuable to others in context outweigh any possible challenges.

Second, studying activities of mobile learners in naturalistic settings or contexts can be challenging due to the fact that mobile learners operate in constantly changing environments (e.g. on the move), therefore, it is difficult to predict when a learning episode or event will occur or what tools will be in use. AODM addresses these issues by providing support for analysing complex social behaviours through decomposition whilst providing a mechanism for making the inter-relatedness of interaction processes more explicit. Finally, AODM can easily be integrated with other methods that the researcher chooses to use.

References

Balachandran, A., Voelker, G., and Bahl, P. (2003). Wireless Hotspots: Current challenges and future directions. Proceedings of *WMASH'03*. Available at http://research.microsoft.com/~bhal/Papers/Pdf/moneto5.pdf [accessed on 17 March 2008]

Bannon, L.J. (1990). From human factors to human actors: The role of psychology and human-computer interaction studies in system design. In J. Greenbaum, and Kyng, M. (eds), *Design at Work: Cooperative Design of Computer Systems*. Hillsdale, NJ: Lawrence Erlbaum Associates, pp. 25–44

Baudin, V., Faust, M., Kaufmann, H., Litsa, V., Mwanza, D., Pierre, A., and Totter, A. (2004). Lab@Future: Moving towards the future of e-Learning. Technology Enhanced Learning (TeL) Workshop 2004. At the 18th IFIP World Computer Congress (WCC/IFIP), Toulouse, France

Caudill, J.G. (2007). The growth of m-Learning and the growth of mobile computing: Parallel developments. In *International Review of Research in Open and Distance Learning*, Vol. 8, No. 2. ISSN: 1492–3831

Courtiat, J-P., Davarakis, C., Totter, A., Mwanza, D., Faust, M., Kaufmann, H., and Villemur, T. (2004). Evaluating Lab@Future: A collaborative E-Learning Laboratory Experiments Platform. *European Distance and*

E-Learning Network (EDEN 2004). Annual Conference, Budapest, Hungary

Dix, A., Finlay, J., Abowd, G., and Beale, R. (2003). Human-Computer Interaction (3rd Edition). Upper Saddle River, NJ: Prentice-Hall

Engeström, Y. (1987). *Learning by Expanding: An Activity-Theoretical Approach to Developmental Research.* Helsinki: Orienta-Konsultit Oy, Finland

Facer, K., Joiner, R., Stanton, D., Reid, J., Hull, R., and Kirk, D. (2004). Savannah: Mobile gaming and learning? In *Journal of Computer Assisted Learning*, 20, 399–409

Greenhow, C. and Belbas, B. (2007). Using activity-oriented design methods to study collaborative knowledge-building in e-Learning courses. *International Journal of Computer-supported Collaborative Learning* (2), 363–391

Hagen, P., Robertson, T., Kan, M. and Sadler, K. (2005). *Emerging research methods for understanding mobile technology use.* In Proceedings of OZCHI05, the CHISIG Annual Conference on Human-Computer Interaction 2005, pp. 1–10

Jones, A. and Issroff, K. (2007). Motivation and Mobile Devices: exploring the role of appropriation and coping strategies. *ALT-J: Research in Learning Technology*, Vol. 15, 3, pp. 247–258

Kadirire, J. (2007). Instant messaging for creative interactive and collaborative m-learning environments: *International Review of Research in Open and Distance Learning*, Vol. 8, No. 2. ISSN: 1492–3831

Kaptelinin, V. and Nardi, B. (2006). Acting with Technology: Activity Theory and Interaction Design. Cambridge, MA: MIT Press

Kjeldskov, J. and Graham, C. (2003). A Review of MobileHCI Research Methods. Proceedings of the 5th International conference on Mobile HCI, Mobile HCI 2003, Udine, Italy. LNCS, Springer-Verlag, pp. 317–335

Kukulska-Hulme, A. and Traxler, J. (2005). *Mobile Learning: A handbook for educators and trainers.* London: Routledge

Leont'ev, A.N. (1981). The Problem of Activity in Psychology. In J.V. Wertsch (ed), *The Concept of Activity in Soviet Psychology: An Introduction.* New York: M.E. Sharpe, Inc

Leont'ev, A.N. (1978). *Activity, Consciousness, and Personality*. Englewood Cliffs, NJ: Prentice-Hall

Luckin R., du Boulay, B., Smith, H., Underwood, J., Fitzpatrick, G., Holmberg, J., Kerawalla, L., Pearce, D., Tunley, H., Brewster, D. and Pearce, D. (2005). Building Bridges: Using Mobile Technology to Create Flexible Learning Contexts. *Journal of Interactive Media in Education*. In A. Jones, A. Kukulska-Hulme and D. Mwanza (eds), Portable Learning: Experiences with Mobile Devices Special Issue, 22. ISSN: 1365–893X

Mwanza, D. (2002). *Towards an Activity-Oriented Design Method for HCI Research and Practice*. Unpublished PhD Thesis – The Open University, UK. Available at http://iet.open.ac.uk/pp/d.mwanza/Phd.cfm

Mwanza, D. and Engeström, Y. (2003). Pedagogical Adeptness in the Design of E-learning Environments: Experiences from the Lab@Future Project. In A. Rossett (ed.), *Proceedings of E-Learn 2003*. International Conference on E-Learning in Corporate, Government, Healthcare, and Higher Education, 2, 1344–1347. Phoenix, AZ: Association for the Advancement of Computing in Education (AACE)

Mwanza, D. and Engeström, Y. (2005). Managing Content in e-Learning Environments. In N. Rushby (ed.), *British Journal of Educational Technology* (BJET), Vol. 36(3), pp. 453–463. British Educational Communications and Technology Agency, Blackwell Science Ltd, UK

Mwanza-Simwami, D., Engeström, Y. and Amon, T. (2009). Methods for evaluating learner activities with new technologies: Guidelines for the Lab@Future project. To appear in the *International Journal on E-Learning* (IJEL), Vol. 8(3)

Nabeth, T., Karlsson, H., Angehrn, A. and Maisonneuve, N. (2008). A social network platform for vocational learning in the ITM Worldwide Network. Conference Proceedings of IST Africa 2008, part of the European Commission's Information Communications Technologies (ICT) programme, 7–9 May 2008, Windhoek, Namibia

Parviainen, R. and Parnes, P. (2003). Mobile instant messaging. Proceedings of the 10th International Conference on Telecommunications ICT

Preece, J., Rogers, Y., Sharp, H., Benyon, D., Holland, S. and Carey, T. (1994). *Human-Computer Interaction*. Wokingham, England: Addison-Wesley Publishing Company

Scanlon, E., Jones, A. and Waycott, J. (2005). Mobile technologies: prospects for their use in learning in informal science settings. *Journal of Interactive Media in Education*, 21(5). ISSN: 1365–893X

Scanlon, E. and Issroff, K. (2005). Activity Theory and Higher Education: evaluating learning technologies. *Journal of Computer Assisted Learning*, 21(6), pp. 430–439. ISSN: 0266–4909

Sharp, H., Taylor, J., Löber, A., Frohberg, A., Mwanza, D. and Murelli, E. (2003). *Establishing user requirements for a mobile learning environment*. Conference proceedings of Eurescom 2003, Heidelberg, Germany

Sharples, M. (ed.). (2007). *Big issues in mobile learning: Report of a workshop by the Kaleidoscope Network of Excellence Mobile Learning Initiative*. Nottingham, UK: University of Nottingham, Learning Sciences Research Institute

Sharples, M., Taylor, J. and Vavoula, G. (2007). A Theory of Learning for the Mobile Age. In R. Andrews and C. Haythornthwaite (eds), *The Sage Handbook of E-learning Research*. London: Sage, pp. 221–247

Sharples, M. (2000). The design of personal mobile technologies for life-long learning. *Computers and Education*, 34, pp. 177–193

Taylor, J., Sharples, M., O'Malley, C., Vavoula, G. and Waycott, J. (2006). Towards a task model for mobile learning: a dialectical approach. *International Journal of Learning Technology*, 2(2/3), 138–158

Uden, L. (2007). Activity theory for designing mobile learning. *International Journal of Mobile Learning and Organisation*, Inderscience Enterprises Ltd

Vavoula, G.N. and Sharples, M. (2002). KLeOS: A personal, mobile, Knowledge and Learning Organisation System. In Milrad, M., Hoppe, U. and Kinshuk (eds), *Proceedings of the IEEE International Workshop on Mobile and Wireless Technologies in Education (WMTE2002)*, 29–30 August, Vaxjo, Sweden, pp. 152–156

Vygotsky, L.S. (1978). *Mind in Society – The Development of Higher Psychological Processes*. In Michael Cole, Vera John-Steiner, Sylvia

Scribner, and Ellen Souberman (eds). Cambridge, MA: Harvard University Press

Vygotsky, L.S. (1930/1981). The development of higher psychological functions (in Russia). In J.V. Wertsch (ed.), *Soviet Activity Theory*. New York: M.E. Sharpe, Inc

Wali, E., Winters, N. and Oliver, M. (2008). Maintaining, changing and crossing contexts: an activity theoretic reinterpretation of mobile learning. *ALT-J Research in Learning Technology*, Vol.16, No.1. London: Routledge Taylor and Francis Group, pp. 41–57

Waycott, J. and Kukulska-Hulme, A. (2003). *Students' experiences with PDAs for reading course materials*. Personal and Ubiquitous Computing, 7(1). pp. 30–43. ISSN: 1617–4909

Winters, N. (2007). What is mobile learning? In Sharples, M. (ed.), *Big issues in mobile learning: Report of a workshop by the Kaleidoscope Network of Excellence Mobile Learning Initiative*. Nottingham, UK: University of Nottingham, Learning Sciences Research Institute

Zurita, G. and Nussbaum, M. (2004). A constructivist mobile learning environment supported by a wireless handheld network. *Journal of Computer Assisted Learning*, 20, 235–243

7. Exploring Novel Learning Practices through Co-Designing Mobile Games

DANIEL SPIKOL

Overview

Co-design practices have been the focus of current research efforts in the field of educational technologies but not as prevalent in mobile games to support learning. Setting the design focus on the entire learning experience including game based activities can provide richer opportunities for evaluation for informal activities. The flow of mobile activities can be captured by using techniques such as tagging technology that combine users' active contributions and reflections with the exchange of data between devices and systems. This chapter presents how co-design offered insights to the design and evaluation of a mobile game called Skattjakt (Treasure Hunt in Swedish) and the benefits it can have for future learning activities. Two completed trials over the last year and a third trial in progress have provided us with valuable results that can help us to bridge learning in informal and formal settings. Moreover, we believe that involving children in the design process for mobile games may give us new perspectives regarding the nature of their learning practices while learning with these games.

1. Introduction

New forms of mobile communication and collaboration are rapidly being adopted and integrated into young people's everyday lives on a global scale. Multimedia capable mobile phones, MP3 music players, digital cameras, and GPS devices are merging into single powerful units that rival the computational power of laptops at a fraction of the cost with genuine portability. These devices have provided new opportunities for researchers, educators, and enterprises to explore how mobile activities can be used to support learning practices. Recently mobile games have begun to be considered within the educational arena. The recent proliferation of mobile games such as Frequency 1550 (Raessens, 2007) and the COLLAGE project (Sotiriou and Chryssafidou, 2007) makes them a fertile ground for the development of new resources to support learning (Facer et al., 2004). Mobile games can promote children's involvement in different tasks such as exploration, content generation, collaboration, problem solving and navigation; all these activities can be seen as important components that support the development of a wide variety of cognitive and social skills.

One possible way to support this type of involvement is through co-design which can be defined as a highly facilitated, team based process in which students, teachers, researchers, and developers work together in defined roles to design an educational innovation, realise the design in one or more prototypes, and evaluate each prototype's effectiveness in addressing an educational need (Penuel et al., 2007) This design approach takes into consideration the different contexts that mobile technologies enable across different learning ecologies. The flow of these mobile activities can be captured by using techniques like automatic and collaborative tagging technology that combine users' active contributions and reflections with the flow of data between devices and systems. A simple example of this is recording the longitude and latitude positions of where and when the content is created while the learners are moving about, which is commonly known as "geotagging". These tags can help to visualize activities by connecting the location and time to content while placing them into applications like Google Earth. These types of technologies that add additional information to created learning artefacts during activities can offer new opportunities for the design and evaluation for learning.

The current research presented in this chapter has approached design through iterative cycles where the mobile applications are one of the tools in the overall learning activity. This chapter focuses on the value of co-design of mobile learning activities as a way to analyze and understand the nature of informal learning activities. The chapter is structured as follows: section

2 presents a brief background on the theoretical considerations and methods, section 3 describes the game and the technology; section 4 presents the design process, and section 5 presents the assessment. The chapter concludes with a discussion about evaluation methods and co-design for mobile games in section 6.

2. Background

The pedagogical design of Skattjakt has been inspired by recent social constructivist perspectives (Jonassen et al., 2002) that regard learning as enculturation, the process by which learners become collaborative meaning-makers among a group defined by common practices such as language, use of tools, values and beliefs. Social constructivism (Jonassen and Land, 2000) asserts that a particularly effective way for knowledge-building communities to form and grow is through collaborative activities that involve the design and construction of meaningful artefacts as well as the exchange of information. Mobile technologies can provide effective and meaningful learning experiences by expanding learning beyond the four walls of the classroom, allowing interaction in the real world and bringing new interactions back into the classroom (Hooft and Swan, 2007). Thus, designing and implementing learning activities that support truly innovative educational practices is a challenge.

One way to support innovation is through co-design. Penuel and colleagues (2007) describe co-design as a highly facilitated, team based process in which key stakeholders, including teachers, researchers, and developers work together in defined roles to design an educational innovation. The design is realized in one or more prototypes, and each prototype's educational effectiveness is evaluated. The process relies on the teachers' ongoing involvement with the design of educational innovations that typically employ technology as a critical support for practice. Co-design can be seen as a collaborative effort that places importance on designs that reflect the core values of the users.

The process relies on the teachers' ongoing involvement with the design of educational innovations that typically employ technology as a critical support for practice. Co-design can be seen as a collaborative effort that places importance on designs that reflect the core values of the users.

Over the last two decades design approaches that involve stakeholders, users, and designers in the design process have been developed in the area of workplace technology design (such as participatory design, user centred design, and scenario-based design (Penuel et al., 2007)) and in the educational domain (such as learner-centred design and design-based research). Co-design differs from exploratory research on learning innovations in that it depends critically on whether the team of people working on the project meets a specific pre-defined challenge, whereas exploratory research has no pre-defined design target. Co-design generally, like all the aforementioned design approaches, involves iterative cycles of development where concepts are tested and refined, ranging from paper prototypes up to the final system.

In such approaches as co-design and learner-centred design, the design process plays a key role in the effort to foster learning, create relevant knowledge, and advance theories of learning and teaching in complex (mobile) settings. These concepts are also consistent with the ideas behind design-based research, an approach that combines the intentional design of interactive learning environments with the empirical exploration of our understanding of these environments and how they interact with individuals while keeping innovation in focus (Hoadley, 2004).

By taking this iterative approach as a point of departure, we can investigate through design how to develop different learning opportunities for children not only to learn through experience, but also to learn by becoming game designers based, in our case, on the ideas behind Skattjakt and working with the teachers. Co-design can provide us with ways to gather insight on the design requirements of challenging and novel activities. One of our aims has been to explore how learning innovations that take place outside the formal educational system can be brought to schools and how children can gain new and different insights on the nature of their learning practices as they become members of the design team. Even though the design process followed here is a blended approach, our pre-specified goal to create a game and process inside a formal environment working with the different stakeholders brings it closer to co-design.

3. Game Description

This section presents Skattjakt (Treasure Hunt in Swedish), a game that has been conceived and implemented to promote physical activity and collaborative problem solving. The game is inspired by the ideas behind treasure hunt activities and the sport of orienteering, a traditional Scandinavian running sport involving navigation with a map and a compass. The orienteering competition is a timed race where individual participants need to navigate through diverse terrain (generally wooded) and in order visit control points indicated on the map. A detailed topographic course map with the control points is handed out revealing the course at the start of the competition. The competitors are required to perform all navigation by themselves and start at staggered intervals, while timing is individual.

The activities in the Skattjakt support informal learning about topics such as local history, the environment, navigation, and physical activities. The game requires different degrees of collaboration between team members to solve a mystery. Six teams can compete simultaneously using mobile phones for navigation and game interaction. The playing field for the game contains control points and detour points allowing the six teams to start simultaneously at different points. At each control point the players enter a 4-digit code and then need to perform a task that results in a new code they enter into the phone. If they enter the wrong answer they need to go to a detour point before getting the next control point on the phone based map. The mobile handset provides an interactive map that reveals the next control point or detour point as the game progresses. The players can zoom and scroll the map to orient their positions.

In the first two versions of the game the playing field covered the university campus, and in the third game the playing field is located in the city centre. A strong narrative drives the players to help a character to solve a mystery that drives the game play. The mobile interface includes an interactive map with the different marked locations where the players can zoom in, out, and pan to see the entire playing area. Figure 7.1 illustrates the full map of the playing field of the campus with the detours and the mobile game interface on the top row of images. A game server provided the logic and scoring for the game that communicated with the game application on the phone.

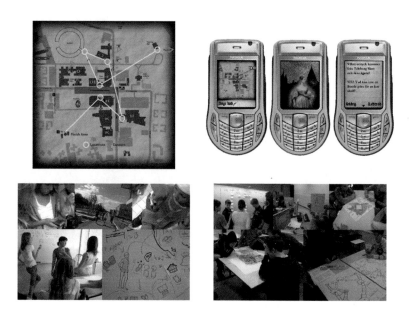

Figure 7.1: The game map with markers and detours with the mobile game interface below.

Skattjakt is part of a larger set of work that investigates creating tools for learning activities that combine mobile and fixed computer technologies (Spikol and Milrad, 2008). This work utilises the Learning Activity System (LAS) that provides the content and the logic for learning activities that bridge indoor and outdoor locations and tasks. The technology is straightforward and relies on a mobile phone application that communicates with the

LAS via General Packet Radio Service (GPRS), commonly known as 3G, a high-speed cellular network. The mobile phone application was developed in Adobe® Flash® Lite™ software. The game starts by sending a message to the LAS with the phone's identity number and the server returns the first location. When the players get to the location they enter a 4-digit code into the phone that is part of the actual landscape (e.g. a house number, opening hours of a store, or the last 4 digits of a phone number) and/or connected to an orienteering flag. This code is sent to the server, which returns the next step for the players, which can be a question, puzzle, or task they must complete. The LAS also keeps track of the teams and their progress, and controls the locations and the detours. In the current version of Skattjakt an additional camera phone is provided to each team, which runs an application that automatically sends the captured image and its geo-information to the LAS. The LAS then combines meta-data that identifies the device, the team, the photograph and the location and renders it on to a map into the web browser for mobile phones or PCs. Since several children make up each team, providing a device and specific tasks for each player works well with the low cost and mobile nature of the devices and the game.

4. Design Process

The game has evolved over two main trials during 2007 and it has been a central part of informal learning activities outside of school for 13 to 16 year olds. The first version was developed iteratively as a proof of concept in the context of a co-design task during a university course on mobile games. Fifteen students (aged 13–16) played this initial version of the game in February 2007 as part of after-school activities. The second version was developed over a co-design task for girls aged 13–15 who were taking part in a weeklong summer school course on digital technology in June 2007. The girls played the original game on campus on the first day. The game experience acted as a starting point for a 2-day workshop and the outcome was a number of student-created game concepts. Based on the summer school experience, the game workshop became an elective class at a local middle school for the fall of 2007. This class used co-design to bring together researchers, teachers, the local orienteering club and the students. The goal of this class was to jointly develop a new version of the game to be played by another local school in January 2008. The game has acted as a catalyst to get the students and teachers involved in the design process, providing a bridge to more formal learning activities like environmental science, physical education, and mathematics.

In Skattjakt we are investigating how to promote collaborative tasks that explore physical activities across different subject matters like history and environmental science. Table 7.1 illustrates the tasks and the related skills across the different game versions. Mobile informal learning presents a chance to situate the learners in the physical world where they need to navigate, negotiate, and make decisions together as a team with physical consequences in the game, such as detours.

These tasks and skills have raised some key questions about how and what to evaluate during the iterative development of the games. In order to investigate what to assess we have written field notes, have been "hanging around", collected documents used in the different learning situations, and in addition have conducted in-depth interviews with teachers and learners. Over the course of developing and trialling the three game versions, we have used surveys for the players and stakeholders, simple observation forms for researchers, we provided additional mobile phones for the players for photographic self-documentation with GPS tagging, and collected simple data files generated by the game system. These different observations, notes, and interviews were loosely triangulated using a mixed method approach to gather wide perspectives for the next phase of design (Denscombe, 2007).

The aim of using these mixed methods has been to "come closer" to learning in real settings and to find out how learning is taking place – how artefacts are used, how the content of learning is established, and what the interaction between the participants looks like. In the summer 2007 trial this content was visualized and reviewed to create new content for future games by the team, through paper-based prototypes and the making of traditional board games to test concepts. See Figure 7.1 for images of the workshops and prototyping sessions.

Collaborative Tasks	Skills	Game Version
Navigation	Map reading	Spring 2007, Summer 2007, Fall 2007
Narrative	Comprehension	Spring 2007, Summer 2007, Fall 2007
Problem Solving	Math and logic	Spring 2007, Summer 2007, Fall 2007
Coordination	Decision making	Spring 2007, Summer 2007, Fall 2007
Strategy	game actions	Fall 2007
Creative / expression	photo taking	Summer 2007, Fall 2007
Critical Thinking & Reflective	Game Design	Summer 2007, Fall 2007
across course curriculum (history, physical education, math, & sciences)		

Table 7.1: Collaborative Tasks and skills.

5.   Assessment

The game with the tasks and related skills presented above has provided us with different ways to assess informal learning practices during the co-design process, and has enabled the team to further develop the game features and subject matter. Following Vavoula and Sharples' (2008) recommendations, mobile learning should be evaluated at 3 levels: a *Micro* level, assessing the user's experience of the technology including usability aspects and utility of functions; a *Meso* level, looking at the user's learning/educational experience; and a *Macro* level, in which the evaluator tries to understand the impact on learning/teaching practice as well as the appropriation of the new technology and emerging practices. All these different levels can help to understand some of the on-going learning processes and they can also assist us to identify problems and further requirements.

Figure 7.2 presents how different data was captured and used during the co-design process to explore how design and evaluation can be used to capture the flow of the learning activity. The figure illustrates how the team, the games, and the assessment evolved over the different versions of the game with the co-design process and the game features. The fall 2007 activity (yet to be analysed at the time of writing this chapter) presents a new game story and new features introduced by middle school students. Another local school played the game and as part of the game play were photographic tasks with an additional mobile phone coupled to a Bluetooth GPS receiver that automatically uploaded geo-tagged images to the LAS and placed them into a Google map. The post-game reflective space generated from these photographs was also viewable as the game unfolded, allowing real-time observations of the game.

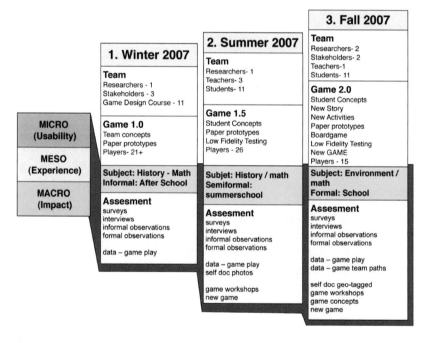

Figure 7.2: How co-design is used across the learning activity.

Interview data came from six girls randomly chosen from the summer 2007 game trial, four of which also participated in the subsequent co-design workshop activity. The interviews were conducted during the workshop the day after the game. We also used observation and procedures sheets that helped the observers to look at aspects such as attitudes, engagement, collaboration, and understanding of the task, the game experience, and roles of players. The six observers were a mixed group of researchers, university students, and members of the local orienteering club that were briefly trained. The primary purpose of the observations was to report critical incidents.

Reflecting on the co-design practices has provided additional information beyond the data we collected from the surveys and interviews. While working with the students in the post-game activities we could see how learners want to become engaged in the activities by connecting the skills of playing games to making games, and relating this knowledge to other learning domains. The preliminary indications of our results offer promises for understanding how informal mobile games can be used as learning tools in traditional educational settings through the active involvement of students in the design of their own learning activities. This can provide ways to understand the learning practices of the students by utilizing the different assessment techniques. The process promotes digital competence of game design and production, provides students with more authentic experiences, and helps the teachers with integrating these practices into the classroom. The game with the surrounding activities has provided us with a way to look at informal learning practices that improve our understanding of the different aspects of mobile learning and its outcomes when learners are involved in the design process.

6. Discussion

The analysis of the different games illustrates the high value of collaboration between players in the teams and in the co-design workshops. During the summer school course the students expressed the interest to learn more about technology in order to extend the game features, and viewed the running and problem solving as positive. Being able to participate in designing the game in combination with actually playing the game is described in the interviews as an enjoyable, creative challenge for the students. The combination of designing new games and creating tasks for the players is something that the students said could be used in integrating different school subjects, such as physical education, environmental education, mathematics, and science studies. Skattjakt has shed light on our research by enabling richer evaluation opportunities that can help the design of future mobile learning games and learning activities with the involvement of learners and teachers.

We have found that a co-design approach looks promising in alleviating some of the challenges faced, such as designing activities that take advantage of mobility and context, have value beyond traditional learning, and begin to address some of the new literacies afforded by this technology (Lankshear and Knobel, 2006). Skattjakt's game-based learning approach integrated with co-design has provided children with powerful opportunities not only to learn through experience, but also to develop meta-level reflections on strategies for learning by making new games (Facer et al., 2004). At the same time, the inclusion of students in the design process provides additional insight for design and evaluation of novel learning processes with mobile technology. In terms of innovation the Skattjakt co-design has moved from an informal activity involving researchers and after-school clubs to a more formal setting of school-based activities involving teachers and students in the design of new games.

Acknowledgements

This work has been partially supported by the Swedish Knowledge Foundation and Växjö University under the ICT and Teacher Training program, project Young Communication. Additional funding has been provided by the Internet Infrastructure Foundation of Sweden, project MeMiMo. Additional in kind support received from Mapping Växjö, NätverketSIP, Norregaard School, and Kronoberg School.

References

Denscombe, M. (2007). *The good research guide for small-scale social research projects*, (3rd ed.). Maidenhead: Open University Press

Facer, K., Joiner, R., Stanton, D., Reid, J., Hull, R. and Kirk, D. (2004). Savannah: mobile gaming and learning? *Journal of Computer Assisted Learning*, 20(6), pp. 399–409

Hoadley, C.M. (2004). Methodological alignment in design-based research. *Educational Psychologist*, 39(4), pp. 203–212

Hooft, M.v.t. and Swan, K. (2007). *Ubiquitous computing in education: invisible technology, visible impact*. Mahwah, NJ: Lawrence Erlbaum

Jonassen, D., Hernandez-Serrano, J. and Choi, I. (2002). Integrating Constructivism and Learning Technologies. In *Integrated and Holistic Perspectives on Learning, Instruction and Technology*, 103–128

Jonassen, D. and Land, S. (2000). *Theoretical Foundations of Learning Environments*. Lawrence Erlbaum Associates

Lankshear, C. and Knobel, M. (2006). *New Literacies: Everyday Practices and Classroom Learning*. Columbus, OH: Open University Press

Penuel, W.R., Roschelle, J. and Shechtman, N. (2007). Designing formative assessment software with teachers: An analysis of the co-design process. *Research and Practice in Technology Enhanced Learning*, 2(2), pp. 51–74

Raessens, J. (2007). Playing history: Reflections on mobile and location-based learning. In Hug, T. (ed.), *Didactics of Microlearning: Concepts, Discourses, and Examples*. Waxmann Verlag

Sotiriou, S. and Chryssafidou, E. (2008). *Collage Implementation Guide*, Ellinogermaniki Agogi, 48

Spikol, D. and Milrad, M. (2008). Combining Physical Activities and Mobile Games to Promote Novel Learning Practices, in *Proceedings of IEEE International Conference on Wireless, Mobile, and Ubiquitous Technology in Education*, pp. 31–38

Vavoula, G. and Sharples, M. (2008). Challenges in evaluating mobile learning. In *Proceedings of MLearn 2008*, Ironbridge, UK, 8–10 October

8. The Fleeting, the Situated and the Mundane: Ethnographic Approaches to Mobile Language Learning (MALL)

CRISTINA ROS I SOLÉ

Overview

This chapter discusses research approaches for researching Mobile Assisted Language Learning (MALL). It draws from research on both traditional Computer Assisted Language Learning (CALL) and recent theoretical and case study research into mobile learning.

The discussion around MALL I present here will allow me to challenge some of the assumptions underlying how Information and Communication Technologies (ICT), e-learning, and networked language learning have traditionally been constructed and reproduced in language pedagogy, and its lack of concern with learners' social and academic practices. In doing this, I will be arguing for an orientation to MALL that situates the learner in a variety of contexts, and looks at the constant flow of experience and activities the learner engages in.

In this chapter I will argue for an approach to researching Mobile Assisted Language Learning (MALL) that has as its focus the learner experience rather than an evaluation of his/her learning. I will propose that such an approach would benefit from adopting an ethnography-as-an-episte-mology methodology (Blommaert, 2005) which questions the assumptions we make about language learning, how we define this knowledge and who owns it (Roberts, Byram, Barro, Jordan and Street, 2001). As a result, I will be arguing for a research methodology that opens up two important avenues. On the one hand, the shift of focus from the technology itself to its embeddedness in the social aspects of the learner; on the other, I will be arguing for a new role for the learner, as a research collaborator, who with the help of technology, accompanies and allows the ethnographer to access fragmented, fluid and multiple sites of learning. Finally, I discuss the implications of such a research agenda for mobile learning in general.

1. Introduction

Doing language learning outside the safe space of the classroom provides students with opportunities for expanding and exploring new aspects of their language learner experience and creates new challenges. Castells, Fernández-Ardévol and Linchuan Qiu (2007) raise an interesting question about the significance of mobile devices in contemporary life when they ask: "Are mobile phones expressions of identity, gadgets of fashion, tools of life, or all of these things?" This question signals that technologies may be regarded as having greater significance for our lives than merely a tool that allows us to perform an activity more effectively. Despite the fact that new technological advances in education are often talked about in terms of their technical capabilities, such as its portability, their interactivity, immediacy, context sensitivity (Naismith et al., 2004), or, indeed, its mobility, we often forget that learning technologies are also embedded in the learners' social worlds and practices. By viewing MALL as a site and a tool for engaging with context and transformative practices rather than just a medium, we acknowledge the much greater import these devices may have for the way we live our lives, our patterns of behaviour and how we make sense of our selves.

When researching the impact of mobile devices in language learning we do not necessarily need to investigate their suitability for a particular pedagogical language learning agenda or for measuring their effectiveness for teaching. Instead, a more ambitious agenda can be set that challenges current conceptions of language learning and addresses questions about social habits and the resulting sense of the language learning self.

The discussion around MALL I present here will allow me to challenge some of the assumptions underlying how Information and Communication Technologies (ICT), e-learning, and networked language learning have traditionally been constructed and reproduced in language pedagogy, and its lack of concern with learners' social and academic practices. In doing this, I will be arguing for an orientation to MALL that situates the learner in a variety of contexts, and looks at the constant flow of experience and activities the learner engages in: "Language as emerging from a person's situatedness and participation in a physical and social world" (Kramsch, 2002, p. 11). In this way, MALL is not taken merely as an aid for the acquisition of language, which can be measured at a particular point in time, but rather, as a continuous engagement with linguistic activity in a variety of contexts.

Indeed, although language learners have mostly been imagined fixed in particular contexts whether abroad or at home, learning languages can involve a succession of activities, set in a multiplicity of sites, which involve a variety of forms of travel between them. Sharples et al. (2007) propose a theory of mobile learning which underlines such a view "we learn across space as we take ideas and learning resources gained in one location and apply or develop them in another. We learn across time, by revisiting knowledge that was gained earlier in a different context, and more broadly (...)" (p. 2).

In today's fragmented, fluid and *liquid* world in which we have changed our solid, fixed lives for more flowing and constantly changing ones (Bauman, 2000), the spaces of the language learner have also diversified and become more fluid: university corridors, community centres, ethnic cafés, Internet meet-ups, and students' bedrooms can all be connected through mobile technology. Language learning settings and routines are under constant transformation and mobile language learning connects these fleeting and ordinary moments in capricious and unpredictable ways. Whether they are public or private spaces, formal or informal ones, the multiple sites of the language learner become the field in which the language learner casts her wide net and constructs new meanings in the target language.

The language learner does not only do language learning in the "domesticated" (Bachelard, 1964) spaces of the institutionally-bound classrooms and residence abroad programmes. Language learners' experiences are also located and travel through a range of informal spaces. Regimented and structured language learning may be defined by rigid educational ideologies, teachers' pedagogical agendas and expectations, and pre-established roles for the learner. In contrast to this, as Sharples et al. (2007) contend, mobile learning subverts this order, e.g. the privileged role of teachers and the regulated educational environment (i.e. the curriculum and examinations which help shaping the learning) in which they operate.

In such a fluid mobile world, away from the traditional educational constraints, language learners may be less bound by the rules and learned behaviours of the language classroom. Instead, mobile language learning may open up new opportunities to perform learning that is mediated by the personal experiences and environments that resonate with each individual. As Kramsch (2002) puts it, language learners engage with the language from a subjective and perceptual point of view, they "do not just learn the language, they are constantly engaged in judging the relevance, validity, pertinence, or usefulness of this or that bit of knowledge" (p. 11). In this way, language learners' knowledge of themselves and others is inflected by the "lived space", the artefacts used, and the meaning attached to them. Mobile devices are not only neutral tools, but artefacts that predispose, embody and shape learners' desire to relate and communicate in another language in specific locations and networks of locations: from the public space of the classroom, or the private world of the bedroom, to the social space of the university cafe; all with their specific audiences and sets of expectations.

Indeed, many authors are beginning to recognise how individuals interact with space when engaged in communication and other meaning-making practices. Individuals are not bound to a particular space, but they are mobile and dynamic, continually exploring and interacting with the physical spaces around them to construct an understanding of themselves and the world around them (Bachelard, 1964; Benwell and Stokoe, 2006; Hall and Du Gay, 1996). In this way, spaces are not just the backdrop where the action takes place, but they become part of the lived experiences, they become personally experienced spaces.

Physical spaces are not arbitrary neutral sites where linguistic resources are deployed, rather, they are the venues where the individual engages in his/her learning. Whether these spaces are used to listen to audio files in the foreign language, to record and rehearse private thoughts into the mp3 recorder, or to take a picture with a mobile phone of an intimate or mundane event, the use of mobile devices for language learning can open new possibilities to experiment with different environments, and the social practices involved in them. The identity of the language learner cannot be studied in isolation from its social and spatial environment, as it is adapted and moulded across time and space, by the different spaces inhabited outside the four walls of the language classroom.

Not only are mobile technologies firmly embedded in space, but they have the power to connect and combine different spaces in complex networks and information flows. As Castells et al. (2007) point out "Mobile communication devices link social practices in multiple spaces" (p. 171) and that "people are here and there, in multiple heres and theres, in a relentless combination of places" (p. 172). Little has been written, however, about what the implications of moving from mainly sedentary learning practices to nomadic ones are for the language learner.

Mobile technology has been hailed as a convenient tool that allows learners to move around as they please, the often heard phrase that mobile devices allow people to operate "anytime, anywhere" is now a well known leitmotif. But mobile learning is also mobile in terms of its ability to permeate different areas of life (Naismith et al., 2004). Indeed, the fluidity of space goes beyond the physicality of a change of location and has implications for how research on the use of these devices could be conducted. And, above all, the multiplicity of spaces and the mobility of the language learner challenge the appropriacy of exclusively positivist and context-independent methodologies for conducting research into mobile language learning.

2. A need for a new methodology

We should then ask ourselves: what is the most appropriate methodology to investigate issues concerning MALL's personal experiences and social practices? Before I go on to describe the methodology proposed here and its practical consequences, I will give a brief review of the methodological approaches which have been used in the past to investigate CALL and discuss what epistemologies and research orientations underlie them.

2.1   A brief history of methodological approaches to CALL research

It has often been assumed that educationalists and researchers know best how to apply knowledge to the outside world. Indeed, the popular belief is that knowledge resides with the experts and the academia and that they are the ones dispensing and applying it to the outside world. Such a view is based on positivist methodological approaches in which knowledge and patterns of behaviour can be detached from the spatio-temporal context in which they occur (Lantolf and Pavlenko, 2000). In this paper, I will challenge such an assumption and take the view that the integration of new ICT tools and Computer Mediated Communication (CMC) media, such as social networking and mobile technology, are not only bringing new tools that make some tasks more effective, but they also bring with them new learning cultures whose description and research focus may require different epistemological orientations rooted in context, space and social practices.

Studies in CMC over the last few decades have made use of both quantitative and qualitative methodologies which are underpinned by similar approaches to language learning. Although meta-studies charting research topics and methodologies in this field have shown that these studies adopt both experimental and more descriptive methodological approaches (Lamy and Hampel, 2007), these have been mostly rooted in a vision of language learning that focuses on language acquisition rather than on learners themselves and how they relate with their environment.

Thus, most CALL and CMC research to date has been characterised by hypothesis-testing approaches and empirical methodologies. Such research orientations have the focus on linguistic outcomes rather than accounting for the unpredictable and the contingent in language learning. As Debski (2003) points out in his survey of CALL research from 1980 to 2000, most studies on CALL started from some level of *a priori* expectations, which were expressed as research questions.

Although some authors recognise that CALL is not only a technological medium that acts as the conduit for information and social practices, but the very site where these practices are shaped and produced (Lamy and Hampel, 2007; Pettit and Kukulska-Hulme, 2006), a great deal of the studies found in CALL are still rooted in outcomes-based methodologies. As a result, there is a tendency in CALL research to interfere with context and setting by creating artificial conditions for conducting the research, rather than researching a naturalistic context, the social practices that develop in it, and the experience of the language learner.

Whereas a common position has been that new technologies should just be seen as a medium that should be interjected, normalised and made invisible in the language classroom (e.g. Bax, 2003), new methodological research orientations are starting to voice the need to investigate the learning experience provided by new technologies, for example, as the sites where new literacies are developed (Kress and Van Leeuwen, 2001; Richards 2000; Ros i Solé and Mardomingo, 2004) and as the springboard for a "transformative" role which endows the learners a stronger agency (Burnett et al., 2007).

My position here is that the focus of MALL research should be one that observes and learns together with the learner, across the learner's activities and sites of learning. An ethnography-as-epistemology approach could help us describe these situated routines and practices of the MALL user by questioning past assumptions about CALL practices, the nature of knowledge acquired through it and the role of the learner in creating it.

2.2 A possible way forward: Using ethnographic approaches to study MALL

There is a new wave of research in new media in sociolinguistics (Androutsopoulos, 2008), educational technology (Goodfellow and Lea, forthcoming) sociological studies (Hine, 2000), and applied linguistics (Chambers, 2000; O'Dowd, 2005) which is introducing ethnographic approaches to CMC. Indeed, recent research studies in computers and education are beginning to shift the emphasis of e-learning as technology and as learning tools, to explore the social uses and practices that they introduce in the fabric of society (e.g. Bates, 2005; Burnett et al., 2007;

Goodfellow and Lea, forthcoming). Pettit and Kukulska-Hulme (2006) believe that there is a need to integrate innovative uses of technology into existing behaviours to the point that mobile devices "come to symbolize a greater focus on students and users" (p. 1).

Ethnography allows the researcher to be an observer of the learning culture of mobile use and how it is shaping the socio-technical agenda. At the same time, it allows us to take a reflexive, critical stance. As Roberts et al. (2001) point out "Only by exposure to another medium – 'taking the fish out of water' – can we identify the nature of the medium we take for granted: the outside ethnographer, by dint of distance from the culture can draw attention to its fundamental tenets and epistemological presuppositions" (p. 91). In this way, if we want to investigate technology, we will acquire an analytical distance and explore how meanings and practices are established in this new medium. The stress here lies in how patterns of behaviour already exist out there, and how research can analyse and make sense of those patterns. The researcher becomes a participant-observer by "hanging around" and documenting the mundane activities that learners engage in. The boundaries between the observable and the observed become blurred as the participant-investigator strikes a close relationship with the informants.

We must be aware, however, of the tension there is in ethnography, between the distance the researcher needs to acquire, and the familiarity and intimate knowledge of the culture s/he must acquire (Roberts et al., 2001). The consequence of this for the study of mobile technology is that the researcher needs to become familiar with language learners' daily practices whilst at the same time remaining reflexive of his/her own practices. Such an intimate knowledge of the learner needs to be coupled with a good dose of reflexivity, where the researcher questions and relativises her own knowledge, i.e. her own assumptions about the nature and use of new technologies for language learning. Indeed, her pedagogical knowledge must be put to one side and be prepared to "view the knowledge of other societies with a more open mind" (Roberts et al., 2001). The researcher will need to put aside her knowledge of how past technologies have been used for language learning and get into the head of the mobile user and his/her beliefs and norms to make sense of the practices, incidents and events in which s/he makes sense of his/her language learning.

2.3 Focusing on ordinary mobile practices

An ethnographic methodology allows the researcher to avoid making generalising statements on the way individuals learn a language, and instead, it tells a story of a particular group of language learners with its variations, particularities, and context dependent features. In doing this, it gives a thick description of their ordinary language learning social practices in a variety of settings, spaces and social contexts and looks for emerging patterns of behaviours. The need for changing the lens through which to research mobile learning practices follows parallel methodological attempts in research on technological settings.

In order to tease out the practices of the "digitally mobile" language learner, the ethnographer will not create an artificial environment or task, but rather, she will try to observe what is going on in the "natural" environment. With mobile technology this can be achieved either directly through traditional participatory observation in which the researcher goes "native" and tries to integrate and participate in the culture under study, or by using technology as an "impartial" observer, and participants themselves as research "collaborators". Such participatory observation will help us experience, bring to the fore, and discover the implicit participant meanings in certain social and local mobile learning practices. After all, the meanings that the ethnographer wants to uncover are not the extraordinary but rather those of ordinary life, e.g. the mundane and fleeting language learning activities learners engage with mobile devices on a daily basis.

As Okabe and Ito's (2006) ethnographic study on the use of mobile phone cameras reports, such an approach and methodology allows us to observe mobile uses in naturalistic settings and everyday practices across a range of contexts. The ubiquity of mobile camera use in Tokyo in 2000, enabled these researchers to record participants' habits and practices rather than designing a new experimental setting for the purposes of the research. In their study, they asked participants to note in diary form the physical and social contexts in which they engaged in. This information, together with information provided in the pictures they had taken un-prompted with their mobile devices, was then used as a resource to co-construct the meaning and patterns of their "techno-social" habits with the researcher. The cameras on the mobile phones were used to record the social events digitally, with the participants themselves acting as a kind of research collaborator. The results of the study showed that mobile-photo practices are often more personal, intimate and mundane than traditional camera usage. Their conclusion that "camera phones captured the more fleeting and unexpected moments of surprise, beauty and adoration in the everyday" (Okabe and Ito, 2006, p. 17) is also a telling justification of the ethnographic method.

Similarly, ethnography could allow researchers to approach language learning as practice rather than as a body of knowledge to be transmitted from the teacher or the prescribed texts (e.g. textbooks, grammar books) to the students. From a socio-cultural approach to language learning knowledge is not something that exists in the abstract or just living inside the brain of our students. Language knowledge is not information that migrates from one place to another; rather, it consists of the way knowledge and structures are presented, encountered and deployed in specific language (learning) contexts and socialisation practices, such as those involving the use of mobile devices. By looking at the use of mobile devices for language learning from such a point of view, i.e. ordinary day-to-day practices situated in a social world, we could explore issues that go beyond a specific scene or pedagogical site. To summarise, by using ethnographic methods for researching language learning we are doing two things. One the one hand, we are concentrating on the characteristics of the technology to focus on the mundane, the fleeting and the private of social events, or as Wali et al. (this volume) have put it, the procedural aspects of mobile learning and the data it generates across multiple contexts, both social and physical. And, on the other, we are using the technology to access fragmented, fluid and multiple sites of learning which would be otherwise beyond our reach. As Hooft (this volume) states "collecting data can and should no longer be an issue of concern for the researcher alone. Involving the learner and his/her technology is essential" (Chapter 10, p. 3).

3. Conclusion: Proposing a new research methodology agenda

Most research to date on the use of CALL has limited its field of enquiry to the educational sphere and within a view of learning in which the fluidity of learners' social actions and their meaning making practices are not accounted for. In this article I have argued that in order to do justice to the potential of new technologies for language learning, we need to start looking at how language learning is situated in ordinary social life and practices, its physical spaces, as well as critically reflecting on them. Most of the research in the last twenty years or so has concentrated either on the pedagogical use of various technologies and how to normalise them into specific pedagogical and "domesticated" spaces, or to study independent and outcome-driven learning variables. The advent of mobile learning, however, is a strong reminder that learning does not happen in neutral, aseptic places that just act as the background of learning, but that technology, as well as the places in which it is situated, open up new possibilities for learner's agency and the creation of new social practices in language learning.

This paper proposes to change our perspective on what counts as communication in the language learning context. The use of digital mobile devices takes us outside the classrooms and into the social worlds and communicative practices of our students. I hope that this chapter will help to set out a new agenda for technology-enhanced language learning methodology, based on the belief that we need to shift our attention from technology as a tool to seeing it as a site that shapes social practices and identities.

At the same time, such an approach to MALL has wider implications. It shows how mobile learning research opens up exciting new avenues for re-configuring what learning means and for how we go about exploring new research approaches to investigate it. It questions prevalent views on learning by widening the contexts in which learning takes place, by including more mundane and social aspects and redefining what counts as learning, and by emphasizing the fluidity and connectivity between multiple learning spaces. It also challenges the ways in which we conceive research by requiring methodological epistemologies which place the learner and its social world at the centre. In order to do this, such a methodology requires that the roles of researcher and researched are democratised and re-defined by inviting the learner to take place in the research process.

References

Androutsopoulos, J. (2008). Potentials and limitations of discourse-centred online ethnography. In J. Androutsopoulos and M. Beisswenger (eds), *Data and methods in computer-mediated discourse analysis: new approaches.* Special Issue of Language@Internet http://www.languageainternet.de

Bachelard, G. (1964). *The Poetics of Space.* Boston, MA: Beacon Press

Bates, A.W. (2005). *Technology, e-learning, and distance education* (2nd ed.). New York: Routledge

Bauman, Z. (2000). *Liquid Modernity.* Cambridge: Polity Press

Bax, S. (2003). CALL– past, present, future. *System* (31) 1, 13–28

Blommaert, J. (2005). Bourdieu The Ethnographer. *The Translator*, 11(2), pp. 199–236

Benwell, B. and Stokoe, E. (2006). *Discourse and Identity.* Edinburgh: Edinburgh University Press

Burnett, C., Merchant, G. and Myers, J. (2007). English and ICT: Moving towards transformation of the curriculum. Available at http://www.ite.org.uk/ite_readings/english_and_ict_20071130.pdf [accessed on 9 June 2008]

Castells, M., Fernández-Ardévol, M., Linchuan Qiu, J. (2007). *Mobile Communication and Society: a Global Perspective.* London: MIT Press

Chambers, A. (2000). Current Practice in CALL: Teachers' Attitudes and other Factors that Limit the Potential of CALL. MA dissertation, Canterbury Christ Church University College, UK

Debski, R. (2003). Analysis of Research in CALL (1980–2000) with a reflection of CALL as an academic discipline. ReCALL 15(2) pp. 177–188

Goodfellow, R. and Lea, M. (forthcoming). Challenging e-learning in the university. Maidenhead: McGraw Hill Education/Open University Press

Hall, S. and Du Gay, P. (1996). *Questions of Cultural Identity.* London: Sage

Hine, C. (2000). *Virtual ethnography.* London: Sage

Kramsch, C. (2002). Language acquisition and language socialization: ecological perspectives. London: Continuum

Kress, G. and Van Leeuwen, T. (2001). Multimodal Discourse: The modes and media of contemporary communication. London: Arnold

Lamy, M.N. and Hampel, R. (2007). *Online Communication in Language Learning and Teaching.* London: Palgrave McMillan

Lantolf, J. and Pavlenko, A. (2000). Second language learning as participation and the (re)construction of selves. In J. Lantolf (ed.), *Sociocultural Theory and Second Language Learning.* Oxford: Oxford University Press

Naismith, L., Londsdale, P., Giasemi, V. and Sharples, M. (2004). Literature Review in Mobile Technologies and Learning. *Futurelab.* Available at http://www.futurelab.org.uk/resources/documents/lit_reviews/Mobile_Review.pdf [accessed on 14 November 2007

O'Dowd, R. (2005). The Use of video-conferencing and e-mail as mediators of intercultural student ethnography. In Belz, J.A. and S.L.Thorne (eds), *Computer Mediated Intercultural Foreign Language Education.* Boston, MA: Heinle and Heinle

Okabe, D. and Ito, M. (2006). Everyday contexts of camera phone use: steps toward techno-social ethnographic frameworks. In Joachim R. Höflich, Maren Hartmann (eds), *Mobile Communication in Everyday Life – Ethnographic Views, Observations and Reflections.* Berlin: Frank and Timme

Pettit, J. and Kukulska-Hulme, A. (2006). Going with the grain: mobile devices in practice. ASCILTE Conference, Sydney, October 2006

Richards, C. (2000). Hypermedia, Internet communication, and the challenge of redefining literacy in the electronic age. *Language Learning and Technology*, 4(2), pp. 59–77

Roberts, C., Bryam, M., Barro, A., Jordan, S. and Street B. (2001). *Language Learners as Ethnographers*. Clevedon: Multilingual Matters

Ros i Solé, C. and Mardomingo, R. (2004). Trayectorias: a new model for on-line task based learning. *ReCALL* 16(1), pp. 145–157

Sharples, M., Taylor, J. and Vavoula, G. (2007). A Theory of Learning for the Mobile Age. In Andrews, R. and Haythornthwaite, C. (eds), *The SAGE Handbook of E-learning Research*. London: Sage, pp. 221–247

9. Mobile Learning Evaluation: The Challenge of Mobile Societies

JOHN TRAXLER

Overview

This chapter looks at the apparent difficulty of the mobile learning community to develop an adequate portfolio of rigorous and appropriate research methods with which to support the evaluation of mobile learning. The chapter tentatively proposes that this difficulty lies not wholly in a failure of the imagination or the confidence of the community to develop these tools and techniques but rather in the gulf between modernism represented by the expectations of much evaluation and postmodernism represented by societies increasingly transformed by mobility.

1. Efforts to date

Recent publications (Kukulska-Hulme and Traxler, 2005; JISC, 2005) and conference proceedings (for example, Ally, 2006; Attewell and Savill-Smith, 2004; Oliver, 2007) have put a large number of case studies documenting trials and pilots (and their evaluations) into the public domain. They show that mobile learning is poised to break through the barriers of scale, embedding and durability and to deliver greater inclusion, opportunity, participation and equity in learning.[1] However, evaluation that

---

[1] Other initiatives, such as the Microsoft Mobile Learning Summit in Seattle in August 2007, the launch of MoLeNET in London in September 2007 and the establishment

is rigorous in the eyes of the necessarily increased range of stakeholders is becoming a prerequisite for securing the necessary resources, funding and support. The tools and techniques for such evaluations are part of the wider repertoire of research tools and techniques explored elsewhere in this book. Several recent papers by Traxler and Kukulska-Hulme (2005, for example) explore and assess the current philosophies and practices of evaluation in mobile learning and highlight a number of concerns. One of these concerns is the tension between the trustworthiness of established tools and techniques for educational evaluation on the one hand and their appropriateness to the novel mobile environment on the other; a related concern is the small number of evaluations that use techniques and tools indigenous to mobile learning. So there are challenges to the development of credible and authentic tools and techniques for the current generation of pilots and trials.

The evaluation of mobile learning must however also address the challenge of moving from informal and impressionistic accounts to the sort of large-scale and longer-term studies that are the prelude to sustained and widespread deployment supported by sector-wide institutions and by government agencies. These are the prelude to the move into the domain of evidence-based decision-making.[2] To recognise this challenge is to recognise that of course evaluation always has an implied readership and audience and begs question about why and how to align the methods of evaluation, and any underlying methodology and philosophy, to the expectations of the readership and audience. How far should an evaluation attempt to shift or

of the International Association for Mobile Learning in Melbourne in October 2007, corroborate this impression.

2   "Evidence-based decision-making" is itself problematic. As Sanderson (2004) points out in an article entitled "Has evidence-based policy any evidence base?", there is no evidence for it! Espousing it as the basis for decision-making is arbitrary and no more rational than resorting to expertise or religious faith. It does however characterise a modernist approach. In the context of evaluation as an evidence-generating practice, especially evaluation in relation to funders and funding, we should bear in mind that "evidence-based policy formulation" is, in the words of Ian Gibson's MP Chair of the Committee Science And Technology Committee remark (Hansard, 2004) in the UK Parliament increasingly derided as "policy-based evidence formulation".

challenge the expectations of its readers? When readers are project funders and evaluators are the project workers themselves, these are not merely "technical" questions but ones that have a very real impact. One respected evaluator (Somekh, 2001, p. 101) recognises this when she says,

> Evaluation is a fascinating, socially useful, morally demanding and highly politicised activity. Its future depends on the uses we put it to, and the role it is given by sponsors and politicians.

These are all major challenges but the purpose of this current chapter is rather different.

2. A different perspective

In looking at evaluation efforts to date and seeing a picture of only partial success in terms of rigour and credibility, it is possible that what we see is not purely the outcome of insufficient confidence and inadequate imagination in meeting the challenges of researching mobile learning and of developing evaluation techniques and tools local to mobile learning, be it innovative or large-scale. We may be seeing something more profound, a mismatch between the (implicit) ethos of much mobile learning and the (implicit) philosophy of its research (and specifically, evaluation) methods.

Mobile devices, systems and technologies are the symptoms and causes of societies and cultures in motion (not just literally). These societies and cultures are changing profoundly, they are in fact becoming recognisably *postmodern* societies in many aspects and therein lies the root of the difficulties with evaluation, not only at the technical level but at the philosophical level. Evaluation however, specifically in terms of its philosophy and methods, is a *modernist* project taking place in a progressively more postmodern environment, in a postmodern environment catalysed and propelled by ubiquitous connected personal mobile devices, systems and technologies. This is of course to over-simplify. The diffusion, absorption and effect of these devices, systems and technologies are by no means uniform. Even if it were possible to treat them as a stable, monolithic and homogeneous whole, their impact and interaction differs across regions, classes, gender, generations and across sub-cultures.

Before proceeding, it is sensible to outline some of the characteristics of these philosophical ideas. At a recent conference, I thought it would be useful to provide the "headlines" of modernism and came up with:

- history is going somewhere – progress is a good thing

- science will give us the answers – technology will help

- reality is real – language can describe it

- education improves people – society is generally benign

- morality and causality are fairly straightforward.

Not profound but hopefully sufficient for our purpose! Modernism is the cultural and intellectual climate in Western Europe arising out of the Enlightenment and characterised by logical positivism, empiricism, rationality *etc*. By comparison, postmodernism has been characterised as the loss of confidence and faith in these tenets, often referred to as an "incredulity at meta [grand] narratives" (Lyotard, 1999), or referred to as a questioning. There is not, of course, any assumed or necessary progression from pre-modern through modern to postmodern. As my headlines hint, postmodernism questions science, history and the possible teleology or purpose behind them:

> In postmodernity we are now also re-examining the Enlightenment idea of history as being capable of being guided towards a single ideal goal, the establishing throughout human societies of a universal model of reason, embodied in a hopefully triumphant agent or subject, whether this be the working class or the state or European Reason itself. (Docker, 1999, p. 109)

> Lyotard is perhaps best known for his critique of what he calls Grand Narratives. In the postmodern age we no longer have a positivistic science that claims to know the truth; rather, science, as in the new quantum mechanics associated with Chaos Theory, now tells stories, competing stories, as in any other area of knowledge. We can no longer call on a tradition of speculative philosophy, as in Hegel, that claims to see history and society in their totality. (Docker, 1999, p. 109)

> Another Grand Narrative Lyotard says in the Postmodern Condition we should disregard is that of teleology, a story of progress for the whole of humanity. In "Answering the Question: What is Postmodernism?", Lyotard tells us that in the era of postmodernity we must severely re-examine the Enlightenment idea of a unitary end of history and of a subject. (Docker, 1999, p. 111)

All this does not make postmodernism an easy concept to competently define, because its many manifestations are linked only as a reaction to modernism, and to a range of cultural and intellectual movements growing out of a century of global warfare and the perceived inadequacy of the dominant "isms" of the preceding two centuries. Butler (2002) gives some insight into the problem of definition, saying:

> postmodernists ... do not simply support aesthetic "isms", or avant-garde movements such as minimalism or conceptualism ... They have a distinct way of seeing the world as a whole, and use a set of philosophical ideas that not only support an aesthetic but also analyse a "late capitalist" cultural condition of "postmodernity". This condition is supposed to affect us all, not just through avant-garde art, but at a more fundamental level, through the influence of that huge growth in media communications by electronic means .... And yet, ... most information is to be mistrusted, as being more of a contribution to the manipulative image-making of those in power than to the advancement of knowledge. The postmodernist attitude is therefore one of suspicion .... (p. 3)

and

> A postmodernist view of the social changes that have most affected contemporary society would therefore ... emphasise such matters as the extraordinary compression of time and space through the new media. (p. 117)

A related movement, poststructuralism is a further complication and could be characterised as a philosophical (that is, epistemological, ethical and ontological and hence methodological), response to the condition of postmodernity. Belsey (2002, p. 5) explains it as follows:

> Poststructuralism names a theory, or a group of theories, concerning the relationship between human beings, the world, and the practice of making and reproducing meanings. On the one hand, poststructuralists affirm that consciousness is not the origin of the language we speak and the images we recognise, so much as the product of the meanings we learn and reproduce. On the other hand, communication

changes all the time, with or without intervention from us, and we can choose to intervene with a view to altering the meanings – which is to say the norms and values our culture takes for granted.

So for poststructuralists, language is an important agent in making our world rather than just the passive vehicle for describing it.

A final complication is the debate about whether societies are indeed becoming postmodern. Alternative formulations include Giddens' (1990) "high modernity", a formulation that seems to recognise the changes ascribed to mobility but not to label them as emergent postmodernism, and Bauman's (2000) "liquid modernity", his term for the present condition of the world as contrasted with the "solid" modernity that preceded it, a world in which nothing keeps its shape, and social forms are constantly changing at great speed, radically transforming the experience of being human.

3. The pointers

There is already exploration of the relationships between mobility and learning and this chapter looking at evaluation should be seen in that wider context. There is for example the well established conference series based in the Hungarian Academy of Sciences (see for example Nyiri, 2005) though this is perhaps still uncovering a shared language and so betrays its origins as the sociologists of mobility engage with the technologists and pedagogues of mobile learning. The purpose of this chapter is to explore the possible relationships between mobile learning and postmodernity insofar as they raise issues for evaluation and research tools and techniques. Some relevant aspects of this emergent and patchy postmodernity are discussed below.

Mobile technologies are reconfiguring the relationships between public and private spaces, and the ways in which these are penetrated by mobile virtual spaces. Virtual communities and discussions had previously been mediated by static networked PCs in dedicated times, places and spaces; now mobile technologies propel these communities and discussions into physical public and private spaces, forcing changes and adjustments to all three as we learn to manage a more fluid environment. This is increasingly documented in the literature of mobilities (see for example Plant, 2000; Katz and Aakhus, 2002; Ling, 2004; and Brown et al., 2002, for a range of accounts and instances). Cooper (2002, p. 22) remarks that the private "is no longer conceivable as what goes on, discreetly, in the life of the individual away from the public domain, or as subsequently represented in individual consciousness". Sheller and Urry (2003, p. 1) argue "that massive changes are occurring in the nature of both public and private life and especially of the relations between them"; and Bull (2005, p. 344) says that "the use of these mobile sound technologies informs us about how users attempt to 'inhabit' the spaces within which they move. The use of these technologies appears to bind the disparate threads of much urban movement together, both 'filling' the spaces 'in-between' communication or meetings and structuring the spaces thus occupied."

Mobile technologies are redefining discourse and conversation. Rather than conversation being set aside as something one does at certain moments, for a delimited stretch of time, usually in a private space (or semi-private phone "box" or "booth"), there is now "a constant flickering of conversation" (Sheller, 2004, p. 5). See the sources mentioned above and for example, Murtagh's (2002) account of the use made of a wide set of non-verbal actions and interactions with the mobile phone in public. In order to maintain discourse and connectedness across different spaces we are devising and learning new protocols. We are, for example, devising new "tie-signs" (Goffman, 1971) in order to manage simultaneous conversations in real and virtual space.

Mobile technologies are eroding established – and largely Western European, perhaps Protestant – notions of time as the common structure for scheduling, co-ordinating and organising activities and events. Plant (2000) talks about the "approx-meeting" and the "multi-meeting", Sørensen and colleagues (2002) about "socially negotiated time", Ling (2004) about the "microcoordination of everyday life" alongside the "softening of schedules" afforded by mobile devices and Nyiri (2006, p. 301) says, "with the mobile phone, time has become personalized". Whereas previously our social and business relations had to be organised and synchronised by absolute clock time, now mobile technologies allow us to renegotiate meetings and events on-the-fly. Mobile technologies are also eroding physical place as a predominant attribute of space. Gergen (2002) talks about "absent presence", and Plant (2002) says that mobile phones have created "simultaneity of place": a physical space and a virtual space of conversational interaction, and an extension of physical space, through the creation and juxtaposition of a mobile "social space". Mobile technologies now enable us to carry our various virtual communities with us but physical communities – the family, the town, the school, the cohort – may be devalued.

Mobile devices, systems and technologies, as the media and containers of knowledge and information, are creating new and highly individualised ontologies – consumer choice turned into what has been called the "neo-liberal nightmare" – and creating fragmented learners in a "fragmented society" to use Bauman's (2001) phrase in an accurate but narrower sense than he intended. Benedek (2005, p. 1) said, "knowledge shaped by mobile communication is also more individualized than knowledge gained at school because its actual content presupposes the infrastructure of socially relevant cognitive achievements."

Mobile devices, systems and technologies are creating virtual communities and groupings, sometimes transient ones, arguably at the expense of existing and traditional ones (captured in Howard Rheingold's (2003) defining book on "Smart Mobs") and creating new norms, expectations, ethics and etiquettes, including languages, obviously "textspeak" and also the "missed call" phenomenon around the world (Donner, 2007). More are described in Ling (1997, 2004). These technologies are possibly shifting ideas about the self and identity. Geser (2004, p. 11) points out that, "the cell phone helps to stay permanently within the closed social field of familiar others: thus reinforcing a unified, coherent individual identity."

Mobile technologies are converging with social software, accelerating the growth of user-generated content, and decentralising and fracturing the production and control of ideas and information. The growth of citizen-journalism (Owen, 2005) is one example; the recent migration of Facebook, Google, Google Maps and YouTube onto mobile devices being others. They are creating new politics and political groupings, and are creating new and transformed notions of exclusion and disadvantage; the modernist notion of the "digital divide" is revealed as problematic (Traxler, 2008). Rheingold (2003) gives accounts of some of these groupings, for example creating and co-ordinating the protest actions against President Estrada in the Philippines.

Mobile technologies provide increased levels of surveillance and oversight, even in the course of delivering and supporting learning. Many of the current authors cite Lyon (2001) in the wider context of a surveillance society. Foucault took Bentham's image of a prison equipped with pervasive and perfect surveillance, the "panopticon", as a metaphor for postmodern society, a society where such surveillance need not actually be exercised because it becomes internalised and habitualised, forever changing our relations with each other and ourselves through what he calls "technologies of the self". In his words, "there is no need for arms, physical violence.... Just a gaze. An inspecting gaze, a gaze which each individual under its weight will end interiorizing that he is his own overseer, each individual thus exercising this surveillance over, and against himself" (Foucault, 1977).

Mobile technologies facilitate the generation of new knowledge, intruding a new dimension into the debate and dichotomy between utilitarian and liberal views of education, and challenging the notion of education as a modernist meta-narrative, a universal canon and a common curriculum, and they deliver knowledge and information in ways that challenge formal learning, its institutions and its professionals, specifically in their roles as gate-keepers to both learning and technology. Less privileged individuals can now access information of their choosing using their own devices without needing to accept the constraints and conditions that were historically imposed on them. At the same time, these technologies facilitate people's direct experience of – "messy", "noisy" – "reality", challenging the reductionism and foundationalism of established educational orthodoxy that manages and controls how "reality" is represented within the classroom as subjects, curricula and levels, and as lectures, lessons, demonstrations and simulations.

These observations suggest that our society is better characterised as postmodern than as modern, or more precisely, that those parts of our society best characterised as postmodern are those where these characteristics of mobility are most evident; clearly parts of our society are characterised by neither mobility nor postmodernity, and nor even modernity in some parts. On the other hand, the evaluation of mobile learning seems to be still basically modern in its approach. Traxler and Kukulska-Hulme (2005) suggest this may be the unreflective default or the "common-sense" position rather than an informed and deliberate choice. They remark, for example, that there is little evidence of researchers engaged in evaluating mobile learning taking an explicit position on epistemology or ethics or other aspects of philosophy.

Furthermore, if we look at a recent taxonomy of mobile learning (Kukulska-Hulme and Traxler, 2007) we see a possible division between, on the one hand, types of mobile learning that are easy to evaluate, for example "technology-driven mobile learning", "the connected classroom" and "miniature but portable e-learning" and "mobile training/performance support", and, on the other hand, the one type that is likely to be much more challenging to evaluate, namely "informal, personalised, situated mobile learning". This may be a purely technical methodological problem due to the likely presence of too many confounding variables, too much "noise" and too little "signal", or it may reveal a division between those types of mobile learning that grow out of modernism and those that grow out of mobility and post-modernity.

4. Conclusions and recommendations

The implication of the misalignment and confusion that we have described is that the mobile learning community need to recognise their under-lying philosophical assumptions, affiliations and preferences, in order to explore the research practices that grow out of postmodernism (and perhaps poststructuralism) (see Denzin and Lincoln (2005) for one of the most authoritative accounts of these themes) alongside their existing practices. This should not however be taken as a call for more techniques or new methods but for an exploration of the philosophical foundation of techniques and methods in general. One specific example might serve as a point of departure and an example of the direction that the mobile learning community should explore. Grounded theory is an established social research technique; it is however established around a "realist" or modernist perspective (Strauss and Corbin, 1998) and this is only now challenged by a constructionist (that is, loosely poststructuralist) alternative (Charmaz, 2002). Whilst these various approaches to Grounded Theory use the same techniques, the established and original approach adopted a "scientific" position in relation to qualitative data gathered by researchers who apparently "bracket off" their subjectivity and partiality. Some of the subsequent approaches challenged the rhetoric of science and (alleged) objectivity and built a different conception of evidence and outcomes. This might be a model for revisiting other accepted techniques and tools and examining their relationships to underlying but perhaps tacit philosophies and for revising how the evidence and outcomes of mobile learning evaluation are positioned and understood.

In conclusion, this account is a quite modernist critique of modernism; it presents a problem and it attempts to provide a solution; it "essentialises" by bundling all sorts of activities and artefacts under the title of "mobile devices, systems and technologies" and it shows a residue of faith and optimism in society, knowledge, technology and learning!

References

Ally, M. (2006). *mLearn2006 Book of Abstracts*. Available at www.mlearn. org.za/CD/BOA_p.07.pdf

Attewell, J. and Savill-Smith, C. (eds). (2004). *Proceedings of MLEARN2003 Conference*. London: LSDA

Bauman, Z. (2001). *The Individualized Society*. Cambridge: Polity

Bauman, Z. (2000). *Liquid Modernity*. Cambridge: Polity

Benedek, A. (2005). New Vistas of Learning in the Mobile Age. In K. Nyiri (ed), *Proceedings of Seeing, Understanding, Learning in the Mobile Age*, 28–30 April 2005. Budapest: Hungarian Academy of

Sciences. Available at http://www.socialscience.t-mobile.hu/2005/
Benedek_abst.pdf

Belsey, C. (2002). *Poststructuralism – A Very Short Introduction*. Oxford:
Oxford University Press

Brown, B., Green, N. and Harper, R. (2002). *Wireless World – social and
interactional aspects of the mobile age*. London: Springer

Bull, M. (2005). No Dead Air! The iPod and the Culture of Mobile
Listening. *Leisure Studies*, 24(4), 343–356

Butler, C. (2002). *Postmodernism – A Very Short Introduction*. Oxford:
Oxford University Press

Charmaz, K. (2002). Grounded Theory – Objectivist and Constructivist
Methods. In J.F. Gubrium and J.A. Holstein (eds), *Handbook of
Interview Research – Context and Method*. London: SAGE Publications,
pp. 509–535

Cooper, G. (2002). The Mutable World: Social Theory in The Wireless
World. In B. Brown, N. Green and R. Harper (eds), *Wireless World:
Social and Interactional Aspects of the Mobile World*. London:
Springer

Denzin, N.K. and Lincoln, Y.S. (eds). (2005). *The SAGE Handbook of
Qualitative Research 4th Edition*. London: Sage

Docker, J. (1999). *Postmodernism and popular culture – a cultural history*.
Cambridge, UK: Cambridge University Press

Donner, J. (2007). The rules of beeping: Exchanging messages via intentional "missed calls" on mobile phones. *Journal of Computer-Mediated
Communication*, 13(1)

Foucault, M. (1977). Power/knowledge: selected interviews and other writings 1972–1977, trans. and ed. by Gordon, C. New York: Pantheon

Gergen, K.J. (2002). The challenge of absent presence. In Katz, J.E. and
Aakhus M.A. (eds), *Perpetual Contact. Mobile Communication, Private
Talk, Public Performance*. Cambridge: Cambridge University Press,
pp. 227–241

Geser, H. (2004). Towards a Sociological Theory of the Mobile Phone.
University of Zurich

Giddens, A. (1990). *The Consequences of Modernity*. Stanford, CA:
Standford University Press

Goffman, E. (1971). *Relations in Public*. Harmondsworth: Allen Lane

Hansard. (2004). Science And Technology Committee, Committee Office, House of Commons, No. 81 of Session 2003–04, 8 November 2004. Available at http://www.parliament.uk/parliamentary_committees/science_and_technology_committee/scitech081104.cfm

JISC. (2005). Innovative Practice with e-Learning: a good practice guide to embedding mobile and wireless technologies into everyday practice. Bristol: Joint Information Services Committee

Katz, J.E. and Aakhus, M. (eds). (2002). *Perpetual Contact – Mobile Communications, Private Talk, Public Performance*. Cambridge, UK: Cambridge University Press

Kukulska-Hulme, A. and Traxler, J. (eds). (2005). Mobile Learning: A Handbook for Educators and Trainers. London: Routledge

Kukulska-Hulme, A. and Traxler, J. (2007). Design for Mobile and Wireless Technologies In H. Beetham and R. Sharpe (2007). *Rethinking Pedagogy for the Digital Age*. London: Routledge

Ling, R. (2004). *The Mobile Connection – the cell phone's impact on society*. San Francisco, CA: Morgan Kaufmann Publishers

Ling, R. (1997). One can talk about mobile manners! The use of mobile telephones in appropriate situations. In L. Haddon (ed.), *Communications on the Move: the experience of mobile telephony in the 1990s*, COST 248 Report. Farsta: Telia

Lyon, D. (2001). *Surveillance Society – monitoring everyday life*. Buckingham, UK: Open University Press

Lyotard, J-F. (1999). *La Condition postmoderne: Rapport sur le savoir (The Postmodern Condition: A Report on Knowledge)*. Trans. G. Bennington and B. Massumi (1979) from *La Condition postmoderne: Rapport sur le savoir*, Paris). Minneapolis: University of Minnesota Press and Manchester: Manchester University Press

Nyiri, K. (2006). Time and Communication. In F. Stadler and M. Stöltzner (eds), *Time and History: Proceeding of the 28 International Ludwig Wittgenstein Symposium*, 2005. Kirchberg am Wechsel, Austria

Nyiri, K. (ed.). (2005). *Proceedings of Seeing, Understanding, Learning in the Mobile Age*, 28–30 April 2005. Budapest: Hungarian Academy of Sciences

Murtagh, G. (2002). Seeing the "Rules": Preliminary Observations of Action, Interaction and Mobile Phone Use. In B. Brown, N. Green and R. Harper (eds), *Wireless World: Social and Interactional Aspects of the Mobile World*. London: Springer

Oliver, C. (2007). mLearn2007 Conference Proceedings. Available at http://www.mlearn2007.org/files/mLearn_2007_Conference_ Proceedings.pdf

Owen, J. (2005). London bombing pictures mark new role for camera phones. *National Geographic News*. Available at http://news.nation-algeographic.com/news/2005/07/0711_050711_londoncell.html [accessed on 15 June]

Rheingold, H. (2003). Smart Mobs: The Next Social Revolution. Perseus Books

Plant, S. (2000). On the Mobile. The Effects of Mobile Telephones on Social and Individual Life. Available at http://www.motorola.com/ mot/documents/0,1028,333,00.pdf

Sanderson, I. (2004). *Is it "What Works" that Matters? Evaluation and Evidence-Based Policy Making*. Belfast: Economic Research Institute of Northern Ireland Ltd. Available at http://216.239.59.104/ search?q=cache:FTLz6DYzdlgJ:www.qub.ac.uk/nierc/documents/ SandersonPaper.pdf+policy-based+evidence+formulation&hl=en

Sheller, M. (2004). Mobile Publics: Decoupling, Contingency, and the Local/Global Gel. *Environment and Planning D: Society and Space*, 22, 39–54

Sheller, M. and Urry, J. (2003). Mobile Transformations of "Public" and "Private" Life. In *Theory, Culture and Society*, Vol. 20, pp. 107–125

Somekh, B. (2001). The Role of Evaluation in Ensuring Excellence in Communications and Information Technology Initiatives. *Education, Communications and Information*, 1, 75–101

Sørensen, C., Mathiassen, L. and Kakihara, M. (2002). Mobile Services: Functional Diversity and Overload, presented at *New Perspectives On 21st-Century Communications*, 24–25 May 2002, Budapest, Hungary

Strauss, A. and Corbin, J. (1998). Basics of Qualitative Research – Techniques and Procedures for Developing Grounded Theory. London: Sage

Traxler, J. (2008). Modernity, Mobility and the Digital Divides, *Proceedings of ALT-C 2008*. Leeds: Association for Learning Technology

Traxler, J. and Kukulska-Hulme, A. (2005). Evaluating Mobile Learning: Reflections on Current Practice, *Proceedings of MLEARN2005: 4th World Conference on mLearning*, Cape Town, South Africa, 25–28 October 2005. Available at http://www.mlearn.org.za/CD/BOA_p.65.pdf

PART III

Methods

10. Researching Informal and Mobile Learning: Leveraging the Right Resources

MARK VAN 'T HOOFT

Overview

Researching learning is a challenging undertaking and the possibility of learning while mobile only complicates matters. As changes in learning are forcing us to take a closer look at process, rather than product, the research tools we have in our arsenal are no longer sufficient. Changes in learning should be complemented with changes in the research questions we ask, the methods we employ, and the data we collect. Mobile devices can aid us in the latter. Two examples of learning while mobile (Frequency 1550 in Amsterdam, the Netherlands; and the use of a context-aware guiding service at the National Museum of Natural Science in Taichung, Taiwan) are employed to demonstrate what research could look like in an environment that is characterized by mobility and enhanced with digital tools. The examples also show issues and challenges to be addressed during the research design phase, including access v. privacy, ownership of information and related issues of data security, and control over the research setting. In sum, when leveraging mobile technologies to study mobile learning we need to reconsider the entire research process, not just new and different data collection techniques we should use.

1. Introduction: Rethinking research

Educational research is tricky business because learning is a construct that is difficult to measure. Many tried-and-true research methods and data collection strategies often fall short in getting us the data we want and need. Even in relatively controlled environments such as "traditional" classrooms or research labs it is difficult to isolate individual variables and establish causal or correlational relationships between interventions such as digital technologies and learning outcomes (Schenker et al., 2007).

Introducing the concept of mobility and the possibility of learning while mobile only complicates matters (see e.g. Sharples; and Livingstone in this volume). Mobility expands learning across space and time and opens up many opportunities for learning that is neither sequential nor consistent. Mobile, networked, and digital tools broaden it even more by providing increased connectivity to people and information (Roush, 2005), augmenting physical environments with digital layers (e.g. Price, 2007), allowing for customization of learning, and offering tools to create, manipulate, and share a wide variety of electronic artefacts (see also Sharples, Taylor, and Vavoula, 2007; Walker, 2006).

In order to study learning in such a flexible and volatile context, we need to rethink what we research and how we do it:

- The changing nature of learning is forcing us to look more at process, not necessarily just product. Learning is a lifelong endeavour that doesn't just happen in formal educational settings, and is increasingly seen in that way by a larger population. Consequently, we should carefully reconsider what kinds of research questions we ask;

- We can no longer just rely on tried and tested ways of doing research to get the data and answers we need. As the nature of learning and learners changes, so should learning research methods and strategies;

- We should consider how we can leverage digital and mobile technologies used by learners to get a better insight into what it means to learn while mobile.

2. Reconsidering the questions we ask

Good learning research starts with solid research questions based on established theories or aims to develop new ones. Too many times we end up with invalid answers because we don't ask the right questions. This has resulted in a substantial amount of research concluding that digital tools produce "no significant difference", because it is implied in the research questions that learning is either "a high-tech or no-tech phenomenon" (Oblinger and Hawkins, 2006, p. 14). *Especially in the area of learning while mobile,* it is obvious that learning occurs as a result of a lot more than merely the infusion of digital tools. As Sharples, Taylor, and Vavoula (2007) describe, learning while mobile is "the processes of coming to know through conversations across multiple contexts amongst people and personal interactive technologies" (p. 224). This type of learning is characterized by an active process, interaction with others, and transfer of learning to/learning in real-world situations. Research questions should be adjusted to accommodate this complexity. As the two examples below show, questions of outcome are no longer sufficient. Questions related to process are more important now than ever before.

3. Adjusting research methods and strategies

Research methods and data collection strategies should be reconsidered as well. We often fall victim to two common pitfalls in research procedures (Tinker, 2007). One has been dubbed the "hobbled horse race", a strategy in which the perceived better intervention is handicapped for the sake of research "fairness". When this is applied in mobile learning research, everything would be held constant except for the presence of mobile devices. As a result, unique affordances of and opportunities created by mobile devices would be eliminated, or at least minimized, before the research has commenced. One could reasonably expect that in such a scenario the chances of finding a significant difference in learning between experimental and control groups are small.

The other pitfall has been described as the "trivial treatment", i.e. a minimization of the intervention to the point where it has no real impact, for example using mobile devices 20 minutes per week in a classroom environment. It should come as no surprise that when such research methods are employed, a statistically significant difference is rarely the result, let alone a practically significant one.

Employing either one of these approaches when studying the effect of technology on learning is senseless. Instead, maybe we should be asking different types of questions that go beyond digital technologies and get at the affordances that these tools provide. As the two learning scenarios later on in this chapter show, these questions may still include those aimed at measuring learning outcomes. However, questions about the learning *process* seem to carry increasing weight.

Data collection strategies that are most common in learning technology research include surveys and pre/post tests which are often complemented by observations, interviews, artefact analysis, and more recently self-reports by learners such as reflective journals. While useful for researching learning that happens in relatively fixed locations, do they hold up when studying learning in mobile and unpredictable environments? According to Taylor (2006), research strategies in the area of learning while mobile need to be more adaptive, and include alternative approaches such as analysis of interaction logs and learner contributions to externalized constructions, such as a wiki, for example.

4. Using mobile technologies to capture mobile data

Mobile and digital technologies can be used to capture a wide variety of data that can help us get (better) answers. Key questions to ask include

- What (combination of) information is of most worth, i.e. what types of data should we collect given the research questions we ask? When investigating learning while mobile, at a minimum the following types of data should be considered:

◊ Spatial data: Where are devices being used by learners? (e.g. by collecting GPS data)

◊ Temporal data: When are they being used? (time stamping of application use or artefact creation)

◊ User data: What are they being used for? (patterns of use of particular applications)

◊ Learner data: What content is being accessed? What artefacts do learners create?

◊ Connectivity data: Who do learners communicate with? What do they share?

◊ Assessment data: How do learners know that they are learning and what they are learning?

- How do we most effectively use technology to gather this data? If learners are using mobile digital tools for learning, research can and should leverage these same tools for data collection purposes. All of the data sources listed above can be captured using mobile devices, usually with a combination of a wireless mobile device, some kind of capturing application, and a database server to which the data is sent via a wireless network. The question is how to get the data to the researcher in ways that don't impede the learning process.

- To what extent should learners be involved in the research design? Learners are becoming increasingly independent, active, and unpredictable. Because of their mobility, it is much more difficult to collect data such as observations or have face-to-face conversations. Therefore, collecting data can and should no longer be an issue of concern for the researcher alone. Involving the learner and his/her technology is essential. One example of this is the co-design as described by Spikol in his chapter on designing mobile games.

Let us apply what has been discussed so far to two examples of learning while mobile: Frequency 1550 (Amsterdam, the Netherlands) and the

context-aware guiding service at the National Museum of Natural Science
(Taichung, Taiwan).

5. Frequency 1550

Frequency 1550 is a city game using mobile phones, GPS technology, and
an ultra high-speed broadband mobile phone network in Amsterdam,
the Netherlands. It takes learners out of the classroom as they take on the
role of pilgrims in medieval Amsterdam anno 1550, competing to find a
special relic. Students roam the city, using GPS-equipped mobile phones
and an ultra high-speed broadband mobile phone network (UMTS) to
download challenges, complete location-based media assignments on the
city's history, and create their own knowledge. They are supported by other
groups of students at a central location who can see the overall picture and
work out the team's strategy in order to outwit their opponents. Their tasks
include collecting the pilgrim's multimedia artefacts, checking out historical references, providing players in the field with relevant information, and
figuring out ways to slow down the other teams' progress. At the end of
each day of playing, all teams gather to see not only who did the best, but
also to collectively reflect on the media produced, the answers given, and
the strategic decisions taken during the game (Waag Society, 2007).

5.1   Reconsidering the research questions

A "traditional" approach to researching learning in Frequency 1550 would
look for end results and employ questions along the lines of, "Is learning
about Amsterdam's history with mobile devices more effective than without them?" or "What is the impact of mobile phones on student achievement in history when learning about Amsterdam's history?" As discussed
earlier, these questions are difficult to answer in a controlled environment
like a classroom, let alone in a much larger and open space. In addition,
while a focused and more precise research question is easier to work with
for purposes of data collection, this type of question tends to overlook the

fact that when infusing mobile technologies in teaching and learning, the nature of teaching and learning changes. Therefore, other questions to be considered, at a minimum, should focus on the learning process and include such inquiries like, "How does teaching and learning of history change when learning while mobile as opposed to learning in more traditional settings?" and "How do learners assimilate their learning of Amsterdam's history into their own lives?"

5.2 Adjusting research methods and strategies

Given the research questions, we can now decide on data collection strategies. With regards to changes in learning, we could utilize tried and true data collection tools such as surveys, interviews, and reflective journals. However, these data sources will be much more valuable if we can augment them with spatial, user, learner, and connectivity data. In fact, the latter can be used to help structure the former (Zhang, 2002). Finally, we should consider the level of learner involvement in the research design, which would probably focus on the learning experience and learner expectations.

5.3 Leveraging mobile technology

Much of the "new" data can be unobtrusively collected by mobile devices and synced up with a remote database while learners are engaged with their devices, their context, and their learning. Examples of applications include Rubberneck, which aggregates time-stamped application use data on handheld devices; RedHalo[TM],[1] remote storage for artefacts that learners create; and Mobile Tools' eTaitava[TM],[2] a mobile feedback system for vocational, on-the-job training. Note that in each of these instances the technology used includes wireless mobile devices and a remote, centralized database for data storage. In our example, we would probably want to collect spatial, user, learner, and connectivity data (and maybe temporal

---

1   http://www.redhalo.com/.
2   http://www.mobiletools.fi/en/?page=etaitava.

data), which could be analyzed for patterns and be used to probe learners for a deeper understanding of these patterns. For example, do learners use particular applications in a specific location or at a regular time? Do learners' connectivity habits exhibit particular patterns in relation to location or application use? If so, these patterns could be visualized (e.g. using maps, graphs, or graphics), and this information could in turn be shown to the learners in an interview or on a questionnaire, in order to get their take on potential patterns that may exist or get insights into the data that a researcher may not see without the input of the learner.

6. National Museum of Natural Science

The context-aware mobile guiding service in the National Museum of Natural Science in Taichung, Taiwan is a good example of informal and personalized learning on-the-go. Visitors can create their own learning experiences that start before they step through the museum doors and continue long after they've left. The museum's website allows users to create unique itineraries that can be saved in an online database and be downloaded to a wireless mobile device that is provided by the museum upon admission. Visitors can also choose to follow a recommended learning tour or freely explore exhibits on their own. No matter what visitors choose to do, the museum's context-aware system automatically determines the visitors' location and delivers corresponding and relevant information to their mobile devices. Following the visit, the web-based system provides additional learning content and recommends further resources according to an individual's on-site learning behaviours and preferences. These can be accessed whenever and wherever it is convenient for the learner.

6.1 Reconsidering the research questions

Compared to the first example, we have to take a different approach here, as we are dealing with learning that is not tied to a formal curriculum. Therefore, we should not merely look for learning outcomes like we would in a traditional classroom environment, and we may want to consult some of the research literature in the area of informal learning for direction. Before we can even consider specific learning outcomes, we would need to find out what kind of learning took place, when and where it took place, and how it took place (again, like in the first example, these are process questions). In addition, we would probably want to investigate what learners do with what they've learned (application in real-life situations), and how this type of learning affects future learning (i.e. whether and how it is part of a broader, life-long learning process). Finally, we would need to consider how the digital tools employed were a help or hindrance in the entire process.

6.2 Adjusting research methods and strategies

Data collection in our hypothetical research scenario here would be fairly similar to that of the Frequency 1550 example, but in this case we would probably want to start by collecting the spatial, temporal, user, and connectivity data in order to create additional and more detailed questions that can be used in surveys, interviews, or focus groups. For example, if we were to find spikes in certain data types (e.g. more usage in certain areas of the museum, preference of certain applications or content over others) we could ask users why this is occurring. We could also look at combinations of data sources and create questions based on patterns we may find, such as "Why did learners tend to use a certain application in a certain location?" In addition, there is room for some interesting pre/post experience comparisons with regards to learner expectations of the experience and actual learning.

6.3 Leveraging mobile technology

Mobile technologies would be used for data collection in much the same way as in our first example, vouching for the versatility of wireless mobile devices for data collection purposes in a variety of everyday situations. Again, data collection should go unnoticed by the learner so as not to interfere with the learning experience.

7. Issues and challenges in data collection with mobile devices

Researching learning while mobile also creates unique issues and challenges that should be addressed during the research design phase. Some of these issues include but are not limited to:

7.1 Access v. privacy

Here the question is what data can researchers have access to without infringing on the privacy of the learners under study, and when do they have access to it? Do learners have control over researcher access to the data they generate as they are learning? Privacy is an increasingly important issue when considering the types of data we can and should collect, and the ways in which we can aggregate and mesh them. For example, think about the combination of spatial, temporal, user, and learner data, and the types of scenarios a researcher could (re)create from that (see, for example, Pachler, Cook, and Bradley; and Wali, Oliver, and Winters in this volume).

7.2 Ownership of information/data and related issues of data security

Whose data is it, really? Does it belong to the creator? The service that stores it? The researcher who collects, aggregates, and analyzes it? In an era in which digital information can be effortlessly created, duplicated, changed, and shared, ownership of data is becoming an increasingly complex concept. Changes in copyright (think Creative Commons) are trying to address this issue to some extent. Obviously, when data is shared between people and across wireless digital networks, issues of data storage and security are paramount.

7.3 Control over the research setting

Both examples describe learning and research settings that cover large amounts of physical space and time, and are therefore uncontrollable. Even when learners are expected to participate in structured activities as is the case in Frequency 1550, they are more independent and unpredictable in their actions. In contrast, the digital tools we employ should be dependable, wireless connectivity being especially important for data gathering purposes.

8. Conclusion

The original objective of this chapter was to take a brief look at how we can leverage mobile technology to study learning that moves across space and time. However, we cannot look at particular data collection techniques in isolation. If we are going to re-examine them, we also need to reconsider everything that drives data collection in educational research, which includes the theories that frame our thinking, the questions we ask, and the methods we employ. Only then will we have a better chance of getting the data we need to yield the answers we are looking for. In addition, it is increasingly important to consider social and cultural dimensions in which learning (and therefore learning research) takes place. As learning is becoming ever more personalized yet collaborative, our research should reflect that (Balacheff, 2006).

Within this changing context, portable digital technologies can play an important role in the mobile learning research we do, and we should take a closer look at how we can leverage them to help us in our work.

References

Balacheff, N. (2006). *10 issues to think about the future of research on TEL.* Kaleidoscope Collective Working Paper #147. Grenoble, France: Laboratoire Leibniz-IMAG

Oblinger, D., G. and Hawkins, B.L. (2006). The myth about no significant difference. *Educause Review*, 41(6), pp. 14–15

Price, S. (2007). Ubiquitous computing: Digital augmentation and learning. In N. Pachler (ed.), *m-learning: Towards a research agenda*. WLE Centre occasional papers in work-based learning. London, UK: Institute of Education, pp. 33–54

Roush, W. (2005). Social machines. *Technology Review*, 108(8), pp. 45–53

Schenker, J., Kratcoski, A., Lin, Y., Swan, K. and van 't Hooft, M. (2007). Researching ubiquity: Ways to capture it all. In M. van 't Hooft and K. Swan (eds), *Ubiquitous computing in education: Invisible technology, visible impact*. Mahwah, NJ: Lawrence Erlbaum Associates, pp. 167–186

Sharples, M., Taylor, J. and Vavoula, G. (2007). A theory of learning for the mobile age. In R. Andrews and C. Haythornthwaite (eds), *The Sage handbook on e-learning research*. London, UK: Sage, pp. 221–247

Taylor, J. (2006). Evaluating mobile learning: What are appropriate methods for evaluating learning in mobile environments? In M. Sharples (ed.), *Big issues in mobile learning: Report of a workshop by the Kaleidoscope Network of Excellence Mobile Learning Initiative*. Nottingham, UK: University of Nottingham, Learning Sciences Research Institute, pp. 26–28

Tinker, R. (2007). Potholes in the road to proving technology. *@Concord*, 11(1), pp. 2–3

Waag Society. (2007). *Frequentie 1550: Mobile city game*. Available at http://www.waag.org/project/frequentie [accessed on 14 November 2007]

Walker, K. (2006). Introduction: Mapping the landscape of mobile learning. In M. Sharples (ed.), *Big issues in mobile learning: Report of a workshop by the Kaleidoscope Network of Excellence Mobile Learning Initiative*. Nottingham, UK: University of Nottingham, Learning Sciences Research Institute, pp. 7–11

Zhang, Y. (2002). An empirical study of children's source use for internet searches. *Proceedings of the American Society for Information Science and Technology*, 40(1), pp. 548–550

11. The Case for MobileHCI and Mobile Design Research Methods in Mobile and Informal Learning Contexts

MARK A.M. KRAMER

Overview

This chapter examines the applicability of MobileHCI and Mobile Design research methods in mobile and informal learning research. The purpose of the chapter is to summarize the most commonly used and emerging research methodologies deployed by MobileHCI and Mobile Design, and to suggest that these might be suited to help mobile learning researchers and practitioners to gather essential data to inform the design of learner-centred experiences.

1. Introduction

Understanding the human factors surrounding the use of mobile devices and applications is central to the design of usable mobile technology. The fields of Mobile Human Computer Interaction and Mobile Design research (hereafter collectively referred to as M-HCI/D) employ various research methodologies to gather and analyse quantitative and qualitative data on mobile usability. Ultimately, the research conducted enhances the users' experience by highlighting the aspects that could be improved upon with the technology and/or applications that are examined.

According to Jensen and Skov (2005) it is useful within a discipline to investigate research methods derived from different disciplines, as these can help inform future directions and influences on the field. The flexibility and scalability of M-HCI/D methodologies posit them ideally to gathering large sets of quantitative and qualitative data within natural settings and contexts, like those encountered in mobile informal learning.

In fact, one of the greatest challenges facing mobile and informal learning research is gathering data about various observable and non-observable phenomena within contexts or settings in which Individuals and groups of learners engage in "real-world" learning. Examples of real-world learning contexts include daily commutes, individual or group journeys, family holidays and class field trips. The ubiquitous and pervasive nature of these contexts makes learning difficult to observe and document for evaluation or research purposes. Therefore, it is imperative to devise new, or enhance existing approaches and methods that will help researchers observe and gather data on informal and mobile, everyday learning.

An example of such a methodological "novelty" is to use the very mobile technologies that enable these modes of real world learning, to gather data on informal and mobile learning. M-HCI/D researchers already utilize methods that harness the technologies themselves and engage users as active assistants in the evaluation of mobile devices and services. Mobile learning research can do the same: make use of mobile technologies to help gather quantitative and qualitative data in real world mobile and informal learning contexts. Indeed, some chapters in this volume present examples of such use of the technology (see the chapters by Hooft; Trinder et al.; Pierroux; and Wali et al.)

In the following we will explore the potential for further methodological transfer between these fields. Ultimately, such exchange of methods will help to broaden the choices mobile learning researchers have, and will also enhance their current methodologies. With this objective in mind we will consider which M-HCI/D research methods and approaches might transfer fruitfully into mobile informal learning research. The methods cited within the chapter have been chosen on the basis that they will assist in collecting data, such as recordings that document the learning process or trace-logs of contextual information that can help to measure the effectiveness of mobile learning tools and technologies. Such data can inform research decisions about current and future designs of learner-centred informal and mobile learning environments and scenarios.

The chapter is exploratory in nature, and thus, will not cover in depth the methodologies, concepts and topics surveyed. It is helpful to view this work as a means to encourage thoughtful discourse and to initiate an ongoing dialogue regarding how M-HCI/D research methodologies can be adopted by mobile learning research to help inform how individuals learn in mobile, informal learning contexts.

2.   Harnessing MobileHCI/MD research methods

The research methods highlighted in this chapter are grounded within the methodological approaches of *Action Research, Ethno-methodology, Participatory Design* and *User Centred Design.* Research methods are always adapted by the research projects that deploy them. It is important to understand how research methods have been adapted by different disciplines; this potentially informs us on possibilities of adaptation in our discipline (Kjeldskov and Graham, 2003).

Wynekoop and Congor (1990) present a review of software engineering research methods in which they created a classification scheme to help in their analysis. The classification examines research methods in terms of the environment in which the research takes place and distinguishes between methods in natural settings, in artificial settings, and environment-independent. Kjedskov and Graham (2003) and Jensen and Skov (2005) have adapted this scheme to classify mobile HCI and children's technology design research methods respectively. Table 11.1 presents a further adaptation of the classification, to highlight the strengths and weaknesses of the methods for mobile learning research.

Table 11.1 presents existing methods that are commonly used within the M-HCI/D communities, where they are evaluated, reflected upon, and enhanced or augmented as needed in order to yield greater value and use. In this way, new methods emerge, adapted to changing conditions and situations.

ENVIRONMENT	METHOD	STRENGTHS	WEAKNESSES	USE
Natural Setting (*Real-world learning*)	Case Studies	• Natural setting • Rich data	• Time consuming • Cannot be generalized	• Descriptions • Explanations • Developing hypothesis
	Field Studies	• Natural Settings • Replicable	• Difficult data collection • Unknown sample bias	• Studying current practice • Evaluating new practices
	Action Research	• First-hand experience • Applying theory to practice	• Ethics • Bias • Time consuming • Cannot be generalized	• Generation & testing of theories / hypotheses
Artificial Setting (*lab-based artificial learning task*)	Laboratory Experiments	• Control over variables • Replicable	• Limited realism • Cannot be generalized	• Controlled experiments • Theory/ Scenario testing
Environment Independent	Survey research	• Easy • Low cost • Reduce sample bias	• Context insensitive • No variable manipulation	• Descriptive data from large samples
	Applied Research	• Learning scenarios can be evaluated	• May need further design to make learning scenario applicable	• Scenario development, testing hypothesis and concepts
	Basic Research	• No restrictions on solutions • Solve new problems	• Costly, time demanding, may produce no solution	• Theory building
	Normative writings	• Insight into first-hand experience	• Opinions may influence outcome	• Descriptions of practice • Building frameworks

Table 11.1: Summary of existing MobileHCI / Mobile Design research methods. (Adapted from Kjeldskov and Graham, and Jensen and Skov).

Hagen, Robertson, Kan and Sadler (2005) demonstrate how this emergence of new research methods has taken place within M-HCI/D through extending and/or combining existing methods. They identify three categories of emergent data collection techniques, which "represent various approaches to accessing and making available data about different aspects of mobile technology use, [and] entail different roles and responsibilities for both researchers and participants" (Hagen et al., 2005). The three categories are:

1. Mediated Data Collection: In which participants [learners] and mobile technologies mediate data collection about use in natural settings [of situated learning].

2. Simulations and enactments: simulations and enactments are used to make available experiential information sensitized to real contexts of use.

3. Combinations: existing methods, and/or mediated data collection and/or simulations and enactments are combined to allow access to complementary data. (Hagen et al., 2005, p. 4)

Hagen et al. (2005) further present general descriptions of these emerging techniques and the three categories, and identify their origins in existing, well-established techniques. Table 11.2 is an adaptation of those descriptions for mobile learning research contexts.

3. Future work

One of the primary goals of mobile learning research is to evaluate the learning and developmental outcomes of individuals and groups of learners. M-HCI/D methods may be more suited to informing and evaluating aspects of usability and accessibility, which have an impact on the effectiveness of the embedded pedagogy of mobile learning scenarios (Squires and Preece, 1999). Furthermore, M-HCI/D methods can be used to capture

TECHNIQUE	DESCRIPTION	DERIVED FROM
Mediated Data Collection	Where access to data about actual use practices is mediated by both learner & technology	
Learner-captured	Learners actively conduct the data collection using mobile devices.	Self-reporting, Diaries, Probes
Technology-captured	Learners engage in mobile learning while data about technology use, content and metadata is logged automatically	Use/Data logs
Learner-Technology-captured	Learners go about their everyday learning while wearing sensors or cameras	Video-observation, Use/Data logs
Simulations & Enactments	Methods for allowing immersive scenarios in which data about existing or potential use is accessed through some form of pretending.	
Simulations	Physical, ergonomic or environmental props are used within a controlled environment in order to simulate mobile learning scenarios.	Lab tests, Scenarios, Heuristics, Prototypes, Emulators, Simulators
Enactments	Mobile learning scenarios are played out through visual imagery or storytelling in order to observe potential outcomes.	Prototyping Scenarios, Role-playing, Work shopping, Storyboarding
Combinations	Various established and/or new methods are combined to enable access to complementary data.	

Table 11.2: Mapping Hagen et al.'s (2005) emerging MobileHCI data collection techniques onto mobile learning research.

the learning experience and the learner's interactions over long periods of time, reflecting different stages of the learning process.

The chapter has presented a broad pallet of methods and techniques that allow for customisable and flexible research designs. In order to determine if they could effectively be transferred to mobile learning research, it is important to examine the specific context and settings of the studies that have employed them. Each study will have its own unique circumstances, which would directly affect the methods chosen and how they are employed. Transferability, then, is directly linked to the study variables, including environment, context, approach, and research questions. Of course methods and techniques are available for evaluation and customisation according to the circumstances of an individual study. Further work in this direction could aim to develop a framework that guides such transference and customization of methods and techniques from other disciplines.

Hopefully this chapter will inspire such further research and will encourage thoughtful discourse on how M-HCI/D research methods can help mobile learning researchers to gather the data they need in order to understand how individuals learn in mobile and informal learning contexts.

References

Hagen, P., Robertson, T., Kan, M. and Sadler., K. (2005). Emerging Research Methods for Understanding Mobile Technology Use. *Proceedings of OZCHI 2005*, Canberra, Australia. 23–25 November 2005

Jensen, J. and Skov. M. (2005). A Review of Research Methods in Children's Technology Design. In ICD 2005, 8–10 June 2005. Boulder CO: ACM Press, pp. 80–87

Kjeldskov, J. and Graham, C. (2003). A Review of MobileHCI Research Methods. In *Proceedings of the 5th International Conference on Mobile Human-Computer Interaction (MobileHCI03)*, LNCS: Springer-Verlag, pp. 317–335

Squires, D. and Preece, J. (1999). Predicting quality in educational software: Evaluating for learning, usability and the synergy between them. *Interacting with computers*, 11, pp. 467–483

Wynekoop, J.L. and Congor, A.A. (1990). A Review of Computer Aided Software Engineering Research Methods. In *Proceedings of the IFIP TC8 WG8.2 Working Conference on the Information Systems Research Arena of the 90's*, Copenhagen, Denmark

Bibliography for Further Reading

Axup, J., Bidwell, N.J. and Viller, S. (2004). Representation of self-reported information usage during mobile field studies: Pilots & Orienteers 2. *Proceedings of OzCHI 2004: Supporting Community Interaction: Possibilities and Challenges*, Wollongong Australia
Consolvo, S. and Walker, M. (2003). Using the Experience Sampling Method to Evaluate Ubicomp Applications. In *IEEE Pervasive Computing*, 2(2), pp. 24–31
Gabrielli, S., Mirabella, V., Kimani, S. and Catarsi, T. (2005). Supporting Cognitive Walkthrough with Video Data: A Mobile Learning Evaluation Study. In *Proceedings of MobileHCI 2005*. ACM Press, pp. 77–82
Intille, S.S., Tapia. E.M., Rondoni, J., Beaudin, J., Kukla, C., Agrwal, S., Bao, L. and Larson, K. (2003). Tools for Studying Behavior and Technology in Natural Settings. In *Proceedings of Ubiquitous Computing 2004*, pp. 157–174
Intille, S.S., Bao, L., Tapia, E.M. and Rondoni, J. (2004). Acquiring in situ training data for context-aware ubiquitous computing applications. In *Proceedings CHI*, 1–8
Intille, S., Larson, K., Beaudin, J., Nawyn, J., Tapia, E.M., Kaushik, P. (2005). A living laboratory for the design and evaluation of ubiquitous computing technologies. In *Proceedings of CHI Extended Abstracts*, 1941–1944
Johnson, P. (1998). Usability and mobility: interaction on the move. In *Proceedings of First Workshop on Human-Computer Interaction with Mobile Devices*, Glasgow, UK
Kjeldskov, J. and Stage, J. (2004). New Techniques for Usability Evaluation of Mobile Systems. *International Journal of Human Computer Studies* (IJHCS) Elsevier

12. In-Sights into Mobile Learning: An Exploration of Mobile Eye Tracking Methodology for Learning in Museums

EVA MAYR, KRISTIN KNIPFER, DANIEL WESSEL

Overview

Mobile eye tracking provides insights into cognitive processing of visual information while a learner moves around. This chapter presents a case study in a small museum exhibition that was conducted to explore the suitability of mobile eye tracking for researching mobile learning. The study showed both potentials and limitations of mobile eye tracking methodology for research on mobile learning in general and in science exhibitions in particular: Mobile eye tracking provides rich, non-reactive data from the learner's perspective which can be further analysed qualitatively and quantitatively. Concerns were raised with respect to interrelations of object fixations and underlying cognitive processes. Limitations also include obtrusiveness, accuracy, selective sampling, ethical concerns, financial effort, and effort of data analysis. These limitations suggest that, to increase validity, eye tracking is best used in combination with other methods. Nonetheless, mobile eye tracking can be a powerful data collection method in research on mobile learning.

1. Mobile eye tracking

Why are eye movements interesting for mobile learning? Our eyesight is our most important sense: most daily tasks involve visual input, and people need to look at objects to acquire information about them. Eye movements are not only important for research on natural human behaviour but especially on mobile learning. We define *mobile learning* in the context of this chapter as learning by integrating information that is spatially distributed in natural environments and, therefore, requires movement of the learner. This book chapter deals with a special case of mobile learning, namely informal learning in science museums (see also Lelliott and Sharples in this book). Most information in exhibitions is represented visually as exhibits with corresponding text labels. The spatial distribution of exhibits requires that learners move around. We argue that methods to examine learning in these visually dominated and spatial environments should be chosen carefully in order to address the specifics of the setting, especially the high mobility of the learner. This paper discusses the suitability of tracking visitors' eye movements as a method to explore mobile learning in museums.

1.1   A short history of eye tracking

Research on eye movement dates back to the early 20th century. Historically, it focused on scene perception (see Henderson, 2007) and reading (see Rayner, 1998). Stationary eye trackers were used for the limited purpose of laboratory studies employing rather simple tasks requiring information processing. Only in recent years has the development of light-weight, mobile eye tracking technologies (Pelz et al., 2000) allowed the assessment of daily activities in a natural environment (e.g. Land and Hayhoe, 2001). This research has still, however, been limited to rather simple tasks.

1.2   How does mobile eye tracking work?

There are different designs of eye trackers and methods of analysis to determine the location of fixations. However, most mobile eye trackers use two cameras. One camera records one eye of the participant, on which three invisible (infrared) dots are projected, while the other camera records the scene from the subject's perspective. These two cameras must be calibrated to give accurate data about eye movements and fixations of each individual. Both images are saved as alternate frames using a video recorder. The most useful output format of mobile eye tracking data is a video that combines the scene view and the position of the fixation indicated with a marker (e.g. small red cross). It provides insight into the perspective of the participant and the point where his or her tracked eye is fixated at a certain moment. This video can be analyzed via conventional video-analysis software.

Fixations and saccades are the basic objects of the analysis of eye tracking data (Rayner, 1998). During fixations, eyes are focused on one location and visual information is obtained. Saccades are rapid eye movements between fixations when visual input is reduced or even totally suppressed.

2. Re-viewing the museum visitor's view: An explorative study

The aim of this study was mainly an exploratory one: We wanted to examine the potentials and limitations of mobile eye tracking for research on informal learning in museums. Mobile eye tracking allowed us to "re-view" the visitors' view – beyond observational or questionnaire methods. In this way, we hoped to literally "see" what eye movements can tell us about exploration behaviour in exhibitions and information processing of exhibition content. To supplement our observations, we performed a literature review on mobile eye tracking. However, in the literature we only found mobile eye tracking studies which examine well-structured, temporally restricted tasks like making a sandwich, finding a specific door, or washing one's hands (e.g. Hayhoe and Ballard, 2005; Land and Hayhoe, 2001; Pelz et al., 2000; Turano, Geruschat, and Baker, 2003). Our study, in contrast, took place in a complex setting with a more open-ended task: the exploration of a science exhibition. This is an example of a setting in which informal learning is likely to take place. As the exhibition was designed to communicate the basic facts and figures, chances and risks, and areas and concrete applications of nanotechnology, we consider the exploration of the exhibition a learning task. However, as with many informal settings, the subjects had not been instructed "to learn", nor were they provided with other concrete instructions concerning the exploration of the exhibition (like learning goals, time restrictions, predefined learning activities; see for example the chapter by Sharples in this book). Corresponding to the "open" nature of this task, a broad range of visiting behaviour was found: for example, the duration of the visits ranged from 17 to 57 minutes.

2.1 Method

Setting. We had the opportunity to present a small exhibition about nano-technology at our research institute. In this way, we ensured a fair amount of external and internal validity: The research setting was designed to be as close as possible to a "normal" visit for participants and at the same time as controlled as possible to reduce the impact of interfering variables.

  Technical equipment. For this study we used an ASL MobileEye eye tracker (see Figure 12.1).

Figure 12.1: ASL MobileEye eye tracker (initial design October 2004).

  Sample. Two male adults and one female adult with normal vision were asked to explore the exhibition with an eye tracker.

  Procedure. First, the purpose of the study and the function of the eye tracker were explained to the subjects. Then, the eye tracker was calibrated to a distance that visitors would normally keep while looking at exhibits (which varied interindividually and ranged between 30 and 60 cm). The study participants were instructed to explore the exhibition as they would normally do in a science museum. After exploration of the exhibition, a structured interview provided insight into visitors' subjective experiences and introspective thoughts on reasons for exploration behaviour and on cognitive processes. For example, the participants were encouraged to report on criteria and reasons for information selection (e.g. "Which exhibits were particularly interesting for you and why?") and their spatial orientation and sequence of exhibit exploration ("Did you explore the exhibits in a certain order or randomly?").

Analysis. Eye movement recordings were transformed to .avi-files and analyzed with the video analysis software Videograph©. Similarly to Turano et al. (2003), we did not analyze eye movements based on xy-coordinates (examining which points on a wall are fixated independent of their denotation), but based on elements and categories (examining which exhibits on a wall are fixated). For our purposes, fixations of similar elements or within the same object category were of higher interest than proximity of fixations. Also, elements and categories are more easily adjusted to background changes than xy-coordinates would be. This makes them better suited to analyze complex mobile eye movement recordings. The categories were developed according to information elements of the exhibition (see Figure 12.2). Each exhibit or text unit was an element. Elements were grouped in larger categories like "exhibits with corresponding labels" or "exhibits on the same concept".

2.2 Exemplary results of the study

This exploratory study on mobile eye tracking provided information both about the way a visitor explores the exhibition and about the usefulness of this method for gaining insight into mobile, informal learning. The following exemplary results may illustrate the kind and quality of information that is obtained by means of mobile eye tracking.

Intra-individual analysis of each visitor's eye tracking recording revealed that exhibits belonging together conceptually are more likely to be fixated successively and also several times alternately (see Figure 12.2 for an example) than adjacent but unrelated exhibits. This may indicate

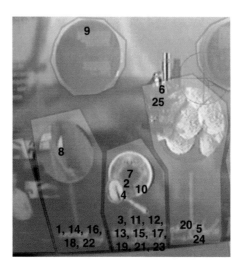

Figure 12.2: Episode of 17 seconds from one participant's scan pattern. Ascending numbers show the scan path (fixations 1–25). Grey overlays highlight object categories. Attend to the fact that the participant fixated different objects conceptually belonging together several times alternately (fixations 13–24, where three subcategories were fixated that compare different size measurements, here from cm to μm).

that people integrate multiple information units into an underlying concept (Rayner, Rotello, Stewart, Keir, and Duffy, 2001) or at least that they do not process these information units independently from one another (Schwonke, Berthold, and Renkl, 2007). However, in one case, our postvisit interview revealed a different explanation for alternate fixation of objects: One participant stated that he was not comparing the content but the design of the exhibition elements. Both explanations of the participant's eye movements indicate that conceptually intertwined exhibits were processed together. However, eye movement recordings alone cannot reveal which information is being processed (in our case: semantic information or information about design) or what cognitive processes exactly are going on.

Analysis across all three participants showed that, overall, some exhibits were less likely to be explored than others. This might be due to limitations in exhibition design: research has shown that the probability of visual exploration depends on the visual salience of objects (e.g. Holsanova, Rahm, and Holmqvist, 2006). An alternative explanation is that these parts of the exhibition were attended to without direct fixations (Treisman, 2006).

All participants first scanned each exhibition wall as a whole (the exhibition consisted of four exhibition walls arranged as a circle). They then began to explore single exhibits in their vicinity. Research suggests that the first process serves as initial selection of information and visual search – and is rather automated (Holmberg, 2004). During early processing stages, pictorial information or text is quickly skimmed and scanned, so that a viewer gets the gist of a scene very quickly (see for example Rayner, 1998, p. 398f).

In a second step, late processing like reading text or exploring details of objects occurs. However, there are multiple exploration patterns for the same scene: in his review on eye tracking, Rayner (1998) states that exploration patterns are especially heterogeneous in scene perception. This is even more likely in our natural setting, as the circular arrangement of the exhibition elements did not trigger a certain exploration path but provided multiple entry points and exploration directions. An exhibition also easily allows for multiple changes between the exhibition elements.

2.3   Discussion of the study

Our results from three visitors' eye tracking data are difficult to generalize for three reasons. First, the sample size is small; further subjects are needed to allow generalization of our results. Second, the ill-structured task of visiting an exhibition resulted in highly diverse inter-individual behaviour, which is difficult to compare across subjects. To identify common patterns across subjects, more clearly defined tasks or at least reduction of the amount of data per visitor would be necessary. Third, data analysis was not based on a-priori hypotheses; we tried to find explanations for patterns a-posteriori. To validate the presented results from this study, further research has to be conducted with larger samples and pre-defined tasks.

Still, the results of this study provide a first insight into informal mobile learning in museums: We were able to identify common eye movement patterns, which allowed us to generate hypotheses about information processing in an exhibition (conceptually heterogeneous exhibits are fixated successively; an exhibition wall is first skimmed then explored in detail). These hypotheses can be tested in further studies. We also identified elements in the exhibition that are less likely to be explored. This result could be used to improve the design of exhibitions by changing salience, position, and information density of less popular exhibition elements.

3. Potentials and limitations of mobile eye tracking

Based on mobile eye tracking literature and our own exploratory study, we identified several potentials of mobile eye tracking for research on mobile, informal learning. Though the advantages of mobile eye tracking for examining mobile learning are more apparent and also very appealing, we would also like to allude to some limitations which might be easily overlooked or underestimated.

3.1   Potentials of mobile eye tracking

Data richness. Eye tracking provides rich, continuous data of natural viewing behaviour and – in the case of mobile eye tracking – also the context of this behaviour. In contrast to other tracking methods (e.g. log file analyses, see for example Trinder, Roy, and Magill; and Wali, Oliver, and Winters in this book), eye tracking can additionally provide insight into planning behaviour that requires visual input but does not result in easily observable action. For example, a visitor visually explores two different walls from a distance and then moves to one of them to explore it in detail. External observation (e.g. by video surveillance) can only show the visitor's actual movements towards one of the walls but not his or her prior visual exploration of *both* walls.

Data validity. Since the actual fixations are recorded objectively by means of a camera, the validity of mobile eye tracking is higher than the validity of external observation: External observation can only determine the direction in which a person turns his or her head and moves but not the point on which his or her eyes are fixated. Since eye tracking data is obtained from the acting subject's perspective, it reduces perspective errors as well.

In contrast to retrospective questionnaires/interviews, eye tracking gathers data *online*, that is, during actual behaviour. If one considers the amount, the immediacy, and the objectiveness of measurement – no error-prone memory or verbalization is needed (e.g. Nisbett and Wilson, 1977) – it becomes apparent that eye tracking can provide insights into unconscious information processing that lies beyond introspectively accessible processing (Pelz et al., 2000).

Mobile eye tracking by means of light-weight head-mounted cameras brings eye tracking out of the laboratory into the natural environment. Behaviour can be measured where it naturally occurs, providing data with high external validity.

Non-reactive measurement. Data-collecting methods like questionnaires and interviews are considered to be highly reactive (Fritsche and Linneweber, 2006). In contrast, eye movements are natural behaviour that can hardly be manipulated by the tracked subject, especially not over longer periods of continuous measurement. While participants might report in an interview that they *did not* see a particular piece of information, mobile eye tracking can reveal that they *did at least look at it* – even if they say otherwise for any reason or simply do not remember it.

Statistical analysis. Similar to other tracking methods, data from eye tracking is highly structured and allows for further statistical analysis. Relevant data that can be extracted from the raw data are, for example, fixation durations, saccade length and degree, occurrences of specific events, holding power of exhibits or navigation sequences (to determine scan patterns, see for example Henderson, 2003). Eye tracking can also reveal interesting details about information processing: for example, which information has been missed, which information is fixated longer than other information, what gaze patterns occurred overall, or what differences in gaze patterns across participants and/or experimental groups exist.

3.2 Limitations of mobile eye tracking

Covert attention and mental spotlight. The first and most important limitation is the limited interpretation of a location of a fixation with respect to attention processes. Treisman (2006, p. 4) stated that "the window of attention set by the parietal scan can take on different apertures, to encompass anything from a finely localized object to a global view of the surrounding scene". Therefore, eye tracking in fact delivers accurate data about eye fixations, but this data does not always lead to correct conclusions regarding the focus of attention. For informal learning in museums, this means while a participant's eye is fixating a specific exhibit, he may actually be attending to the whole exhibition wall without devoting attention to the fixated exhibit itself or he may be thinking about something completely different while his gaze still lingers on that specific exhibit.

Limited conclusions about cognitive processing. A related problem is the limited validity of the interpretation of eye movements. "Whereas a given cognitive event might reliably lead to a particular fixation, the fixation itself does not uniquely specify the cognitive event" (Hayhoe and Ballard, 2005, p. 190). Interpretations of eye tracking data are often based on assumptions and heuristics about underlying cognitive processes. We may have an objective recording of a person's eye movements, but the cognitive processes that take place in the meanwhile are subject to interpretation.

One problem here is that eye movements are determined by two processes, namely bottom-up, stimulus-led processes triggered by salience of stimuli and top-down, cognitively-led processes based on prior knowledge and goals of the subject (Henderson, 2003). Whereas the influence of bottom-up processes can be modelled (Turano et al., 2003), data on a person's reasons for specific behaviour cannot be obtained by eye tracking. Cognitive processes cannot be observed directly through eye movements. Such top-down processes might be modelled more easily for clearly defined tasks, but only with great difficulty for open tasks like those involved in mobile, informal learning.

The example from our explorative study – when our interpretation of a participant's eye movement was proven to be incorrect by the interview

– illustrates the limited validity of conclusions from eye tracking data on underlying cognitive processes.

Obtrusiveness of measurement. In contrast to static eye tracking embedded into computer monitors, a mobile eye tracker is obtrusive for both the subject wearing the camera(s) and his or her environment: Participants wearing goggles know that their gazes are tracked, and the unfamiliar feeling may bother them. Other people can clearly see the eye tracker and, thus, they might interact differently with the person wearing it. This holds especially for informal settings like museums, which are highly social settings (Gammon, 2004). While this was not relevant for our study, since we allowed only one visitor in the exhibition at each time, this might be a major problem in more natural settings.

Selective sampling. Mobile eye tracking devices are difficult to calibrate for persons with glasses or corneal irregularity. Therefore, usually only people with normal vision are invited to participate in eye tracking studies. This might impair the generalization of results from eye tracking: If visual impairment is correlated with other relevant variables, this restriction leads to a biased sample.

Limited temporal and spatial accuracy. The temporal resolution depends on the recording of eye tracking images. A 50 Hz PAL DVCR tape in a mobile recorder saves two camera images by alternating frames. This results in a resolution of 25 Hz. Given that short fixations of about 33 ms were observed (Pelz et al., 2000), this means that some fixations can easily be missed.

Eye tracking works best if the system is calibrated to a specific fixation distance. Yet fixation distance is not constant in mobile settings but rather changing constantly. As a consequence, spatial accuracy of mobile eye tracking systems is worse than that of stationary systems. We tried to reduce this problem by calibrating the device at a distance the participants would typically keep to an exhibit wall. However, in other settings with an even wider range of fixation distances (e.g. a museum with large rooms and exhibits with a broad range of sizes) this limitation becomes a problem for mobile eye tracking.

Laborious data analysis. With a stationary eye tracker and a given background (e.g. a website), software for automatic data analysis is available. However, in mobile eye tracking, automatic analysis is limited: the background changes constantly and the participants' behaviour and eye movements are very inter-individually variable. Therefore, each eye tracking recording has to be analyzed manually. To automate the process, software would be necessary that can recognize the elements on the video frame and combine this information with eye tracking data. As far as we know, there is currently no software capable of doing so. Thus, many studies use only short tasks where inter-individual similar eye movements can be expected (e.g. Land and Hayhoe, 2001), which unfortunately limits the generalization of eye tracking data to more complex (learning) tasks.

Price. Mobile eye trackers are expensive; for example, the version used in our study costs about 24000 €. The price of the equipment limits the number of simultaneous measurements within dyads or groups that could be useful in order to explore collaborative learning and social engagement. However, instructions on how to build mobile eye trackers using off-the-shelf components at a cost of about 350 USD have been presented recently (see for example Li and Parkhurst, 2006).

Ethical concerns. As eye tracking also gathers data about unconscious or uncontrolled eye movements, participants have no control about the information they reveal during eye tracking. Even if they have previously agreed to the study, participants might be embarrassed by a confrontation with their eye tracking videos. The videos might reveal information they would rather have kept private.

We propose the following procedure to meet these ethical concerns: Study participants should be briefed which data will be gathered and how it will be analyzed, and be informed about the general purpose of the eye tracking study prior to data collection (e.g. via a sample video). When participants are confronted with their video feed during data analysis, only the interviewing researcher should be with them. Before publication of image or video files for any audience, participants must be asked for permission. Regarding the privacy of the people who are recorded on the eye tracking video, the same conditions as in photography should be applied.

4. Conclusions

Given the described limitations, eye tracking should be combined with other methods to increase the validity of interpretations. Such triangulation is recommended for other data gathering methods – see for example the chapters by Lelliott; Sharples; and Wali et al. in this book. Conclusions from eye movements about underlying cognitive processes are error-prone (Hayhoe and Ballard, 2005). To reduce interpretation bias, clear a-priori hypotheses about cognitive processes and their influence on eye movements are indispensable. Interview and questionnaire data about a person's interests and prior knowledge can be used to examine hypotheses with the data at hand, like in the exploratory study presented. A combination of eye tracking with Personal Meaning Mapping (see Lelliott in this book) could be interesting for the purpose of explaining changes between Personal Meaning Maps before and after a museum visit. An alternative is to confront visitors with their own eye movement record after the visit and ask them to think aloud.

An important question is whether data should be analyzed intra- or inter-individually. As eye tracking data are very rich, large samples are rarely used (for an exception, see Wooding, 2002), while the degree to which results from small samples can be generalized is limited. Especially in the context of complex, ill-defined problems (like visiting an exhibition), comparisons across subjects are restricted because of highly inter-individually variable behaviour. To be able to generalize results, pre-defined tasks should be used. Still, exploratory case studies – like the one presented here – can provide important insights into how information is processed and how informal learning happens on the move.

Further technical development of mobile eye tracking devices will probably eliminate some of the technical and pragmatic constraints of mobile eye tracking (e.g. fixation distance, costs, temporal and spatial accuracy). Development of software that supports automated analysis of real-world-videos with changing angles, views, distances, and objects is needed to reduce the complexity of the analysis of eye tracking data.

Despite some limitations, mobile eye tracking is a powerful data collection method in mobile learning research. Previous research has used mobile eye tracking to study behavioural planning, coordination of vision and action, and visual search (Hayhoe and Ballard, 2005; Land and Hayhoe, 2001; Pelz et al., 2000; Turano et al., 2003). The study presented here is the first to address information processing within the context of mobile learning by means of mobile eye tracking. In our exploratory study, we gained valuable in-sights into the information processing performed by museum visitors. Although the presented interpretations of our results need further validation, we would have hardly gained these findings otherwise. For this reason, we would like to encourage further research on mobile learning using mobile eye tracking.

Acknowledgements

This research was conducted within the research project "Learning in museums: The role of media" (see http://www.iwm-kmrc.de/museum/), funded by the "Pact for Research and Innovation" of the German Federal Ministry of Education and Research.

We would like to thank Viktoria Schuster for her help in analyzing the data.

References

Fritsche, I. and Linneweber, V. (2006). Nonreactive Methods in Psychological Research. In M. Eid and E. Diener (eds), *Handbook of Multimethod Measurement in Psychology*. Washington, DC: American Psychological Association (APA), pp. 189–203

Gammon, B. (2004). *Design for Museum Visitors*. Paper presented at UK Usability Professional's Association. Available at http://ukupa.org. uk/events/presentations/science_museum.pdf [accessed on 2 April 2007]

Hayhoe, M. and Ballard, D. (2005). Eye Movements in Natural Behavior. *TRENDS in Cognitive Science*, 9, pp. 188–194

Henderson, J.M. (2003). Human Gaze Control during Real-World Scene Perception. *TRENDS in Cognitive Science*, 7, pp. 498–504

Henderson, J.M. (2007). Regarding Scenes. *Current Directions in Psychological Science*, 16, pp. 219–222

Holmberg, N. (2004). *Eye Movement Patterns and Newspaper Design Factors: An Experimental Approach*. Master Thesis, Lund University. Available at http://theses.lub.lu.se/archive/2006/04/12/1144841530 -20432-695/NilsHolmberg.pdf [accessed on 25 June 2007]

Holsanova, J., Rahm, H. and Holmqvist, K. (2006). Entry Points and Reading Paths on the Newspaper Spread: Comparing Semiotic Analysis with Eye-Tracking Measurements. *Visual Communication*, 5(1), pp. 65–93

Land, M.F. and Hayhoe, M. (2001). In What Ways Do Eye Movements Contribute to Everyday Activities? *Vision Research*, 41, pp. 3559–3565

Li, D. and Parkhurst, D.J. (2006). OpenEyes: An Open-Hardware Open Source System for Low-Cost Eye Tracking. *Journal of Modern Optics*, 53(9), pp. 1295–1311

Nisbett, R.E. and Wilson, T.D. (1977). Telling More than We Can Know: Verbal Reports on Mental Processes. *Psychological Review*, 84(3), pp. 231–259

Pelz, J.B., Canosa, R.L., Kucharczyk, D., Babcock, J., Silver, A. and Konno, D. (2000). Portable Eye Tracking: A Study of Natural Eye Movements. In B.E. Rogowitz and T.N. Pappas (eds), *Human Vision and Electronic Imaging V* (Proceedings of SPIE, Vol. 3959). SPIE, pp. 566–582

Rayner, K. (1998). Eye Movements in Reading and Information Processing: 20 Years of Research. *Psychological Bulletin*, 124, pp. 372–422

Rayner, K., Rotello, C.M., Stewart, A.J., Keir, J. and Duffy, S.A. (2001). Integrating Text and Pictorial Information: Eye Movements when Looking at Print Advertisements. *Journal of Experimental Psychology: Applied*, 7, pp. 219–226

Schwonke, R., Berthold, K. and Renkl, A. (2007, August). *How Do Learners Actually Use Multiple External Representations? An Analysis of Eye Movements and Learning Outcomes*. Paper presented at the 12th Biennial Conference of the European Association for Learning

and Instruction (EARLI). Budapest, Hungary. Available at http://
earli2007.hu/nq/home/scientific_program/programme/proposal_
view/&abstractid=189 [accessed on 10 November 2007]

Treisman, A. (2006). How the Deployment of Attention Determines What
We See. *Visual Cognition*, 14, pp. 411–443

Turano, K.A., Geruschat, D.R. and Baker, F.H. (2003). Oculomotor
Strategies for the Direction of Gaze Tested with a Real-World Activity.
Vision Research, 43, pp. 333–346

Wooding, D.S. (2002). Fixation Maps: Quantifying Eye-Movement Traces.
In A.T. Duchowski, R. Vertegaal and J.W. Senders (eds), *Proceedings
of the Eyetracking Research and Application Symposium, ETRA 2002*.
New York: ACM Press, pp. 31–34

13. Using Personal Meaning Mapping to Gather Data on School Visits

ANTHONY LELLIOTT

Overview

There are a number of difficulties in assessing the outcomes of informal and mobile learning. In formal learning situations there is normally a clear teaching activity involving specific objectives which can be assessed prior to and after the intervention. These do not necessarily apply in informal situations such as museum[1] visits (Hein, 1998), and with a shift towards more constructivist learning in these contexts, new techniques are worth investigating. Personal Meaning Mapping (PMM) is a variation of concept mapping developed by John Falk, of the Institute for Learning Innovation, Maryland, USA (Falk, 2003) for use in informal learning environments. While concept mapping requires the technique to be taught to learners, PMM can be used with no prior experience on the part of the learner, and has uses both within and outside the classroom, thus providing a useful technique for assessing learning in informal and mobile learning environments. This chapter is based on an empirical study of school groups visiting an astronomical observatory in Gauteng, South Africa (Lelliott, 2007). The data collection involved structured interviews with students on astronomy concepts such as stars, the Sun and gravity, the students drawing Personal Meaning Maps as well as interviews based on their Maps. The chapter provides an account of a useful technique for data collection which is available to both practitioners and researchers of informal and mobile learning, and which can be carried out with the simple tools of pen and paper.

---

1   In this chapter, museum is used as a generic term encompassing traditional museums, science centres, zoos and other institutions.

1. Theoretical basis

The technique of Personal Meaning Mapping (PMM) is informed by the concept maps developed by Novak and collaborators in the 1980s (Novak and Gowin, 1984; Novak and Cañas, 2007). Concept maps have their roots in Ausubel's theory of meaningful learning (Ausubel, Novak, and Hanesian, 1978), which emphasized the importance of learners' prior knowledge. In concept mapping, a subject is taught how to map out their own understanding of concepts on a sheet of paper, and join these concepts with appropriate connectors. In this technique there is sometimes a "correct" concept map, drawn by an expert, against which the subject's map can be compared and scored. Much of the concept map analysis that has been developed over the past 20 years is based on this type of comparison (McClure, Sonak and Suen, 1999) and it has proved a useful technique for both pedagogy and the study of conceptual development, especially at school and tertiary levels. There have been a number of variants of concept mapping since the procedure was first developed by Novak and techniques used by Morine-Dershimer (1993) and Leinardt and Gregg (2002) are probably the closest to PMM. In a study of conceptual change, Morine-Dershimer asked student teachers to make a concept map depicting their view of the important components of teacher preparation by providing the phrase "teacher planning". Two semesters later, the students repeated the task, and then compared their post-course map with their original map. Leinardt and Gregg used a similar method with preservice teachers visiting a museum. They counted the number of ideas on each person's pre-visit and post-visit map, and then analyzed the structure of the maps to detect whether they had changed and whether there was any reorganization of information. Like these variants of concept mapping, the method of PMM creates no expectations of what the learner *should* know, either before or after the visit. In this respect it supports constructivist pedagogies whereby prior knowledge is regarded as being valuable to ascertain.

Other mapping techniques used in educational research such as flow diagrams (Davidowitz and Rollnick, 2005) and vee diagrams (Trowbridge and Wandersee, 1998), have not been employed as extensively as concept maps. Critiques of concept mapping have been made by Kagan (1990) and Ruiz-Primo and Shavelson (1996). Kagan noted in his critique that concept maps were used to assess short-term change rather than long-term gain. He also noted that studies often compared the subject's maps with a target "master" map. Many studies made claims that the map reflects an individual's actual cognitive structure, while Kagan suggested that the maps may reflect students' ability to "reproduce the structure of the discipline" (Kagan, 1990, p. 451) rather than show real changes in their cognitive configuration. Ruiz-Primo and Shavelson (1996) sounded warnings about using concept maps for assessment purposes, and stressed the need for further research on the relationship between the maps and students' cognitive schema.

A key difference between many analyses of concept mapping and PMM is that in the latter there is no "correct" map developed at any stage, against which the PMM is scored, and Falk (2003) maintains that such a form of analysis would be counter to the philosophy of PMM in the context of museum learning. This makes the maps more akin to multimodal maps used by semioticians such as Kress and Mavers (Preston, 2007). For Falk, there is no correct answer or series of answers that a museum visitor can be expected to come up with in relation to their visit. Unlike the school classroom, or the university lecture, where the students would be expected to learn particular scientific concepts or facts following pre-set course objectives, the learning which takes place in museums is personal, context-bound and idiosyncratic. A PMM is therefore an individual's personal construct of whatever learning took place as a result of their visit.

Falk (2003) recommends a particular method of analyzing PMMs, which involves looking across four dimensions of learning: extent, breadth, depth, and mastery. Extent examines vocabulary while breadth categorizes concepts used by the learner, and a comparison can be made between his or her pre- and post-intervention learning. Depth measures a learner's understanding of the concepts used while mastery assesses the overall quality of the understanding and how the learner makes use of it. While Falk suggests that PMMs can be analyzed both quantitatively and qualitatively, most of the studies in which they have been used have been dominated by quantitative techniques (e.g. Adelman, Falk, and James, 2000; Falk,

Moussouri, and Coulson, 1998). A recent innovation in the use of PMM has been adapting it for online use in a study of how amateur ornithologists interact with a website documenting bird distribution in the USA (Thompson and Bonney, 2007)

2. How Personal Meaning Mapping is conducted

PMM is a technique developed specifically for museum learning, in which an individual's knowledge and views about a particular topic are investigated prior to the person entering the museum and again after the visit. Specifically, PMM is carried out in the following manner:

1. Prior to the visit to the museum, the person is given a sheet of paper, on which a word or phrase is written in the centre. He or she is then asked to write or draw anything that comes to mind in relation to the word or phrase. This can be factual information, ideas, beliefs, or any other related opinions, and is written in a specific color on the paper (e.g. blue).

2. The investigator then has a short interview with the individual, and, investigates the ideas he or she has already written on the paper, recording any elaboration of ideas in a different color ink from the original (e.g. red).

3. After the visit, the person is given their original paper, and asked to make changes or additions to what they have already written on the paper. According to Falk (personal communication) and Luke (personal communication), it is crucial that the original paper is given back to the person, rather than asking them to fill a new one. It ensures that they do not feel that the investigator is "wasting their time" by asking them to repeat what they have already done, and it allows them to alter their original ideas. This contrasts with methods normally used in concept mapping. The corrections and

additions the individual makes to his or her map use another color ink (e.g. black).

4. Finally, the investigator carries out another interview, based on the alterations and additions carried out in step 3. The investigator writes these (again using the person's own words) in a different color ink (e.g. green).

Examples of PMMs are shown below in Figures 13.2 and 13.3.

3. Personal Meaning Mapping and an astronomy science centre

My study was qualitative, examining 34 grade 7 and 8 students (12- to 14-year-olds) from 4 schools in Gauteng, South Africa. Apart from the fact that I used PMMs to demonstrate short-term rather than long-term gain, the criticisms noted by Kagan (1990) and Ruiz-Primo and Shavelson (1996) do not apply to my study, as I used the maps principally as a basis for further questioning rather than as a representation of the children's minds. I chose to use PMM as a technique to complement my other data collection methods of observations and an "oral test". The oral test (conducted at the same time as the PMMs) focused on Big Ideas in astronomy (Lelliott, 2008), and was related to a traditional expectation of cognitive learning.[2] The aim of the oral test was to determine whether the students increased their formal knowledge of astronomy as a result of the visit. In contrast, the PMM revealed students' ideas, stories and feelings about astronomy which *they* regarded as relevant. The questions asked in the interview related to the PMM were prompted entirely by what a student had written or drawn on their map.

---

2   For example, students were asked questions such as "Why does the sun move across the sky every day?" and "What is gravity? What does it do? What would gravity be like on the moon?"

In my study, the environment for data collection was quite different to many studies using PMM. Like Luke (1998), my data was collected in the school classrooms of the selected participants in the study. I initially gained permission from the school Principal and relevant class teachers, and obtained informed consent from the students and their parents. I then addressed the students in class and explained that I am researching their forthcoming visit to one of the study sites. After handing out blue pens to each student, I explained that I wanted them to write whatever they think about when seeing the words in the centre of the sheet of paper. Before giving them the paper, I then showed an example on the chalkboard, using the word "Johannesburg". I asked the class what things came into their heads when they saw that word on the middle of a piece of paper. Using examples from the class, I then wrote their suggestions on the chalkboard, linking the words they suggested to the central word "Johannesburg", or to words they have already put forward, as shown in Figure 13.1.

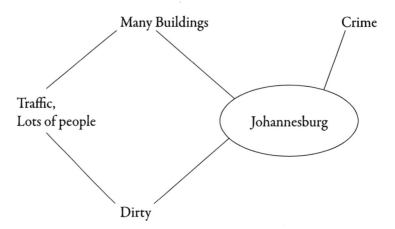

Figure 13.1: Example of initial PMM drawn on chalkboard.

Once I had answered questions, and considered that students had got the idea of the technique, I handed out the PMM sheet that I had prepared in advance for the study. The "prompt" words in the middle of this sheet were "space, stars and planets". Falk recommends that thorough piloting of the prompt is necessary (Falk, 2003), and I did this in one of my pilot schools, using a combination of words including space, Earth and stars before deciding on the final wording, which elicited the most fruitful responses.

I then asked the students to write what they could tell me about these words. I stressed the following, that:

- Even if they were not sure about a particular issue, they should feel free to write about it.

- This was not a test.

- They could use words in their home language if they wanted.

- They could do drawings.

- They could write about their feeling and beliefs

I then allowed students the time they required to complete the PMM. This varied from about 5 minutes, to a maximum of about 30 minutes. Most students would complete the map within 15 to 20 minutes. In order to ensure anonymity, I wrote a number on the PMM as each student completed it, and compiled a class list with the students' names and the PMM numbers. I could then cross reference each student against their own PMM, but anyone seeing a map would not be able to identify which student had completed it. As they completed their PMMs, students handed them to me. I then selected which students I wanted to interview, on the basis of what they had written or drawn in the PMM. Criteria for selection included the extent of student interest and prior knowledge of astronomy, as well as demographic considerations such as gender and race. The oral test was conducted in a quiet room at the school, and was immediately followed by the interview related to the PMM. After this initial data collection, students then visited either a planetarium or the visitors' center of a working radio telescope. Data was collected again back at school after the visit, and Table 13.1 shows the time elapsed between data collection and the visit.

BETWEEN	RANGE IN DAYS	MEAN NUMBER OF DAYS	MODAL NUMBER OF DAYS
Pre-visit PMM and interview	0 to 15	6	4
Interview and visit	1 to 10	4	1
Visit and post-visit PMM	1 to 16	5	6
Post-visit PMM and interview	1 to 16	5	6

Table 13.1: Days elapsed between collection of data before and after the visits.

During the visit to the planetarium, the students attended a live "show" (a tour of the solar system) presented by the planetarium educator. At the radio telescope visitors' center, students were given a tour of the facility during which time they participated in a number of activities including using "Coke" bottle rockets, spinning on a turntable, using a sundial, observing sunspots and attending a slide show of the NASA Moon landings.

4. Analysis

My study being qualitative in nature implied that I forego extensive quantitative analysis, and make individual learners the units of analysis. In this respect the personal meaning maps and accompanying interviews were very helpful, as they provided details of the sort of learning not captured in my structured interviews. Examples of this additional learning are provided in the "Gugu's learning" section below. In addition, although not analyzed for all the dimensions suggested by Falk (see above), I was able to use the PMMs to assist with some descriptive statistical data, such as the number of astronomical vocabulary words ("extent" in Falk's terminology) used by each participant in the study. This involved counting words related to their pre- and post-visit PMMs. More useful was categorising the phrases and ideas students put in their PMMs and following up on these in the PMM interviews based on what they had written. This data was analyzed using the qualitative data analysis software package ATLAS.ti which assisted in organizing the data and in categorization and interpretation.

4.1 Gugu's learning

Here I present the results of one student's learning during her visit to the science centre to demonstrate the sort of data which can be generated by PMM. Gugu is representative of the ten students who did not appear to learn much based on their results in the structured interview, but whose PMM revealed that learning nevertheless did occur. Gugu's personal meaning map (Figure 13.2) drawn before her visit to the science centre was similar to those of several other students in the study. She listed the nine planets together with some brief facts about several of them. For example that Jupiter is the biggest planet and Mercury is the closest planet to the Sun. She referred to stars as being "a lighting thing" created by God, and that they are our "friends, family and negbour (sic)". She also referred to stars being at the galaxy and Milky Way. She stated that space consists of open space, containing planets, stars, galaxy and the Milky Way. When probed about her PMM at the interview, she confirmed that "God created stars so that they can shine at night". Although she knew the term galaxy she was unable to explain its meaning or its relationship to the term Milky Way. She further referred to a spaceship and rocket, although she found difficulty in expressing herself here. She also appeared to have differing ideas on aliens. Having said she doesn't believe in them (in the structured interview) she mentioned that some planets have them (in the PMM).

Figure 13.2: Gugu's Pre-visit Personal Meaning Map.

After her visit to the science centre, Gugu, instead of adding to her PMM as requested, filled the *reverse* side of the paper with numerous facts (Figure 13.3). Several of these facts were a repetition of her pre-visit PMM, such as her reference to the nine planets, Pluto being the coldest, Mercury being the hottest and stars being in the galaxy. However, she wrote down several new pieces of information, including the following:

- She "saw which bottle goes high and low" (details are provided below).
- Additional planets to the nine named ones.
- Additional facts about the nine planets.
- Black spots on the Sun.
- Various features of Mars: water, land, and orbit.
- A description of the Moon landing and the time taken to get there.
- A star bigger than the Sun.

Figure 13.3: Gugu's Post-visit Personal Meaning Map.

All the new information that Gugu provided in her PMM related directly to her experiences at the science centre. For example, the reference to the bottle was the "Coke bottle rockets" which students played with at the centre, while the black spots refers to sunspots which the students observed when the Sun's image was projected on to a small telescope screen. None of these pieces of knowledge emerged from the oral test. In her interview, further probing of several of the ideas in her PMM was carried out but was limited due to time constraints. Her understanding of a galaxy was still minimal: "A galaxy I think is where the stars stay and the moon and the solar system and everything", but she understood that it would contain thousands and thousands of stars. Her belief in aliens appears to have changed on reflection: in the post-visit PMM she wrote that she believed in them, but when questioned she said that this was a mistake, and that although she had read about them in a magazine she really didn't believe they existed. I consider that Gugu's changes to her PMM are incremental additions to her knowledge of basic astronomy resulting from her visit to the science centre, and were elicited by the PMM.

5. Implications for Personal Meaning Mapping in teaching and research

The reason why I considered the additions to Gugu's PMM as important is that when questioned about aspects of space and stars during the oral test data collection, Gugu showed no improvement in her knowledge or understanding. The oral test could be regarded as a more traditional pre- and post-test of astronomy knowledge, which demonstrated a range of ability across the 34 students in the study. Gugu was at the bottom end of this range, suggesting that the visit had made no difference to her knowledge of astronomy. However, the use of PMM, in which there was no expectation of specific prior knowledge, showed that Gugu had acquired several facts about astronomy which might not have been identified by traditional tests.

This suggests that Personal Meaning Mapping might have uses in normal classroom settings, as well as the way it is currently used in out-of-school learning. Teachers could, for example, ask their students to complete a PMM prior to starting a topic, in order to determine the prior knowledge of the class. A relatively brief analysis would enable a teacher to tailor his or her teaching to the class' prior knowledge, as well as target individuals and groups for enrichment or remediation. In this way, using PMM in the classroom could complement or replace other constructivist methods of determining prior knowledge such as diagnostic tests (Cohen, Manion, and Morrison, 2000). However, it is in informal learning environments that PMM has the greatest potential. It has for example been successfully used in youth workshops (Lewis, 2004) and during conference evaluations (James, 2006), where the affective aspects of the method have been most pronounced. As mobile learning develops it is likely that devices such as PDAs might be used to collect the PMM data instead of pen and paper.

PMM is a relatively new technique and little analysis or evaluation of the technique has yet been published. As it involves knowledge of interviewing and time to administer both the written sheets and the interviews, then resources in the form of time and funding are significant (Falk, 2003). It generates a lot of data, and is therefore time-consuming to transcribe and analyse, and requires knowledge of analysis procedures on the part of the researcher. Issues of validity and reliability are similar to other techniques which involve coding during analysis, and require careful attention to the selection of the initial words or phrases used as prompts, and to inter-rater agreement.

Burtnyk et al. (2005) suggest that it needs to be used with caution, especially as the relatively large amount of data it generates is subjected to intense analysis. During my study, I found no particular drawbacks in using PMMs as a data collection method, but I have the following recommendations for their use in research:

1. Where possible, spend adequate time in preliminary analysis of the PMM prior to the initial interview. Similarly, spend adequate time in analysis of the PMM before the second round of data collection, and prior to the second interview. This would allow the researcher to carefully devise questions based on the PMM for use in the interview. Unfortunately, in the sequence of data collection involved in museum visits, this is not always possible.

2. In a pilot study, experiment with the two alternatives of handing the original PMM back to the participants for addition/correction and asking them to complete a new PMM. Falk strongly recommends the former for museum visitors, for ethical reasons due to their time constraints and the inconvenience they are being put to. School groups are "used to" formal and informal testing as part of their school work, and are not likely to object to completing a new map. A comparison between these two alternatives might therefore be of value. It is possible that receiving the original PMM influences the additions and corrections made, and that completing a new map might result in new knowledge or concepts being expressed.

3. It might be worth doing some additional validating of the technique as part of the piloting. For example, if a PMM is given to a group of people, who then repeat the procedure some time later, with no intervention between the two processes, is there any difference between what people complete on the PMM? To what extent does the very act of completing a PMM result in possible changes in people's thinking about the topic? This has wider implications for both informal and mobile learning research, and although methodologically challenging is an important area to investigate.

4. It is possible that mobile devices could be equipped with appropriate software to enable visitors to capture their PMM and edit it during and immediately after the visit. This would provide a more immediate record of their experiences.

In summary, Personal Meaning Mapping is an innovative procedure with considerable potential to assist in the collection of data in informal learning environments. Its use by museum educators and teachers accompanying school groups would enable them to better understand the sort of learning which occurs during museum visits. This could in turn improve the quality of the visits and the experience provided by the informal learning sites themselves.

Draft versions of this chapter were presented at the 2007 SAARMSTE conference, Maputo, Mozambique and the 2007 MIL-RM workshop, London.

References

Adelman, L.M., Falk, J. and James, S. (2000). Impact of National Aquarium in Baltimore on Visitors' Conservation Attitudes, Behavior and Knowledge. *Curator*, 43(1), 33–61

Ausubel, D., Novak, J. and Hanesian, H. (1978). *Educational psychology: A cognitive view* (2nd ed.). New York: Holt, Rinehart and Winston

Burtnyk, K., Foutz, S., Kessler, C. and Kidwell, M. (2005). *Personal Meaning Mapping (PMM): Examples of Methodological Flexibility*. Paper presented at the 18th annual Visitor Studies Association Conference. Available at http://www.visitorstudiesarchives.org/vsa_browse_vsc.php

Cohen, L., Manion, L. and Morrison, K. (2000). *Research methods in education* (fifth edn). London and New York: Routledge-Falmer

Davidowitz, B. and Rollnick, M. (2005). Development and application of a rubric for analysis of novice students' laboratory flow diagrams. *International Journal of Science Education*, 27(1), 43–59

Falk, J.H. (2003). Personal Meaning Mapping. In G. Caban, C. Scott, J.H. Falk and L.D. Dierking (eds), *Museums and Creativity: A study into the role of museums in design education*. Sydney: Powerhouse Publishing

Falk, J.H., Moussouri, T. and Coulson, D. (1998). The Effect of Visitors' Agendas on Museum Learning. *Curator*, 41(2), 107–120

Hein, G.E. (1998). *Learning in the Museum*. London: Routledge

James, A. (2006). Your Place or Mine? Engaging New Audiences with Heritage. Conference Evaluation Report, Manchester

Kagan, D. (1990). Ways of Evaluation Teacher Cognition: Inferences Concerning the Goldilocks Principle. *Review of Educational Research*, 60(3), 419–469

Leinhardt, G. and Gregg, M. (2002). Burning Buses, Burning Crosses: Student Teachers See Civil Rights. In G. Leinhardt, K. Crowley and K. Knutson (eds), *Learning Conversations in Museums*. Mahwah, NJ: Erlbaum, pp. 139–166

Lelliott, A.D. (2007). Learning about Astronomy: a case study exploring how grade 7 and 8 students experience sites of informal learning in South Africa. Unpublished PhD, University of the Witwatersrand, Johannesburg

Lelliott, A.D. (2008). *Massive – the concepts of size and scale addressed by out-of-school learning*. Paper presented at the 16th Annual SAARMSTE Conference, Maseru, Lesotho

Lewis, A. (2004). Personal Meaning Mapping Exercise – "Your Culture". Learning and Culture, Oxfordshire County Council

Luke, J.J. (1998). Art Around the Corner: An Assessment of the Long-term Impact of an Art Museum Program on Students' Interpretations of Art. Unpublished Master of Museum Studies Thesis, University of Toronto, Toronto

McClure, J.R., Sonak, B. and Suen, H.K. (1999). Concept Map Assessment of Classroom Learning: Reliability, Validity, and Logistical Practicality. *Journal of Research in Science Teaching*, 36(4), 475–492

Morine-Dershimer, G. (1993). Tracing Conceptual Change in Preservice Teachers. *Teaching and Teacher Education*, 9(9), 15–26

Novak, J. and Cañas, A. (2007). Theoretical Origins of Concept Maps, How to construct them, and Uses in Education. *Reflecting Education*, 3(1), 29–42

Novak, J. and Gowin, D. (1984). *Learning How to Learn*. New York: Cambridge University Press

Preston, C. (2007). An introduction to Multimodal Concept Mapping: approaches and techniques. *Reflecting Education*, 3(1), 6–23

Ruiz-Primo, M. and Shavelson, R. (1996). Problems and issues in the use of concept maps in science assessment. *Journal of Research in Science Teaching*, 33(6), 569–600

Thompson, S. and Bonney, R. (2007). *Evaluating the Impact of Participation in an On-line Citizen Science Project: A Mixed-methods approach*. Paper presented at the Museums and the Web 2007 Conference. Available at http://www.archimuse.com/mw2007/papers/thompson/thompson.html

Trowbridge, J.E. and Wandersee, J.H. (1998). Theory-Drive Graphic Organizers. In J.J. Mintzes, J.H. Wandersee and J.D. Novak (eds), *Teaching Science for Understanding. A Human Constructivist View*. San Diego: Academic Press, pp. 109–131

14. The Generic Learning Outcomes: A Conceptual Framework for Researching Learning in Informal Learning Environments

JOCELYN DODD

Overview

This chapter will focus on the Generic Learning Outcomes, developed by the Research Centre for Museums and Galleries (RCMG) at the University of Leicester. The Generic Learning Outcomes, (GLOs hereafter) are a conceptual framework rather than a specific research tool developed to capture the impact of museums, libraries and archives on their users' learning. The chapter will explore the context and development of the GLOs to clarify their rationale and frame their underlying values. Examples of research studies will illustrate how they have been used to report on museum learning. These studies combine both qualitative and quantitative research methods to give both the depth and breadth of users' learning experiences, and can help to reveal new opportunities for developing learning in museums. The examples will demonstrate how the GLOs have been used to develop specific questions used in questionnaires, and how the GLOs have also been used to analyse qualitative research data. The chapter concludes by considering how the GLO conceptual framework enables researchers to evaluate informal (and mobile) learning.

1. Introduction

Museums as learning environments are inherently diverse, rich, interactive and physical:

> Museums are sites of spectacle and display, environments that can be rich and surprising. They can be overwhelming and difficult to manage, but equally they can arouse curiosity or inspire new ideas. Museum-based learning is physical, bodily engaged: movement is inevitable, and the nature, pace and range of this bodily movement influences the style of learning. Museums have no national curriculum – each museum may present a different view of specific matter, they have no formal systems of assessment and prescribed timetables of learning. Learning in museums is potentially more open-ended, more individually directed, more unpredictable and more susceptible to multiple diverse responses than sites of formal learning, where what is taught is directed by externally established standards. (Hooper Greenhill, 2007, p. 4)

Museums are typical sites of informal and mobile learning, as is testified by the number of studies that explore mobile learning in museums (see for example the chapters by Pierroux; Sharples; and Lelliott, this volume). This is not surprising: museums as sites for learning offer learning experiences which span both formal and informal learning; they afford highly diverse learning practices; they present a non-traditional learning environment that can host diffused, informal situations, where learning outcomes are unpredictable and individually directed. These are all core characteristics of mobile learning (Sharples; Traxler; Pachler; Vavoula, this volume).

This chapter presents the Generic Learning Outcomes (GLOs), a conceptual framework developed to measure, describe and report on learning in the museum sector and now extensively used across museums. Bridged by the informal character of both museum-based and mobile learning, the chapter suggests that the GLOs might offer opportunities for researching the impact of mobile learning innovations.

2. The context of the Generic Learning Outcomes development

The context of the development of the GLOs is important in understanding their characteristics, quality, features, and shape. The last decade has seen an unprecedented development in the scale, scope and character of learning in museums.

In the UK, the government's focus on education and learning has been part of a desire to create a more inclusive learning society. In this context, government policy and initiatives have been drawing culture much more centrally into government activities, insisting on education in museums being centrally positioned: "The Government believes that education is central to the role of museums today" (DCMS, 2000, p. 4). Museums have responded with a modernisation process through which they are redefining themselves in relation to contemporary issues and needs. Museum modernisation has focused not only on internal processes of curatorship, but also on the complex interpretive processes of creating sophisticated exhibitions and learning initiatives which reflect the needs of audiences, both current and potential, reflecting the rapid social and cultural changes in the late 20th and early 21st centuries.

The policy focus on education was followed by a raft of museum education programme initiatives, for example the Education Challenge Fund, which presented many opportunities for development, but also challenges. To maximise the benefits of these developments, the UK's Museums Libraries and Archives Council (MLA) developed in 2003 the national initiative *Inspiring Learning for All*,[1] which intended to develop a more professional approach to learning in the sector. The initiative endorsed an awareness that alongside substantial streams of funding from central government was a need for organisations to be accountable, and therefore emphasised measuring the outcomes of learning: what learning impact did the programmes have and how could this be measured?

1   http://www.inspiringlearningforall.gov.uk.

These were addressed by the *Learning Impact Research Project* (LIRP) which was carried out under the *Inspiring Learning for All* initiative, between 2001 and 2003. The project, carried out by an interdisciplinary group of researchers at the RCMG,[2] resulted in the GLOs. The development and application of the GLOs is documented in detail in Hooper-Greenhill (2007). A summary of the development process and the GLO framework is presented in the following section.

3.   The Generic Learning Outcomes

LIRP was carried out in a real world context that was complex, fast moving, volatile and highly politicised (Hooper-Greenhill, 2007). The project thus aimed to better understand learning in museums and build a theoretical understanding of this; while at the same time it aimed to translate this understanding into a method to measure learning that could be used by practitioners and also be used to give a national picture of cultural learning, that would be considered robust in terms of government performance measures.

Consultation and piloting with professionals was central to the project, which involved 15 organisations[3] across the sector. The first challenge of the research was to devise a comprehensive definition of learning that would be equally applicable to museums, libraries and archives. There was a lack of common understanding of learning, a common vocabulary, and

2   I was part of this research team and subsequently worked on a number of research projects and professional development programmes using the GLOs. The research team was directed by Professor Eilean Hooper-Greenhill.

3   The organisations involved were: Museum of Science and Industry Manchester, Norfolk Museums, Knowsley Museum, Imperial War Museum, Leeds City Art Gallery, Poole Library, Warwick Museum, Hampshire Museums, University of Sunderland Library, University of Leicester Library, Somerset Archive and Record Service, Essex Libraries and Heritage Services, Warwick Library, Leicestershire Libraries.

broad understanding of the scope and range of learning. However, there was agreement that museums, libraries and archives (a) represent open, flexible environments for learning which worked for both formal learning and informal self directed learning, (b) host learners who varied in age, motivation and types of engagement, (c) do not "test" their users, nor do they set them specific learning standards to achieve. These assumptions framed LIRP's second challenge, to devise a method to measure learning in such organisations, to capture its complexity and open-ended character, and to give an account of their learning impact on individuals and groups in both the long and short term.

4. Defining learning in museums, libraries and archives

Inspiring Learning for All had adopted the UK Campaign for Learning[4] definition of learning:

> Learning is a process of active engagement with experience. It is what people do when they want to make sense of the world. It may involve the development or deepening of skills, knowledge, understanding, awareness, values, ideas and feelings, or an increase in the capacity to reflect. Effective learning leads to change, development and the desire to learn more.

LIRP took this as a starting point to clarify on one hand whether people working in museums, libraries and archives would identify with this definition, and on the other to examine how it related to educational theory and whether it was able to capture the complexity of the learning process and outcomes. A literature review (Mousouri, 2002) showed that whilst a great deal of research had taken place into formal learning, very little had been written about cultural learning, especially in libraries and archives. Learning practice and research were more developed in museums, where it was clear that:

---

4   www.campaign-for-learning.org.uk.

- learning is a complex set of processes in which people are involved in different ways and to different degrees throughout their life,

- learning involves the use of what you already know to make sense out of new knowledge,

- cognitive learning (facts and information) cannot be separated from affective learning (feelings and emotions),

- as Claxton (1999) describes it, learning runs along a continuum from a tight focus like a spotlight to a low focus like a floodlight, so learning may not be purposeful.

The LIRP team concluded that the abovementioned broad and open-ended definition of learning was appropriate for describing cultural learning:

> The understanding or learning that underpinned LIRP acknowledged social and cultural difference and the resulting perspectival character of knowledge. It understood culture as a system of producing meaning, and, from a basis in social constructivism, it perceived "reality" as multiple. It saw learning as integral to everyday life, rather than limited to specific educational moments: as such it adopted a life long learning position. Learning was understood as constructivist and experiential/ performative, involving active minds and bodies. Learning was perceived as one way in which individuals' identities were produced. (Hooper-Greenhill, 2007, p. 43).

5. Capturing learning in museums, libraries and archives

The next challenge for LIRP in measuring the impact and outcomes of learning in museums, libraries and archives, was to get a clear view of what learning outcomes might mean in this cultural learning context. There was extensive literature on learning outcomes in formal education, that showed how learning outcomes are devised in relation to a specific curriculum area at a specific level, and how students can be assessed against that level (Mousouri, 2002). Learning outcomes are prescribed by the curriculum and are managed by the teacher, clearly laid down in advance; after undertaking a particular study the student's progress can be measured against them. It is possible to see how such a process might be implemented in formal taught sessions, for example school sessions in museums or adult education programmes in libraries or archives, where the objectives of the session can be pre-set and an assessment of the impact on the participants can be made.

However LIRP needed to measure the learning impact on a much wider constituency, not only people engaged in formal learning programmes but also those who may learn unintentionally, and a system was required that could capture the learning experiences of anyone using a museum, library or archive. As discussed already, this learning can be infinitely diverse, with varying learning styles and approaches, with user-set rather than institution-set learning agendas that reflect their personal motivations and interests, and with sometimes unexpected learning outcomes. It is clear that it is not possible to set learning outcomes for each individual in advance, nor is it appropriate for the organisation to make a judgement about the level of learning. And thus, the notion of learning outcomes as used in formal education was inappropriate for LIRP purposes.

LIRP's literature review (Mousouri, 2002) also presented examples that took a more generalised approach to learning outcomes, where specific individual outcomes are grouped into generic categories (see for example LTS, 2002), which are not attached to particular knowledge, skills or values. So for example a specific outcome and its corresponding generic outcome from a series of museum workshops on Raphael's *Madonna of the Pinks* might be:

SPECIFIC OUTCOME	GENERIC OUTCOME
Discuss religious images in the painting	Knowledge and understanding
Explain what paints it is made from and their origins	Knowledge and understanding
Draw a mother and child from life	Skills
Describe the painting	Skills

Table 14.1: Specific and corresponding generic learning outcomes from a series of museum workshops on Raphael's *Madonna of the Pinks*.

While it was impossible (and undesirable) for LIRP to (pre)set specific learning outcomes, generic learning outcomes could help to map out what happened when people used museums, libraries and archives. The outcome categories needed to be broad enough to encompass the diversity, richness and complexity of the learning experience. They also needed to acknowledge enjoyment and inspiration as an aspect of cultural learning that had emerged as highly significant in a number of previous studies (Hooper-Greenhill and Dodd, 2002; Dodd et al., 2002).

6. The five Generic Learning Outcomes

The GLOs thus emerged, featuring five broad categories which are diverse enough to encompass all potential learning outcomes, providing a language to talk about the multiple dimensions and outcomes of learning (Hooper-Greenhill, 2002). The five GLOs are:

- Knowledge and understanding
- Skills
- Enjoyment, Inspiration and Creativity
- Attitudes and Values
- Action, Behaviour and Progression

Knowledge and understanding refer to learning new facts and information. *Skills* refer to knowing how to do something and range from intellectual through to emotional, social and physical skills. *Enjoyment* is likely to lead to the development of positive learning, which is itself likely to lead to the motivation to learn further. The open ended nature of cultural learning enables exploration and experimentation, leading to *inspiration* and *creativity*. *Attitudes and values* refer to new information being absorbed and attitudes being developed, which in turn (in)form people's values. *Action* refers to what people will do as a result of learning, possibly leading to changes in *behaviour* and *progression*.

As a conceptual framework the GLOs can be used to develop research questions, design research tools and analyse and interpret research data. They provide a language to describe individuals' experiences where nothing is pre-determined and there is no external target to be met. The learning may be short or long term, deeply significant or quite superficial – but is nevertheless personally relevant. Examples of their use are presented in the next section.

7. Applying the Generic Learning Outcomes

Since their launch, the GLOs have become common currency in museums and have been used in a number of large, complex studies (Hooper-Greenhill et al., 2004a; 2004b; 2006; 2007). For the purposes of illustrating how they can be applied, this section will focus on one specific element of a larger study (Hooper Greenhill et al., 2007), to look at the learning outcomes of community participants who have been involved in museum activities and experiences. The purpose of the evaluation was to identify the learning outcomes of the community projects for children and adults, and to get the views of their community group leaders on the effect of the museum experience. The study wanted to gain a broad view of learning from all the participants, but also wanted to look at the depth of learning experiences of a small number of participants. In addition, the learning outcomes would be compared with the learning outcomes of similar education projects for teachers and pupils.

7.1 GLO-based research tools

The design of the research tools drew heavily on previous studies of similar museum education projects for teachers and pupils. Those studies had used teacher and pupil questionnaires, which were designed to be completed very quickly at the end of a museum visit. The questions for the pupils' questionnaires were selected from a question bank on the Inspiring Learning for All website.[5] For example, the question bank contains the following items, regarding:

- Knowledge and understanding (yes/no/don't know answer)
  - ◊ I felt that I learnt some new information
  - ◊ I have developed an increased interest in something I knew little about before coming here
  - ◊ I have gained knowledge that I can use or have used in my work as a result of my visit(s) here
  - ◊ I have gained a better understanding of other peoples' ideas
  - ◊ I have learnt new things about myself and my family's history
  - ◊ I understand better the community I live in
- Action, behaviour and progression (yes/no answer)
  - ◊ I have developed a new interest during my visit(s) here
  - ◊ I can use the knowledge I learnt here when I visit other similar places
  - ◊ I am thinking about starting some training or a college course as a result of my experience here
  - ◊ I am planning to join a special interest group as a result of my experience here
  - ◊ I achieved my intentions
  - ◊ I intend to come again
  - ◊ Visiting has given me lots of ideas for things I could do
  - ◊ The visit has made me want to find out more

---

5   http://www.inspiringlearningforall.gov.uk/uploads/Question%20Bank.pdf.

The selected questions were made into statements to which pupils were asked to respond with "Yes", "No", "Don't know". Each questionnaire also had a "thought bubble" for children to answer the question "The most interesting thing about using the museum was ..." which enabled pupils to respond using their own words or drawings to something significant about their visit (see Figure 14.1). A teachers' questionnaire was designed similarly, to elicit teachers' responses about their students and the effect of the visit on their class. Questions were included to reflect all five GLOs, and the language was age-appropriate for each version of the questionnaire – the teachers', the young children's (age 7–11), and the older children's (11 and above).

The questionnaires were piloted extensively with museum learning staff and schools in four museums and were refined accordingly. For example, one question relating to skills was not included in the 7–11-year-olds questionnaire as the children could not understand the idea of skills well enough to comment. The following guidelines for the design of GLO-based questionnaires were devised:

- Use separate questionnaires for different age students
- Use fewer questions for younger groups and a space for the student to write or draw
- Ensure questions are written with the age group in mind
- Pilot questionnaires with the age range they are written for
- Present the questionnaires on good quality paper and make the design appealing
- Inform the teacher in advance of the visit about the questionnaire
- Design a separate teacher's questionnaire which can be completed simultaneously
- Invite the students to work together if they like but they need to complete individual forms
- Allow 5–10 minutes to complete at the end of a visit, provide a quiet space and plenty of pens or pencils – if possible ensure the

questionnaires are completed on-site as they are less likely to be
sent back if taken away

For the purposes of this project, the community questionnaires were
carefully considered in relation to the characteristics of the community
audience. As comparisons with the pupils in school groups were to be made,
the schools' questionnaires described above were tested for suitability with
community groups. This testing led to changes in the layout to produce a
more informal feel (for example, the questionnaire for 7–11 year old was
designed in the shape of a mobile phone). The questions in the children's
questionnaires all worked very well and remained unchanged, despite the
community groups participating in quite different sessions from schools.
The questionnaire for community group leaders had to be different from
the teachers', though, as it had to work across a much more diverse group
of people. Again, the GLOs were used to frame part of the questionnaire,
including a question which focused on the five elements of the GLOs. For
example it asked, "How do you rate your experience today in the development of your group's skills, e.g. making and doing, language, social etc."
They were asked to rate these from very important to not at all important.
Consultation and piloting were critical to tailor the questionnaires to the
needs of these different groups.

The study also had a qualitative element, which took the form of case
studies. Data for the case studies came through informal semi-structured
interviews. The GLOs informed the interview questions, but were principally used in the subsequent analysis.

7.2   Procedures and methods

The sample involved in this study all came from community projects
which were part of the UK DCMS/DCSF National/ Regional Museums
Partnership Programme 2006–7. An example project was Social Services,
Manchester City Council, who were working with looked after children
at Manchester Art Gallery on the project "Image and Identity", where
young people explored their own image and identity through practical
workshops and by looking at the way artists have presented themselves.
Three questionnaires were used, one for community group leaders, one

for children 7–11-years-old, and one for children aged over 11 and adults. These were administered by the key workers in the museums, following a briefing from the research team at a research seminar. The questionnaires were often completed after the participants had been involved in multiple sessions in the museum.

Case studies were selected after familiarisation visits to each of the twelve partnerships projects. Four case study projects were selected:

- Engaging Refugees and Asylum Seekers
- Image and Identity
- Journeys of Change
- Creative Canals

The case studies explored the multiple perspectives held by the diverse participants about their learning, and involved interviews with community group leaders, participants, session facilitators and museum staff. This part of the study was exploratory, responding to opportunities to gather useful and relevant information, including personal accounts from participants.

7.3 Analysis of GLO-based questionnaires

The community groups' experiences varied greatly. Many groups did not have a group leader, like for example the Somali Youth Forum in the "Journeys of Change" project. Some museums were reluctant to administer the forms, viewing them too "bureaucratic" and an intrusion into what should be a pleasurable experience.

Thirty five (35) responses from community group leaders were collected – a very small number compared to the 407 of teachers' responses in previous studies. The results show that group leaders value highly opportunities for their group's members to develop their skills (69%) and increase their knowledge (60%). They find enjoyment, inspiration and creativity less important (54%), in contrast to teachers in previous studies who value these most highly (71%). The case studies explored these themes in more depth. For example, for refugees and asylum seekers life skills such as communication (language) and social skills (integration) are very important. For young people in the care system, being able to communicate about their emotions is especially significant. Although the sample for this study was relatively small, the findings raise interesting questions about how the GLOs are valued differently by different groups using the museum for different purposes.

One hundred and eleven (111) questionnaires were completed by children aged 7–11-years-old, 57% of whom were girls and 43% boys (see Table 14.2). Another 391 questionnaires were completed by people aged over 11 years old (see Table 14.3). In this group, 32% were male and 68% female, and their ages varied from 12 to 90 years old; however, the bulk of responses came from the 12–19-years-old range.

Responses from the younger children were very positive (see Table 14.2). The children appeared stimulated by the museum experience, with 84% of them stating it had given them lots of ideas for things they can do. The boys in particular were uncharacteristically enthusiastic: with 98% stating that they enjoyed using the museum, they were much more positive than their peers who had visited with school in previous studies.

The older children and adults were inspired by their museum visit (82%) and were confident that they had learnt in new ways (80%) and said they were now much more interested in the subject than when they started (78%). Moreover, 77% found that the museum is a good place to pick up new skills. A characteristic example comes from Nahla, a 15-year-old who took part in the "Visual Dialogues" programme at Tate Britain (see Figure 14.1); she is very clear about the skills she has learnt regarding how to overcome being shy, and changing her behaviour by being cooperative.

Compared to older children in community groups, previous studies had shown that this age group is less positive when visiting with their school. For example, only 61% of older children in school groups were inspired by their visit, 68% said they learned in new ways, and 58% said they were now more interested in the subject. Community groups are clearly much more positive about their learning in museums. These differences might be due to differences in the programmes the two samples were involved with. Nevertheless, the children in the community groups felt very valued and found the museum a rewarding place to learn in.

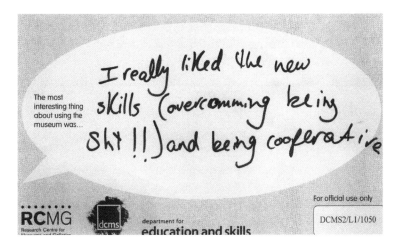

Figure 14.1: Nahla, 15-years-old, was pleased with the new skills she learnt at Tate Britain (Visual Dialogues programme).

GLO	COMMUNITY GROUP MEMBERS – Children 7–11years	YES	NO	DON'T KNOW
Enjoyment, Inspiration and Creativity	I enjoyed using the museum	93%	2%	5%
Knowledge & Understanding	I learnt some interesting new things	83%	3%	14%
Knowledge & Understanding	I could understand most of the things I saw and did	78%	8%	14%
Attitudes and values	Working with the museum was exciting	89%	3%	6%
Action, behaviour, progression	It has given me lots of ideas of things I can do	84%	6%	9%
Attitudes and values	What I learnt will be useful for other things	78%	4%	17%
Action, behaviour, progression	I want to find out more	79%	4%	17%

N=111

Table 14.2: Questionnaire results for 7–11-year-olds in community groups.

GLO	COMMUNITY GROUP MEMBERS – Older children and adults	YES	NO	DON'T KNOW
Enjoyment, Inspiration and Creativity	I enjoyed today	95%	1%	3%
Enjoyment, Inspiration and Creativity	Working with the museum has been very interesting for me	82%	5%	12%
Knowledge & Understanding	I discovered some interesting things	93%	3%	3%
Knowledge & Understanding	I feel I have a better understanding of the subject	84%	7%	8%
Skills	It was a good chance to pick up new skills	77%	7%	12%
Attitudes and values	Using the museum was a good chance to learn in new ways I had not considered before	80%	6%	13%
Knowledge & Understanding	I could make sense of most of the things we saw and did	85%	4%	9%
Action, behaviour, progression	I would like to do this again	80%	3%	15%
Knowledge & Understanding	I am now much more interested in the subject than I was when I started	78%	7%	11%

N=391

Table 14.3: Questionnaire results for over 11-year-olds / adults in community groups.

7.4   GLO-based analysis of qualitative data (case study interviews)

The questionnaires give an overview of learning by community groups. The case studies examined in more detail the impact of the group visits on individuals. Case studies were focused on individual group members, and the case study interviews data analysis was based on the GLOs.

An example case study was that of Lisa, a participant in the "Image and Identity" project at Manchester Art Gallery. Through interviews with museum staff, artists, social workers, residential care workers and Lisa herself, we were able to draw a picture of the impact the project had on her. After a failed adoption and several unsuccessful attempts to place her in a foster home, Lisa now lived in a children's home. We were told that she had an attachment disorder. Her participation in the project had been very important in her life since, vividly summarised in a senior social worker's reflections:

> It has had a holistic effect. The project has impacted on her in every way – emotionally, on her mental health, physically and on her ability to manage situations, it has really impacted on her in every way. Lisa has looked and analysed, and learnt skills which have helped her to express who she is. This has built her confidence, as for example when she has confidently talked to large groups of adults. Her most recent representation of her identity illustrates a considerable move forward, and now she is thriving and achieving in every direction; in school, making friends, doing very well at swimming, cycling and dancing.

Case-study evidence can be categorised using the GLOs as presented in Table 14.4 below.

8. Conclusions

The findings from both the case study and the questionnaires presented in the previous section give powerful evidence of the learning impact of museum visits – in this case, the impact is on community groups. The use of the GLOs enabled comparisons with previous studies. More details about this study and its findings regarding learning in museums can be found in Hooper-Greenhill et al. (2007). In general, the findings of GLO-based studies reflect both the characteristics of the participant groups (e.g. community groups or school groups) and the characteristics of the museum education programmes these groups take part in. For example, school groups value enjoyment, inspiration and creativity most highly, reflecting

GENERIC LEARNING OUTCOMES	LISA, AGE 13 *Image and Identity* programme
Knowledge and Understanding	Self awareness
Skills	Skills to express herself Skills to manage new situations Analytical skills
Enjoyment, Inspiration and Creativity	(not explicitly referred to but implied)
Attitudes and Values	Change in attitudes towards her own experiences and identity
Action,* Behaviour and Progression	Increased confidence Confidence to talk to adults Has enabled her to progress and thrive in new areas: • in school • making friends • doing very well at swimming, cycling and dancing Progression in her representations of herself

Table 14.4: Categorising evidence in interview extracts using the GLOs.
*Action was originally presented as Activity in Inspiring Learning for All,
but subsequently changed to action, the actions people take and the activities
they engage in are seen as interchangeable.

both the importance teachers place on enjoyment on school field trips and the museum school sessions which are designed for learning through fun.

The GLOs have an apparent simplicity, yet they are able to accommodate the complexity of very diverse learning experiences. Their clarity is a reflection of the underlying systematic and rigorous development from which they emerged: they are rooted in theory, and remain an eminently useful tool in practice. The GLOs are now common currency in the Museum sector in the UK, providing a common language that strengthens and allows greater development of museum practice and the sector's understanding of learning.

As a conceptual framework the GLOs provide agreed categories, which can systematise data collection and analysis of individuals' experiences. Learners' accounts of their experiences in museums, libraries and archives, once condemned as anecdotal, can now be categorised and used as evidence of impact. The GLO-based studies have provided a clearer view of learning in museums and the possibilities it offers, nuanced and evidenced by an extensive range of data. The diverse range of research projects that have utilised the GLOs testify that it is a robust and adaptable framework, useful in evidencing the impact of the museums sector for government, as well as in informing and reshaping museum education practice.

The GLOs have been developed specifically to capture the broad range of dimensions of informal learning experiences where outcomes extend beyond cognitive gains, there is no curriculum, there is no clear-cut beginning and end to the learning, and the experience is learner-driven. To the extent that mobile learning experiences share these characteristics, the GLOs can be refined and honed to capture the impact of mobile learning innovations.

References

Claxton, G. (1999). *Wise Up: The Challenge of Life Long Learning.* London: Bloomsbury

DCMS (Department for Culture Media and Sport). (2000). The Learning Power of Museums: A Vision for Museum Education. London: DCMS (Jointly with Department for Education and Employment). Available at http://www.culture.gov.uk/images/publications/musuem_vision_report.pdf

Dodd, J., O'Riaian, H., Hooper-Greenhill, E. and Sandell, R. (2002). A Catalyst for Change – The Social Impact of the Open Museum. Leicester: RCMG. Available at http://www.le.ac.uk/museumstudies/research/rcmg.html

Hooper-Greenhill, E. (2007). *Museums and Education: purpose, pedagogy, performance.* Abingdon, Oxfordshire and New York: Routledge

Hooper-Greenhill, E. (2002). Developing a scheme for finding evidence of the outcomes and impact of learning in museums, libraries and archives: the conceptual framework. Leicester: RCMG. Available at www.le.ac.uk/museumstudies/research/publicationsandprojects. html

Hooper-Greenhill, E. and Dodd, J. (2002). Seeing the Museum through the Visitors' Eyes: The Evaluation of the Education Challenge Fund. Leicester: RCMG. Available at http://www.le.ac.uk/ms/research/pub1107.html

Hooper-Greenhill, E., Dodd, J., Creaser, C., Sandell, R., Jones, C. and Woodham, A. (2007). Inspiration, Identity, Learning: The Value of Museums Second Study An Evaluation of the DCMS/DCSF National /Regional Museum Partnership Programme in 2006–2007. Leicester: RCMG. Available at http://www.le.ac.uk/ms/research/pub1100. html

Hooper-Greenhill, E., Dodd, J., Gibson, L., Phillips, M., Jones, C. and Sullivan, E. (2006). What did you learn at the museum today? Second Study, MLA

Hooper-Greenhill, E., Dodd, J., Philips, M., Jones, C., Woodward, J. and O'Riain, H. (2004a). Inspiration, Identity, Learning: The Value of Museums The evaluation of the impact of DCMS/DfES Strategic Commissioning 2003–2004: National/Regional Museum Education Partnerships. Leicester: RCMG. Available at http://www.le.ac.uk/ ms/research/Reports/Inspiration,%20Identity,%20Learning_The%20 value%20of%20museums.pdf

Hooper-Greenhill, E., Dodd, J., Phillips, M., O'Riain, H., Jones, C. and Woodward, J. (2004b). What did you learn at the museum today? London: MLA

LTS (Learning and Teaching Scotland). (2002). Education for citizenship in Scotland, a paper for discussion and development. Dundee: LT Scotland

Mousouri, T. (2002). A context for the development of learning outcomes in museums, archives and libraries. Leicester: RCMG. Available at http://www.le.ac.uk/museumstudies/research/Reports/LIRP%20 analysis%20paper%202.doc

15. Using Automatic Logging to Collect Information on Mobile Device Usage for Learning

JON TRINDER, SCOTT ROY, JANE MAGILL

Overview

This chapter combines an overview of automatic logging as a means of collecting usage data of mobile devices for learning, with reports on the practicalities and experience of using such logging in real world situations. Problems in data collection encountered during the project highlight difficulties in quantitative measurement of effects in mobile learning. Even after successfully overcoming a number of practical difficulties, there were still subtle interactions between the measurement process and the group dynamics of the student cohort under study, which proved to be disruptive to the collection of mobile learning data.

1. Introduction

Evaluating how a personal mobile device such as a PDA is used presents unique challenges due to the wide variety of possible usage patterns and the spread of locations and circumstances in which it may be used. It is impractical to follow a user around, interviews and questionnaires rely on their memory after the event, and asking them to keep a usage diary adds an overhead that is typically longer than the task itself. Many studies have relied on attitude surveys or interviews (Sharples, this volume) to measure the efficacy of the introduction of mobile learning, but without any objective data to prove even that the devices were actually used.

To provide objective data, and to reduce the burden of manual record keeping, the device can itself be used to automatically record when it is used. Such automated logging has been used in other PDA projects to record cumulative application usage time (Avanzato, 2001) and combined with other techniques by Wali et al. and Hooft (both in this volume).

The initial objectives of the project described in this chapter were to investigate the educational potential of mobile devices with specific focus on mobile Computer Aided Assessment (CAA) and, within that context, to determine how else the devices were used by the students. Before attempting to measure any benefit of the devices it was considered essential to determine if the usage of the devices could be reliably measured and to identify suitable evaluation techniques. The project has developed through four phases to date. In each phase the students used a PDA on which was installed an automatic logging application, a quiz application to provide on-demand formative Computer Aided Assessment (CAA), and additional applications and content. Ethical considerations, such as not unfairly disadvantaging anyone who did not want to use PDA based material meant providing the same content in paper form, and this possibly acted as a disincentive to use of the assessment application, an example of a "hobbled horse race" (Hooft this volume).

The primary focus of the chapter is the final phase of the project. Earlier phases, outlined below, are described in detail in (Trinder et al., 2005a).

Phase 1 ran between February 2003 and June 2003, and involved 14 undergraduate students from a Joint Honours computing and electronics course. This was intended to be a pilot project to test the logging software and to ensure that instrumentation and support were adequate.

Phase 2 ran between June 2004 and August 2004, and involved 5 "summer-school" students. These were school leavers in a university widening participation programme that targets schools from which low numbers of pupils progress to Higher Education. The course was held at the University of Glasgow within the Department of Electronics and Electrical Engineering. Results from phase 1 had indicated that the PDAs would be of benefit to this group of students and in addition phase 2 allowed further refinement of the logging system.

Phase 3 was intended to run for over a year starting in October 2003, with 15 3rd year undergraduate electronic engineering students at the University of Glasgow. However, the students lost interest in the devices very quickly and the study was discontinued after 4 months, in February 2004. Subsequent interviews with students in this group showed that they perceived the style and functionality of the devices to be outdated. The devices were 18 months old at the start of phase 3 and since the students own mobile phones could perform many of the PDA functions there was insufficient incentive to carry an extra device.

Phase 4 ran for 7 months, between October 2004 and mid April 2005. The student group chosen was a cohort of 36 first year foundation level technology students in the Faculty of Education. This course is taken by students who are likely to become technology teachers in secondary schools.

Phase 4 took place at a time when there was growing interest in the use of mobile devices in schools, and the project team believed that future teachers would be intrinsically motivated to experience such developments. Additional funding was obtained for this phase so that new PDAs with a richer feature set could be used.

In previous phases of the project it was discovered that the students did not have a strong incentive to regularly carry the PDA until they identified a personal benefit in doing so. Thus the devices chosen for phase 4 had features that we believed would be attractive and immediately useful to the students. The device chosen incorporated a camera and an MP3 player at a time when most phones owned by students did not provide such functionality. The camera also had educational potential for use in other course work, in particular a design course, for collection of images for a design folio. It was hoped that these features would make the device worth carrying and if the device was with the student most of the time, then this would engender a sense of ownership which would lower barriers to use. The sense of "ownership" of a device extends beyond physically owning the device, a phenomenon referred to by Jones et al. (2005) as "appropriation", and is identified as an important motivating factor in the use of mobile devices.

Prior to distributing the PDAs the course tutor and researcher explained to the students the purpose of the project, what data would be collected, who would see the data and how the data would be used. It was made clear that any personal data on the PDA would not be visible to the research team or their tutors. Many institutions have policies prohibiting the installation of games on university computers, but students were told that they were allowed to install games on the PDAs. The students were asked to complete a short questionnaire, to evaluate their knowledge and competence with mobile technology. The results from the questionnaire suggested that the students were reasonably "technology savvy", with only 2 of the 36 students not owning a mobile phone. The questionnaire was administered to the students at the start of a lecture, and time was set aside for its completion. Similar to the experiences described by Wali (this volume) we had previously experienced very poor rates of return for questionnaires that students had to complete in their own time.[1] In trials where device use is carefully controlled there is a danger that this control will artificially limit the patterns of use and the richness of any results. So despite the advantages of studying mobile device use in controlled situations (for example, it makes analysis simpler), this approach jeopardises one of the main advantages of PDA use for learning, namely the benefits that PDAs are *personal*, and allow users the flexibility to develop their own optimal usage patterns. Our techniques of data collection were therefore constructed to allow usage flexibility for users, whilst extracting a rich data set for researchers. However, our experience has shown that there are major practical hurdles to overcome in collecting data from students outside a carefully controlled environment. These are discussed in detail in the following sections.

1   Either paper or web based.

2. Logging and data collection

Based on experience gained earlier in the project, all practical steps were taken to remove or reduce barriers to data collection. The logging application would be installed on the PDAs and the logs would be collected when the students periodically "synced" their devices to suitably configured lab computers. The process of syncing would perform the necessary unpacking and storage of log data for future analysis; however the reality was somewhat more complex.

2.1 Problems with data collection

In phases 1–3 the problems of collecting the logs from the students appeared to be either technical (data loss due to battery problems) or convenience (a lack of suitably configured machines to which students could sync their devices). In phase 4, the chosen devices could retain data on battery discharge, and an open access computer cluster was available for students to sync. Students were encouraged to sync their PDAs during scheduled labs so that the process could be supervised and any problems identified and resolved.

In the first few weeks, we observed that some of the students had installed games on their devices, indicating that at least some of them were syncing their devices. Downloading a game onto a PDA required either syncing it, or having the game "beamed" from another device. Collection of the logs, however, continued to be problematic as the students did not sync their machines whilst on campus, thus leaving us with no access to the logs.

In order to collect the usage logs it was essential that the students performed the sync of their PDAs whilst on campus but there were no practical or ethical means of forcing them to do so.

The students' interest in games provided an opportunity to offer something tangible in exchange for their cooperation. A weekly prize draw for a commercial game was held for all students who had synced their PDA during the previous week, but this did not produce even a marginal improvement. When the students were asked at scheduled labs to sync their devices most said they did not have the device with them and when asked about this they were vague or evasive. This gave the impression that the students were not carrying the PDAs with them – though we found out later that this was not always true.

As the students were unwilling to sync their PDAs with the lab computers an alternative method was devised. The logging application was modified to enable "beaming", a mode of data transfer using infra-red or Bluetooth, to the tutor's PDA. The beaming session also enabled the tutor to send new materials to the student's PDA, such as additional quiz questions, thus making the process mutually beneficial. After these changes had been made a few logs were successfully collected but the students normally claimed to not have their PDA with them and remaining vague or evasive about the reason if pushed for an answer typical responses were that the device had been forgotten or the battery flat.

Despite the above problems, a number of log files were collected. None of the logs covered the full duration of the project, but there were coincident logs for five users. Initially this data appeared to the research team too thin to be useful, but after recently re-examining the data with the aid of a custom data mining application, richer information than expected was exposed.

2. Data analysis

2.1 The logging

Previous projects utilising logging of PDA use had recorded cumulative application usage times (Avanzato, 2001) but for our purposes a greater level of detail was desired. A custom-made application called AppLog[2] was used to record a far greater detail of PDA usage than any other application available at the time.

---

2   www.ninelocks.com/applog.

AppLog records time-stamped events in a log file on the PDA, which is processed during syncing, to generate a file containing "event descriptors" (referred to as Ninelocks Event Descriptors or NEDs). The event descriptors indicate the time at which an event, such as the launching of an application occurred and how long that session of usage lasted.

From the NED file it is possible to derive other information relating to how a device has been used. Examples of the type of information that can be derived are: number of applications used, distribution of application run times, the intervals between device or application use, and the most frequently used applications. There are important advantages to writing a bespoke logging system or utilising an open source alternative such as knowing with certainty what information is recorded and having the potential for customisation of the application behaviour and being able to dictate the format of the log files to facilitate easy transfer into other applications for analysis.

From the event descriptor file it is possible to derive other factors relating to how a device has been used. Examples of the type of information that can be derived are: number of applications used, distribution of application run times, the intervals between device or application use and the "most used" applications.

Detecting learning activities can be more difficult when the student is using a variety of devices concurrently (such as mobile phones, desktop PCs at home and in the University), unless there are logging facilities on all the devices and then these can be combined for analysis. If, the student is using a single device it may be necessary for them to swap between applications on that device to achieve a particular objective. In these circumstances learning activities can potentially be detected from the pattern of usage e.g. on one device it was seen from the logs that whilst using the quiz application the user had launched the calculator application and then returned to the quiz application presumably to help determine the correct answer. To this effect we utilised the access logs on the university's Virtual Learning Environment (Moodle). These logs do not contain event duration information, but they nevertheless provide indications of a type of resource that was used at a specific time e.g. taking an on line test or downloading lecture notes. Unfortunately there are no indications of the PDA being used at the same time as VLE resources were accessed. From the VLE logs it appears 16 of the students accessed the VLE less than 20 times.

Investigating subtle patterns of device use requires a more immediate and interactive means of exploring, visualizing and filtering the data than a standard statistics package provides. As no suitable applications existed to fit these requirements, an application, called Graaf,[3] was developed to perform these functions. Graaf enables interactive exploration of data files produced by AppLog, and enables log events to be filtered by various parameters including day of week, application name, the number of times an application was used, and the length of usage session. Graaf produces graphical, textual representations of raw data and statistical analyses of the data. An additional experimental feature of Graaf, which is still being refined, is to produce audible representations of the data. When considering mechanisms for locating interesting recurrent patterns there is a temptation to think in purely visual terms. An alternative, surprisingly useful, method that we also used was to convert the data to an audible form and listening for patterns. In its simplest implementation, each application is assigned to a musical note and its duration based on the length of the event. An interesting side effect of this is that it enables analysis of data by users with impaired sight thus adding accessibility to the log data.

3.2   Filtering and usage trends

There were some anomalies in the data caused by user interference and device failure, such as unusually long events when the device had crashed, and events with negative durations due to the user having changed the calendar date on the device. These were identified during the testing of the analysis application and suitable filtering applied to detect and remove these events.

Some operating system characteristics combined with how the device was used also interfered with the data. For example, there were some noticeable peaks in the distribution of session lengths around 120 seconds. These

---

3   www.ninelocks.com/graaf.

are most likely due to the power saving feature of the device which is set by default to switch the device off after two minutes of inactivity. This indicates that users rarely consciously turned the device off but having used it for whatever purpose left the device to power off automatically, leaving us uncertain regarding how long sessions of usage actually were.

There is a greater chance of observing more meaningful patterns once suitable filtering has been applied. Determining the filter parameters and the values of those parameters needs careful consideration. We found that filtering out applications that had been used on less than 10 occasions or with a cumulative usage time of less than 10 minutes significantly reduced the number of applications utilised by our students from 82 to 20. These filter values were determined by experimentation and the examination of which events were removed.

Useful indicators of how much a device or application was used were the average and median values of the duration of usage session and of the intervals between uses. The median value of the length of time for which an application was used ranged between 20 and 40 seconds for the majority of users. Values varying greatly from this may be indicators of spurious data due to system or application faults, e.g. it was found that the camera and image viewer applications sometimes prevented the automatic power off feature from operating and so the device would continue to run until the battery was exhausted.

In some circumstances these values were seriously distorted by the use of applications such as the mp3 player which tended to be used for long periods of time and others such as the clock which are used for very short periods. For filtering purposes, it can be difficult to differentiate short usage events from occasions where an application is launched by mistake. To look at the data from a different perspective, rather than examine how often a device or application was used, we also found it useful to look at the amount of time where there was low usage compared to the rest of the group.

Grouping applications by type (media applications, organiser, document viewers, etc.) can give a broad indication into the users' primary use of the device, i.e. for games, music, reference, organisation etc.

3.3 Identifying areas of interest

In the course of log analysis various techniques assisted in the identification of potentially interesting areas of activity. The simplest view of the log data was an x/y chart showing the time of day on the vertical axes and the date on the horizontal. This gives a good indication of the amount of data collected and how much (or not) the devices were used. Such a plot shows a few obvious time related patterns such as the quiet zone in the early hours of the morning, but to elicit more useful data requires more data filtering and the comparison of different parameters.

Comparing multivariate data for multiple users simultaneously is problematic, whilst the parameters could be plotted on separate charts ideally we wanted to quickly compare multiple parameters (e.g. usage times of each application) for multiple users simultaneously.

The benefit of 3d charting is only fully realised when it is possible to navigate around the view, it does not translate well to the static view of a printed page. Amongst the techniques that we found useful were:

- Simple x/y dot plots with applications on one axis and date on the other. These were useful to highlight busy times of day and busy days. These charts can highlight swapping between applications to achieve a task, which shows as oscillations in the traces.

- Radar charts were especially useful allowing multiple parameters to be shown on one chart. When the parameters are application types the chart shape can indicate the proportion of each application type the user has predominately used: the more symmetrical a user's plot the more balanced their use of the device (see Figure 15.1).

- Animating the data by "playing back" sequences of the logs. Sometimes it was best to combine all users on one chart and at others to have a matrix of charts with one chart per user. This is helpful to show clusters of activity.

- The extent of device use may vary between users and it can be useful to consider parameters of use relative both to the rest of the group and to the user's overall use of the device. For distributions such as the length of a usage session it can be useful to view distribution plots of absolute values (i.e. the actual time durations) and relative percentages of application use (i.e. What proportion of the total time for which the PDA was used can be attribute to the music player). The use of logarithmic scales also helped highlight unusual or extreme values.

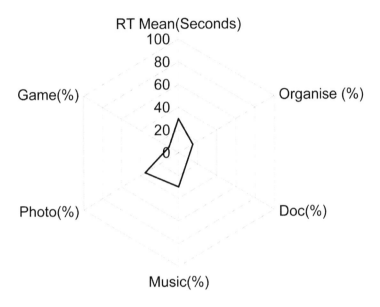

Figure 15.1: Example radar chart of 3 users' application use (percentage of use time devoted to each application) and median of runtime (seconds of application use length).

3.4 Identifying "useful" applications

An area of interest for our project was to determine a means of identifying which applications were *useful* to users and this posed an interesting challenge. By the very nature of personal mobile devices different sets of applications will be considered to be the most useful to different people. The problem is how to determine the useful application from usage patterns.

There are some obvious usage patterns that can indicate an application is useful to someone: e.g. it is used frequently or used for a large amount of time. However there are other patterns of use that may also characterise a useful application that are less easy to detect. For example an application that is only used once per day or less, such as to-do list of goals or objectives, could be invaluable to a user but the importance the user attaches to it may not be obvious from a usage log. Also such events can easily be confused with spurious events, such as launching the wrong application.

The obvious way of determining what application is useful to someone is to ask, though again there are problems with perception and the use of the device may be so transparent to the user that they do not notice they are using it. A classic example is checking the time on your wristwatch/phone.

4. User co-operation

The co-operation of participants in a project cannot be assumed and even when the initial indications are that the participants will be supportive of your research, the reality may be different.

The lack of co-operation during phase 4 surprised us. With so few students appearing to co-operate we considered the possibility of factors that might have influenced the group as a whole. Discussions with researchers in other institutions suggested that students are getting tired of being surveyed and tested, however in our case the students had no history of being involved in previous trials, and we believe the problem was due to the disruption of peer groups and the status of individuals within the group.

The problems of obtaining the students co-operation and involvement was apparent from the early stages of phase 4 when we tried to arrange for a random selection of students to take part in short interviews about the project. To motivate students to participate we offered an incentive (food and drink during the morning lecture). The interviews occurred before the exploration of the log data described in this chapter had occurred. At the time it was our perception that no useful log data had been acquired and the tools to examine the data had not been written.

During the interviews it became apparent that the PDAs were being used and carried by the students more frequently than enquiries and requests to sync had previously indicated. It was also found that some students had found imaginative ways of using the PDAs, such as photographing books to remember their titles and recording concerts to show friends. It was not clear what had inspired these uses, whether they were original ideas or if they had been influenced by each other or from ideas found on the web. The spread of such social practices via the internet is described by Lankshear as "internet memes" (Lankshear and Knobel, 2006). These unexpected uses are a reminder that "the unexpected consequences of technologies always outweigh the expected ones, both positive and negative" (Norman, 2007, p. 101)

In the weeks following the interviews, when we asked students individually if they had their PDA with them, they tended to divert attention from themselves and instead named colleagues who had their PDA with them; the named colleagues often indicated, in turn, that the person who had named them did actually have their own PDA with them. This denial suggests that their actions may have been influenced by sociological factors. Such problems have been predicted in other evaluation situations "Evaluation may raise issues of self-esteem, social standing and status" (Traxler and Riordan, 2003). It is possible that students were nervous about being seen to make mistakes in the use of the PDA in front of either their peers or academic staff. It is also possible that there was a certain element of guilt or embarrassment that they were not fulfilling perceived expectations of using the PDAs for much other than games, even though we had reassured them that our interest in how the PDAs were actually used had no judgmental character. More interestingly, the PDAs were introduced six weeks into the cohort's first term (in order for them to settle into the new course), enough time for initial peer groupings and hierarchies to form. Teaching staff could clearly judge students who were now more often fulfilling leadership, spokesman-ship, or support roles within the cohort by this point. Initial open use of PDAs by those who were competent with the technology was openly perceived by their peers as "geeky", and may have subliminally been felt as threatening to the still fragile hierarchy formed within the cohort – an example of disruptive technology disrupting the group utilising that technology. As noted, interviews and logging showed that PDA use, often novel and imaginative, still occurred, but in a mode more unforthcoming to peers and teaching staff.

An unusual aspect of the students in phase 4 compared with other phases of the project is that they are a relative small group who attended almost all lectures and laboratories together. This may have reinforced the initial peer hierarchy. Small groups can be advantageous for providing peer support but it appears that they may also amplify problems. Strong personalities possibly exert a greater influence on a small group who are always together than they would in a larger group. For example, one strong personality in this group was very dismissive of PDA use, and this may have impeded other students from using the device as its use was difficult to hide. If this is the case, the implications are far reaching, as many pilot projects are conducted with small groups due to budget constraints.

It is difficult within the financial and ethical constraint of many projects to offer the students extra incentive to co-operate in a project. At the outset we had believed that offering them a PDA would itself be an adequate incentive for their co-operation, but it appears that to the students much technology is perceived as cheap and disposable – devices such as phones are treated as throw about, throw away technology. During interviews students revealed they owned multiple phones (sometimes at the same time) and older phones were passed on to other family members.

5. Concluding comments

Whilst logs can provide a useful insight into device usage, detailed analysis often requires additional sources of information. A common source for additional information is directly from participants, either through face to face or online questionnaires, which of course requires user co-operation (see also Wali et al. in this volume). Gaining their cooperation within the bounds of ethical incentives proved to be more difficult than initially expected.

At the outset logging was seen as a solution to the problems of relying on users' memories. It appears that logging, although automatic and transparent to the user, still relies on their co-operation. For some the knowledge that "something" is being recorded can be a barrier. This reluctance to observation is also noted by Wali et al. (this volume), who in one study had only 1 out of 61 students agree to logging software being installed on their device. No matter how innocuous the kind of data that is collected may appear, the user is nevertheless aware that they are being watched. Seemingly innocuous log data can potentially be used to derive other information (the very reason it is being collected) e.g. proving that a user spent an entire lab playing games. This is interesting as almost all web access is traceable but that does not stop students using it. Perhaps for students it is the knowledge that the person who will see the information is someone nearby who has a social or professional relationship with them.

Introducing new technology is problematic in many ways. The use of the devices should not be made compulsory unless the students have been informed of this when they enrolled on the course, and the compulsory use is well integrated with the course.

As the facilities of the mobile devices and the ease and availability of network access improve, the potential richness and immediacy of data that can be collected from mobile devices will increase. Mechanisms and laws put in place to protect confidentiality (such as the data protection law) must be taken into account when determining what to log.

Student now own and use a diverse variety of devices, and this may make the use of logging less practical. Server based applications maintain system logs, but these show only part of the device's usage. The variety of form factors and screen sizes complicates the design of common logging platforms and interchangeable data types.

Our previous work on this project has shown that "the successful introduction of mobile personal technologies is critically based on the very interpersonal networks and skill that are naively assumed to be unimportant when dealing with personal technology" (Trinder et al., 2005b). The final project phase has shown the full extent of the important and subtle social factors at work, setting the stage for further detailed investigations.

References

Avanzato, R. (2001). Student use of personal digital assistants in a computer engineering course. In *FIE '01: Proceedings of the Frontiers in Education Conference, 2001. 31st Annual.* Vol. 2, pp. F1B–F19. Washington, DC: IEEE Computer Society

Jones, A., Issroff, K. and Scanlon, E. (2007). *Affective factors in learning with mobile devices.* In M. Sharples (ed.), Big Issues in Mobile Learning. LSRI, University of Nottingham, pp. 17–22

Lankshear, C. and Knobel, M. (2006). *New Literacies: Everyday Practice and Classroom Learning.* McGraw Hill

Norman, D. (2007). *The Design of Future Things.* Basic Books

Traxler, J. and Riordan, B. (2003). Evaluating the effectiveness of retention strategies using SMS, WAP and www Student Support. *Proceeding of the 4th Annual Conference: LTSN Centre for Information and Computer Science.* Galway, Ireland, pp. 54–55

Trinder, J.J., Magill, J.V. and Roy, S. (2005a). Expect the unexpected: practicalities and problems of a PDA project. In J. Traxler and A. Kukulska-Hulme, (eds), *Mobile Learning: A Handbook for Educators and Trainers,* Open and Flexible Learning. Abingdon: Routledge, pp. 92–98

Trinder, J.J., Magill, J.V. and Roy, S. (2005b). Using PDAs for CAA: Practicalities, disasters, apathy. In M. Danson (ed.), *9th International Computer Aided Assessment Conference,* 5–6 July. Loughborough, pp. 433–438

PART IV

Research Designs

16. Mobile Enabled Research

CHRISTINE DEARNLEY, STUART WALKER

Overview

In this chapter we present a case study investigation into the benefits, barriers and essential specifications of mobile devices used for learning and assessment purposes with disabled students. We discuss the processes of developing a participatory research design using mobile devices to shift the locus of control in data collection processes. We also consider the role of mobile devices in supporting learning for health and social care practitioners, against a background of current UK disability legislation.

1. Background[1]

MEDS (Mobile Enabled Disabled Students) is a research project currently being undertaken at the University of Bradford, funded by the ALPS CETL[2] Research Capacity Investment Fund. MEDS commenced in October 2007 and aims to inform the ongoing work and development

---

1   Please note that the literature review section for this chapter has formed parts of other publications: Dearnley, C.A., Haigh, J., Fairhall, J. (2008). Using mobile technologies for assessment and learning in practice settings: a case study. *Nurse Education and Practice*, 8(3), 197–204. Dearnley, C.A. et al. (2009). Using Mobile Technologies for Assessment and Learning in Practice Settings: Outcomes of Five Case Studies. *International Journal on E-learning*, 8(2), 193–208.

2   Assessment & Learning in Practice Settings (ALPS) is a Centre for Excellence in Teaching & Learning (CETL) funded by the Higher Education Funding Council for England (HEFCE).

of ALPS in relation to the specific needs of disabled students when using mobile technologies for learning and assessment in practice settings. ALPS is a collaborative programme between five Higher Education Institutions (HEIs)[3] and aims to develop and improve assessment, and thereby learning, in practice settings for health and social care students.

The ALPS CETL is working towards an interprofessional programme of assessment of common competences such as communication, team working and ethical practice among health and social care students. Between July and December 2007, ALPS issued 900 mobile devices with unlimited internet access to students undertaking practice based learning and assessment across the ALPS partnership. The assessment tools will be delivered in electronic, mobile format. Five pilot case studies have already been undertaken, with a range of mobile devices used and methods of data collection employed. These informed the current work of ALPS and are reported elsewhere (Dearnley et al., 2008; Haigh et al., 2007; Taylor et al., 2006; Parks and Dransfield, 2006)

The use of mobile technologies by health and social care providers is rapidly increasing. These include a range of devices that can be easily transported and provide easy access to information by either direct storage on the device or internet access. There is reported use of mobile technologies among paramedics (Norman, 2005), doctors (Fischer et al., 2003; Scheck McAlearney et al., 2004) and nurses for such purposes as tracking medication, supporting care planning and research (Miller et al., 2005). The role of mobile devices in improving practice by reducing medical errors is a common theme in the literature (Tooey and Mayo, 2004; Hochschuler, 2001). Thompson (2005) enthuses about the potential of handheld computers and claims that they will transform nursing practice, making it more efficient, safer and of a higher quality. Fisher et al. (2003) published an extensive review of general information about handheld devices and their use in various medical fields. In addition to the data retrieval functions, Sullivan et al. (2001) assert that using this technology can enhance student learning in work based settings.

---

3   Universities of Bradford, Huddersfield, Leeds, Leeds Metropolitan and York St
     John.

A number of studies have demonstrated how mobile devices can be used to enhance interaction, and thereby learning, in different contexts. Naismith et al. (2004) reviewed the literature related to mobile technologies and learning and found such a wide range of activities for which they were being used in education, that they asserted that these technologies are fundamentally changing the nature of learning. Naismith et al. (2004) further assert that mobile devices can support collaborative learning by providing a means of communication without attempting to replace any face-to-face interactions. It is no surprise therefore, given the wide range of work based contexts in which health and social care students undertake learning placements, that the potential of mobile learning is being explored among this group of students.

Within the United Kingdom, the Disability Rights Commission (DRC), now within the Equality and Human Rights Commission (EHRC), has been reviewing the legislation, regulations and statutory guidance within professional occupations. The legal review was carried out as part of the DRC's formal investigation into fitness standards in teaching, nursing and social work. Whilst the focus of the formal investigation was in these three areas, for comparative purposes those governing medicine, dentistry, and the health professions falling within the scope of the Health Professions Council were analysed (Ruebain et al., 2006).

The final report "Maintaining Standards: Promoting Equality" (DRC, 2007), concluded that Disabled People often face barriers to entry and progression throughout large parts of the public sector. It also found that the mass of regulations and guidance often do little to protect the public whilst often deterring people from applying or remaining in these professions (DRC, 2007, p. 24). The recommendations for relevant regulatory bodies across England, Scotland and Wales, included:

- That all requirements for good health or physical and mental fitness that are within their remits should be removed.

- That impact assessments of policies, practices, procedures, and processes for assessing fitness to practice should be carried out.

· That where competence standards were found to have an adverse
impact on disabled people, they should be re-evaluated to try and
enable disabled people to meet the required standards (DRC, 2007,
p. 25).

If such recommendations were enacted one could expect more disabled
students in HE for these fields. Therefore, as in other areas of educational
provision, accessibility will need to be ensured for all forms of teaching.
Indeed, the investigation recommended that there was a need to research
the provision of reasonable adjustments for students to ensure that disabled
people were not disadvantaged (DRC, 2007, p. 26).

The aim of MEDS is to inform the ongoing work and development
of ALPS in relation to the specific needs of disabled students when using
mobile technologies for learning and assessment in practice settings. MEDS
aims to establish what works well for disabled students who currently
use mobile devices and to identify the challenges that mobile technologies present to them. The MEDS team is working closely with ALPS,
recruiting disabled users to trial the use of new assessment tools as they
are developed, to assess their impact and identify changes that need to be
made for disabled users.

It is generally accepted that it is both easier and good practice to build
accessibility at the point of design, rather than have to add this at some
point in the future. Moreover, the principles of the Special Educational
Needs and Disability Act SENDA (2001), directly apply to the provision
of education services. The Act makes it an offence to discriminate against
a disabled person by treating him or her less favourably than others for a
reason relating to their disability. Education services are understood to
include the provision of e-learning materials.

It might be assumed therefore that the needs of disabled people would
be already catered for. However, accessibility for disabled people is often
overlooked. Virtual Learning Environments are currently far more widely
used in HE than Mobile communication devices and their development in
terms of accessibility can inform the development of mobile (m)–learning
because they are also a relatively recent technological addition to learning

processes. Lessons can therefore be learned from research related to this experience.

Dunn (2003) for example, found that inaccessible elements were both within the VLE software itself, and within the content the institutions put into the VLEs. Moreover, the lack of accessibility appeared to stem from a lack of knowledge about designing VLE systems that were accessible by disabled people. Pearson and Koppi (2006) argue that such learning can offer disabled students opportunities in learning and participation that they might not otherwise have had. Yet this is tempered by Papadopoulos and Pearson (2007) stating that this can only happen if the learning activities and resources are designed to be accessible.

The experience of VLEs demonstrates the need for accessible learning environments in order to ensure equality, good practice and reduce the risk of possible litigation. With this in mind we designed a research project to identify good practice when implementing mobile devices and learning activities.

2. Research Design

In order to achieve its aims, MEDS considered a range of exploratory methodologies as a detailed project proposal was developed. An eclectic approach was agreed within the phenomenological paradigm embracing a philosophy of collaboration based on feminist ontology (Letherby, 2003). A feminist ontology was appropriate to this study because it acknowledges the complexity and diversity of societal structures and the people within those structures.

Collaborative research of this nature is often called Action Research (AR) and this project reflected many of the ideals of AR, which according to Russell (1997) is a long way from any idea of research that might imply "distance" or "neutrality" because it is based "where we live our day-to-day successes, frustrations, disappointments, and occasional miracles." Abbott and Sapsford (1998) asserted that AR "arises out of practice and feeds back into practice," whilst Russell (1997) affirms that AR is something we do *with*, not *on*, the students we teach. There is parity here with the ideals of feminist ontology (Harding, 1987; Stanley and Wise, 1993; Stanley, 1997; Maynard, 1994) and what we were hoping to achieve in this project, not simply because our participants were from a marginalized group, but because they were human beings. As Letherby (2003, p. 125) advises, the project team are committed to viewing things from the perspective of the respondents, whilst being cognizant of our "privileged position" within the research relationship.

2.1   Method of data collection

In selecting the methods of data collection for this project we supported the views of Oakley (1998, p. 724) that "the critical question remains the appropriateness of the method to the research question." The research question for the MEDS project is:

> How can mobile devices be used effectively to assist learning and assessment in practice settings among disabled students?

Traditionally, the qualitative methods of data collection available would have been limited to a range of individual or group interviews. We decided to undertake an initial focus group interview to help us identify what works well for disabled students who currently use mobile devices and to identify the challenges that mobile technologies present to them. This was appropriate and was conducted within the framework of our participatory philosophy. The session was attended by the software developers who demonstrated prototypes of the ALPS assessment software. Participants were allocated ALPS mobile devices and encouraged to handle and "play" with them before being invited to provide feedback, both generally and specifically, on how they experienced accessing the software on the mobile devices. Participants could engage to the extent that they felt comfortable and were in no way required or indeed pressured to disclose their impairment, although many chose to share this information alongside personal experiences and seemed to find comradeship through the experience.

We believed we also needed an end point data collection process, with a purposive sample to enable us to develop initial specification guidelines for accessible mobile devices. At the planning stage we thought it likely that this would involve semi-structured interviews, however, we support the views of Letherby (2003) in that it is not always possible to determine from the start the direction in which a study such as this might lead. We therefore ensured that flexibility was built into the study by not committing ourselves to a particular route and regularly reviewing possible approaches to data collection that would enable us to capture the unique elements of the participants' experience.

It was decided that in addition to the more traditional methods of qualitative data collection, we would employ an electronic mobile diary system, in which participants would be asked to record their experiences of using the ALPS mobile devices and assessment software. This approach sat comfortably within the philosophy of the study because it allowed the locus of control in this element of the data collection process to transfer from the researcher to the participant, allowing them choice in relation to when, where, how and what they recorded about their experiential journey.

We were very much aware, however, that mobile devices offer benefits to both researchers and participants during the data collection processes. From the researcher's perspective, this is a tool that allows participants to record their thoughts and feelings as they experience particular phenomena. We anticipated that this would supply us with "live data", capturing the real essence of the lived experience and increasing authenticity as the participants reflect "in action" rather than "on action" (Schon, 1983) with its resulting reliance on recall. In this case the "phenomenon" would be using an assessment document on a mobile device or accessing a web based document to support learning whilst in a practice/work based setting. Potentially however, that phenomenon could be anything that was being researched, for example living with a particular illness/condition or experiencing an event or procedure. This immediacy of access and reduced reliance on recall must increase the validity of data collected. It is also likely to increase the volume of data collected and we acknowledge the challenge therein.

Whilst paper based diary keeping has been used elsewhere in qualitative research, our challenge was to develop a process to facilitate the collection of journal type data on the mobile device, allowing for a wide range of participant impairments. There were several functions of the device that we immediately began to see as exciting opportunities for the qualitative researcher. For example, in its most simple form, the device allowed for reflective note taking anytime, anywhere; participants could potentially take a little time out of a daily routine to jot down a few reminders of what they were experiencing (the researched phenomenon). They could then add to this if they wished at a later time or on a larger keyboard if they synchronized the device with a home or university PC. The devices offer three options for writing notes; a slide out keyboard, an onscreen keyboard and onscreen handwriting recognition. However, for those who found any of these methods unsuitable the devices offered several other options. These included the audio facility, by which participants could record their data, and video capture by which, if they wished, they could maintain a video diary. Whilst these options afford different types of use, for example a video entry could not be augmented at a later time as easily as a written entry could be; we valued the choice they offered to our disabled participants who may have found some options particularly difficult/inaccessible. The wide range of options available to participants to record their experiences enabled greater engagement and therefore increased the validity of this study.

We were particularly enthused by the video diary option and the potential to obtain "talking head" type data, which can be an extremely powerful dissemination tool. However there were of course many issues to consider before that option could become a reality for us. These included technical and ethical issues and will now be discussed.

We had transferred the locus of control in the data collection process, but there were tensions in this, particularly in relation to the volume and content of the data collected and thereby the integrity of the study. Qualitative research commonly generates large quantities of data that can be time consuming and expensive to analyse and we would argue that to collect more data than can reasonably be managed is unethical given the time commitment made by participants. We therefore developed a "diary guide". In addition to technical guidance related to the options of writing, recording or videoing the diary, we also advised on the frequency of entries.

This was difficult because we didn't want to stifle participation and individual choice and therefore the balance had to be right. We stated that the frequency of entries was up to the participant, advised that there were likely to be some times when more entries would be made than other times and requested them to keep entries as brief but as full as possible. We suggested that it would be helpful for them to reflect on the following events:

- when they had used the device for a specific purpose for the first time
- when they had found the device particularly useful
- when they had found specific problems or difficulties with using the device

We also advised in the guidelines that many people find that keeping a reflective learning diary helps them to study and achieve higher grades and that participants might find it helpful to use the device for that purpose. However, we stressed that if they did so, that would be for their own purpose and requested them to keep these recordings separate from those for the research. We did add however, that we would be interested to know if they did find them useful for this purpose.

It was decided to train and support participants on a one-to-one basis; this was possible because MEDS is a relatively small pilot study and only 9–12 participants would be keeping mobile diaries. Three trainers were assigned and participants equally divided. To ensure consistency of training, documents were created (technical guidelines in addition to the diary guidelines) and a plan developed by the three trainers. Participants were offered continuous support throughout the study via email, phone and face to face contact as and when required.

3. Implementing the study

Having developed a robust methodological action plan aimed at increasing research participation to maximum effect, the next set of research processes to consider were implementation processes. These include gaining ethical approval from the University Ethics Committee,[4] establishing a steering committee that reflected the participatory nature of the study and recruitment of student participants. These will now be discussed.

3.1 Ethical Issues.

All research must be set within an ethical framework. Gilbert (2001) suggests that ethics is a matter of principled sensitivity to the rights of others. This is a very broad definition posing a wide range of considerations and potential barriers to research. Yet it accurately portrays the difficulties of research into the area of mobile technologies. In particular, research such as MEDS, that explores issues of human computer interaction in "real world" settings.

A key element of this particular study was that participants were disabled people. Ethically, there are obvious concerns in working with groups that are seen as "vulnerable". There are many ethical issues to be considered; disability is often seen as a "personal tragedy" and disabled people "in need of care". However, as Oliver (2004) notes another position is the social model of disability which views disability as an externally imposed restriction. As researchers we challenge any notion of a "template of normality" as having value and instead believe that mobile technology is potentially emancipatory and should enable, not disable.

---

4   The University of Bradford Committee for Ethics in Research agrees policy with regard to all issues of research ethics which affect the University. Additionally, the Committee delegates authority to grant ethics approval to a subcommittee structure which reviews research proposals, and hears appeals against the decisions of such subcommittees.

As researchers we were aware of the need for transparency, informed consent and the relationship between ourselves and the students who were willing to participate. All student participants were provided with written information about the study and what we were inviting them to do. They were also trained in the use of the technology, which involved them clearly demonstrating their ability to do so. Crucially, making a diary entry to the study was a two stage process; firstly they had to report their experiences using the mobile device and only then did they *choose* to submit the data. This was required for every submission, it was not automated and therefore a conscious decision had to be made for every piece of data submitted and this constitutes informed consent. Frankfort-Nachmias and Nachmias (1991) citing Milgram (1974) outline the difficulties and ethical problems that stem from perceived obedience to authority. All researchers were members of staff at the University of Bradford, there was therefore the potential for hierarchy to affect the research. As with many technologies, training was required to enable participants to effectively use them. Once again the issue of authority appears under the guise of those who teach and / or have expertise. Johnson (2001) notes, the issue of the expert in IT is a complex one and not always clear. Many participants are familiar with and routinely use mobile technologies, often more so than some researchers. There is a danger that researchers inadvertently undervalue, undermine or overlook expertise that a user already possesses, with possible detrimental effects. By raising awareness of this among the team and focusing on the philosophy of participation, we hoped to avoid such occurrences.

Another ethical issue occurred as it was necessary to provide devices for the study. There was a potential danger of coercion, in that some participants, who might otherwise wish to leave the study, could feel that they were unable to do due to the financial outlay on the technology, training etc. This issue was addressed by ensuring all participants were fully aware of their rights.

The technology itself has created ethical issues. All the devices have the ability to take photographs or video. There are potential problems regarding the misuse of these, particularly in relation to their use in practice setting. This issue is being addressed by ALPS, with whom the MEDS team works closely. All devices had internet and email access and it is not difficult to see the beneficence of providing such technology. However, as providers there was also the question of leaving a user open to all the potential abuse and harm to themselves that such entry offers. All such issues were addressed in a contract of use in addition to verbal and written information and consent to participate forms. All correspondence was initially reviewed by a disabled student who is a member of the project steering committee and changes were made based on her suggestions.

3.2 Establishing a steering committee

A steering group was established which included the research team, University teaching advisors, a representative of the research sponsors (ALPS), an independent advisor from Techdis[5] and a disabled student participant. The latter two members were important to ensure that the study reflected the needs of Disabled People.

3.3 Sample selection and recruitment

Focus group volunteers were identified from the University records by the Disability officer who remained the only member of the research team to have access to the records of student participants. Care was taken to provide information in a mode appropriate for each student, clearly stating the aims of the study and the nature of participation requested.

Volunteers to maintain a diary were selected initially from disabled students at the University of Bradford who had been allocated an ALPS mobile device.[6] ALPS allocated 900 mobile devices to student cohorts from the range of Health and Social Care professions across the five HEIs involved in the CETL. Cohort allocation was based on the desire to include

---

5   TechDis is a JISC-funded Advisory Service (Joint Information Systems Committee). It aims to support the education sector in achieving greater accessibility and inclusion by stimulating innovation and providing expert advice and guidance on disability and technology. See http://www.techdis.ac.uk/.

6   All Allocated ALPS mobile devices included ALPS software and unrestricted data access.

the full range of ALPS professions and lecturing staff that were keen to innovate. Additional disabled students were identified and invited to take part in the study to ensure that a range of impairments were represented in the sample (a mixture of convenience and purposive sampling). These participants were also allocated an ALPS mobile device. From this total sample, it is anticipated that six will be selected specifically, based on their impairments and use of the devices (purposive sampling of participants with relevant, informative and valid experiences to share) to be involved in end-stage semi-structured interviews.

We hoped to video record these interviews so that they could stand alone as individual case studies. Such visual "story telling" can be extremely powerful for dissemination purposes. However, there are always ethical dilemmas in requesting research participants to relinquish their right to anonymity by providing a visual recording of them discussing their own experiences. Often it is the sensitive nature of what is being discussed that determines if this methodology is appropriate or not. In this case it was slightly different in that the experience of using mobile technologies in itself is not a sensitive issue, but participants would have to feel comfortable with disclosing their impairment. Clearly this would be easier and more acceptable to some participants than others. However, if some participants are thus excluded, the question of reliability arises. We would argue that as long as all stories are heard and represented in the research outputs overall, this issue can be overcome and therefore support the notion of video recording the final semi-structured interviews with those participants who agree to this, whilst not making it a requirement of taking part.

4. Discussion

Mobile devices offer researchers an alternative method for data collection, which, it could be argued increases the validity and authenticity of the data. This is due to the fact that participants are actively engaged and are able to record experiences in the moment, or very soon after. We would contrast this with traditional research methods, e.g. focus groups where there is a significant temporal displacement between the experience and the recoding by the researcher. The "mobile approach" to data collection shifts the locus of control from researcher to participant by giving them increased freedom to select when, where and which experiences they wish to share. This creates new challenges for the qualitative researcher, as it *assumes* that participants are recording in the moment or soon after and also that the technology will always work and that participants have the skills both related to the technology and recall/reflection. Additional participant support is therefore required, adding another dimension to the participant –researcher relationship. It is also possible that we are creating a kind of dualism in our participants as they become both authentic participants and also their own sort of researcher. The question of research ownership is thereby raised.

5. Conclusion

We have provided an overview of the MEDS case study, which was designed to explore the benefits, barriers and essential specifications of mobile devices used for learning and assessment purposes with disabled students. We have discussed the role of mobile devices in supporting learning generally for health and social care practitioners specifically, against a background of current UK disability legislation. We have provided an overview of the research proposal and how we integrated traditional qualitative research methods of data collection with new and innovative approaches facilitated by the functions of mobile devices. We have outlined both challenges and opportunities that this has created and raised a number of philosophical questions related to the role of the participant, their relationship with the data, the researcher and ultimately ownership of the research. In conclusion we would suggest that using mobile devices for collecting data has enabled disabled students to actively engage in the research process. We feel that the MEDS study has demonstrated mobile information technology can be an effective tool for use in social science research. Our research specifically targeted disabled people, but we would contend that the methods and methodology would be equally applicable in other areas based on its ability to enhance participant engagement and response. There are ethical challenges, which such technologies pose and which we have so far only been able to address tentatively. This research is preliminary and further research is clearly required to explore all these issues in more depth.

Acknowledgements

Sincere thanks to John Fairhall and Jak Radice for their technical support to the MEDS project and to all student participants who have given of their time.

References

Abbott, P. and Sapsford, R. (1998). *Research Methods for Nurses and the Caring Professions*, 2nd edn. Buckingham: Open University Press

DRC (Disability Rights Commission). (2007). Maintaining Standards: Promoting Equality Report of a DRC Formal investigation on Professional regulation within nursing, teaching and social work and disabled people's access to these professions. Available at http://www.maintainingstandards.org/files/Full%20report%20_%20final.pdf [accessed on 8 April 2008]

Dearnley, C.A., Haigh, J., Fairhall, J. (2008). Using Mobile Technologies for Assessment and Learning in Practice. *Nurse Education in Practice*, vol. 8(3), 197–204

Dunn, S. (2003). Return to SENDA? Implementing accessibility for disabled students in virtual learning environments in UK further and higher education. London: City University. Available at http://www.saradunn.net/VLEproject/index.html

Fischer, S., Stewart, T.E., Mehta, S., Wax, R. and Lapinsky, S.E. (2003). Handheld computing in medicine. *Journal of the American Medical Informatics Association*, 10(2), 139–149

Frankfort-Nachmias, C. and Nachmias, D. (1991). *Research Methods in the Social Sciences*, 4th edn. London: Edward Arnold

Gilbert, G.N. (2001). *Researching social life*. London: Sage

Haigh, J., Dearnley, C.A. and Meddings, F.S. (2007). The impact of an enhanced assessment tool on students' experience of being assessed in clinical practice: a focus group study. *Practice and Evidence of the Scholarship of Teaching and Learning in Higher Education*, 2:1. Available on http://www.pestlhe.org.uk/index.php/pestlhe/issue/view/5

Harding, S. (1987). *Feminism and methodology*. Milton Keynes: Open University Press

Hochschuler, S.H. (2001). Handheld computers can give practitioners an edge. *Orthopedics Today*, 21(6), 56

Johnson, D.G. (2001). *Ethics On-Line*. In Spinello, R.A. and Tavani, H.T. (eds), *Readings in CyberEthics*. Boston: Jones and Bartlett Publishers

Letherby, G. (2003). *Feminist research in theory and practice*. Milton Keynes: Open University Press

Maynard, M. (1994). Methods, practice and epistemology: the debate about feminism and research. In Maynard M. and Purvis J. (eds), *Researching women's lives from a feminist perspective*. London: Taylor and Francis Ltd

Milgram, S. (1974). Obedience to Authority: an experimental view. London: Tavistock

Miller, J., Shaw-Kokot, J.R., Arnold, M.S., Boggin, T., Crowell, K.E., Allegri, F., Blue, J.H. and Berrier, S.B. (2005). A study of personal digital assistants to enhance undergraduate clinical nursing education. *Journal of Nursing Education*, 44(1), 19–26

Naismith, L., Lonsdale, P., Vavoula, G. and Sharples, M. (2004). *Mobile technologies and learning*. Available at http://www.futurelab.org.uk/resources/publications_reports_articles/literature_reviews/Literature_Review203/ [accessed on 7 April 2008]

Norman, A. (2005). Handheld Public Services. Available on http:// www.handheldlearning.co.uk/content/view/14/2/ [accessed on 19 September 2006]

Oakley, A. (1998). Gender, methodology and peoples ways of knowing: some problems with feminism and the paradigm debate in social science, *Sociology* 32(4), 707–732

Oliver, M. (2004). The Social Model in Action: if I had a hammer. In Barnes, C. and Mercer G. (eds), *Implementing The Social Model of Disability: Theory and Research*. Leeds: Disability Press

Parks, M. and Dransfield, M. (2006). Mo-Blogging – Supporting Student Learning Whilst in Health Care Practice Settings. *mLearn: Across Generations and Cultures 2006*. 22–25 October 2006, Banff, Alberta, Canada

Papadopoulos, G. and Pearson, E. (2007). *Accessibility awareness raising and continuing professional development: The use of simulations as a motivational tool*. Association for Teaching and Learning, online newsletter. Available on http://newsletter.alt.ac.uk/e_article000735502. cfm [accessed on 19 March 2007]

Pearson, E. and Koppi, T. (2006). A pragmatic and strategic approach to supporting staff in inclusive practices for online learning. Proceedings of the 23rd annual asceilite conference: *Who's learning? Whose technology?* The University of Sydney

Ruebain, D., Honigmann, J., Mountfield, H. and Parker, C. (2006). Analysis of the statutory and regulatory frameworks and cases relating to fitness standards in nursing, social work and teaching Disability Rights Commission. Available at http://www.equalityhumanrights.com/ Documents/DRC/Policy/fitness_regulatory_review_report.pdf [accessed on 8 April 2008]

Russell, T. (1997). Action Research at Queens University. Available at http://educ.queensu.ca/projects/action_research [accessed on 31 January 2002)

Scheck McAlearney, A., Schweikhart, S.B. and Medow, M.A. (2004). Doctors' experience with handheld computers in clinical practice: qualitative study. *British Medical Journal*, 328, 1162

Schon, D. (1983). *The Reflective Practitioner*. San Francisco: Jossey-Bass

Stanley, E. and Wise S. (eds). (1993). *Breaking out again: feminist ontology and epistemology*. London: Routledge

Stanley, E. (ed.). (1997). *Knowing feminisms*. London: Sage

Sullivan, L., Halbach, J.L., Shu, T. (2001). Using personal digital assistants in a family medicine clerkship. Acad Med 2001 76(5), 534–535. In Fischer, S., Stewart, T.E., Mehta, S., Wax, R. and Lapinsky, S.E. (2003), Handheld computing in medicine. *Journal of the American Medical Informatics Association*, 10(2), 139–149

Taylor, J.D., Eastburn, S., Coates, C. and Ellis, I. (2006). Using mobile phones for critical incident assessment in health placement practice settings. *Third Biennial Northumbria/EARL SIG assessment Conference*

Thompson, B. (2005). The transforming effect of handheld computers on nursing practice. *Nursing Administration Quarterly*, 29(4), 308–324

Tooey, M.J. and Mayo, A. (2004). Handheld technologies in a clinical setting: State of the technology and resources. *Critical Care Nurse, supplement*. February 2004

17. Research 2.0: How Do We Know about the Users that Do Not Tell Us Anything?

PATRICK MCANDREW, STEVE GODWIN, ANDREIA SANTOS

Overview

The OpenLearn initiative at the Open University (http://www.open.ac.uk/ openlearn) offers free and open access to online material across a wide range of subjects. This material has been placed in on online environment based on the Moodle learning environment together with additional tools for communicating with other users and creating knowledge maps. One of the design aims of the initiative was to be low barrier to access so all content is available without registration, though some tools and features will only work once registered. The result is that we are seeking to research a site that is publicly accessible and has a majority of users that do not identify themselves, many of whom spend a short time on the site. As a further challenge the content itself is openly licensed using Creative Commons (http://creativecommons.org/) and can be taken and relocated on mirror servers, or accessed remotely through content feeds. The initiative has had to face this challenge and implemented a mixture of tracking, simplified surveys and the gathering of interesting stories. This approach has enabled us to spot interesting trends while remaining unsure about many of our users and their aims. The methods that we find we are using indicate a new style of research that can be related back to Web 2.0 as Research 2.0.

1.   Research challenge

Working as a researcher in a mobile or open environment can mean accepting a loose and remote connection with end users. In an initiative such as OpenLearn, where the aim is to provide free and open access, the definition of who is the user is problematic; our users can be anyone. From a research point of view, the challenge was that, while it would be good to know as much as we could about those users, it was clear that in such an open system we could not expect everyone to provide us with all the data. With more than 2million unique users over two years of operation we also needed to accept that we would not be able to handle full data from all users in any case. Our solution to this problem is to follow a disaggregated approach (Jones, 1999) by breaking down the users into categories, and adopting different strategies for those different categories; building up broad pictures to help us understand results; and, accepting that we were in a dynamic changing research world with realistic methods and aims.

2.   User categories for open research

As a starting point for our research approach we planned an approach where we did not see all users as equal. We developed a three-level approach to studying our users seeing them as enthusiasts, registered users and visitors. These three categories can be considered further as:

The enthusiasts are those who are prepared to tell us what they do. For some of these enthusiasts we have found that simply giving the avenue to report back data to us has enabled us to capture stories and investigate new ways to use OpenLearn. In other cases enthusiast activity has come to our attention through contacts, the impact of their work or through self-descriptions in blogs that mention our site. To help us to do this we have established watches against mentions of our own site using Google's Alert feature (http://www.google.com/alerts), and carried out scans of activity through the technorati blog analysis site (http://technorati.com/).

For registered users we can identify both their activity on the site, through logs in the Moodle system, and we request during registration that they indicate to us if they can be approached for research purposes. In practice about half of those who register on the site give this permission and can then be approached with requests to supply additional information through surveys, email interview, or direct contact. While after over a year of operation there are more than 60,000 registered users of OpenLearn, these represent less than 3% of the overall users as measured by software tracing machine access.

Visitors are the general users of the site, including the 97% of our users for whom we have no direct measure of their activity and are only left with the tracks left from IP addresses and search engine hits. These are crude tools but should not be ignored in analysing use (Harley and Henke, 2007). In the case of OpenLearn, both web analytics software and custom software created to work with the Moodle learning environment logs helped us monitor overall behaviour of visitors.

3.   Spotting patterns in user behaviour

The three-level approach gives us scope to address a variety of research questions and then to shape how our site operates. For example one possible question is "How are people using the OpenLearn site?" OpenLearn does not apply a value-judgement in the access to the content, however content was designed with expectations about user engagement and it is easy to take the view that those who have spent more time on the site, registered and carried out tasks that leave evidence have gained more than those who visit once and do not return.

The evidence that we can use to address this comes first from considering visitor data. For example we can see from our analytics data that over a six month period (February–July 2008) we had approximately 60% of visitors who viewed only one page on the site. The proportion of such "bounce visitors" was highest if users arrived from a search result (66%)

and lowest from direct access to the site (50%). So those who arrive from a search and may have no expectations of the site could well have found the simple answer to some questions, but we also suspect that the site needs to do more to appeal to this sort of visitor.

The next stage is to investigate through registered users actions. Using software developed in the initiative log data stored by the Moodle learning environment is converted into traced visits depending on machine address. The software then enables overall trends to be calculated and also visits to be examined. For all visitors machine addresses indicated by IP (Internet Protocol) numbers provide an approximate way to track continuous usage, for registered users their coded identity allows more reliable tracking while they remain logged in. Log data only enables visit times to be estimated based on the time between page impressions from the Moodle server. A conservative measure is used so that if the user only visits one page no time on site is recorded, though the user could have spent much longer reading that page.

Examining the data for registered users showed that there was a distinction between those who spend a significant amount of time on the site and those who visit quickly. Figure 17.1 below illustrates this for a particular sample over a 6-week period and is indicative of the overall shape of use. The majority of users (more than half of all the registered users in this sample period) spend less than 30 minutes in total using the site, however a significant minority (nearly 10% of registered users) have spent more than four hours on the site. We can expect both the experience of these users and their willingness to report details to be different.

The logged data enabled a division in the sample to target the lower end users from amongst those who are registered with a survey and those with higher time on site users with a more extensive questionnaire and follow up questions. For some of the registered users we also have evidence of their engagement and use of the site through the artefacts that remain after they have made forum entries, enrolled in units and posted to their own learning journal. Clustering the data returned from the questionnaires has enabled us to propose further types of users that are using our sites, for example classifying some as "volunteer students" and others as "social learners" (Godwin and McAndrew, 2008).

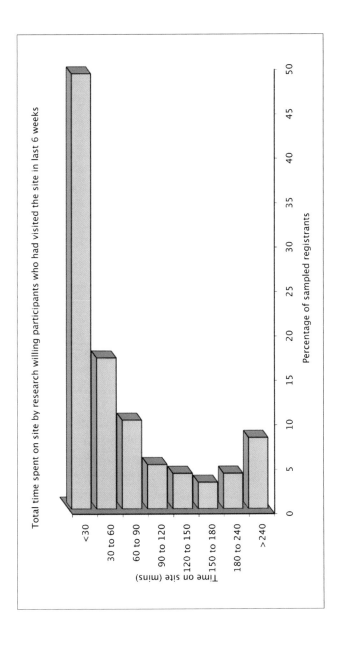

Figure 17.1: Pattern of use of OpenLearn – based on 6-week sample of registered users.

We are now reviewing what it means to be an OpenLearner, and so offer greater reason to register with the site and prepare to more fully use the opportunity to learn. Features associated with social activity are being explored that will separate out the dependence on subject-based content. In particular all users can record interests, collect things that interest them, spot what others like to do. To support this we have added in a personal view of the site, tagging of content and personal interest, and a record of the user's own actions. These changes are primarily designed to further lower the barriers to use and increase the value of the site to learners. However they have the secondary benefit of making user actions apparent to the researcher so that we can understand where interests lie and the paths that users take through content.

4. Learning from the enthusiasts as lead users

OpenLearn offers a "LearningSpace" where we expect users mainly to access the content as learners. At the same time we are giving permission to users to work with the content in any way they wish. This was made explicit in the provision of a separate "LabSpace" with extra facilities and the invitation to users to make changes to the content. What we did not expect was how innovations in use would take place away from our own site. Two examples from outside the OpenLearn team are the extraction of our content for reuse in distributed CDRoms/DVDs to provide local per-sonalised learning environments in remote parts of the world (Esslemont, 2007) and the transfer of OpenLearn content through RSS feeds into other environments (Hirst, 2007).

These enthusiast users provide innovations that we did not plan for or had envisaged having a different purpose. The model of users as inno-vators is considered by von Hippel (2005) as an extension of his view of "lead users" that are going beyond the mass of users. While the number of such users we can identify is small, we have clear examples of such lead users and been able to draw on their experience and change our own work to benefit others. What we do not know is whether we have a greater mass of lead users amongst those who have not made contact with us. Attempts to monitor this have included automated notification of blog entries that refer to "openlearn", encouraging contact and being aware of potential connections, however it remains difficult to make an assessment of the level of participation and identify interesting activities. Direct appeals to draw innovators to the site announced as opportunities and competition have had some success at a small scale to encourage educators to edit materials on the site. The result has been new material of benefit to all of our users, for example a translation into Catalan of an existing unit on genetics, and a connection with users who are trying out new ideas. This suggests a model where we can further our research by offering authentic actions on site that can also provide us with data.

5. Research 2.0

The discussion so far has looked at the particular example of OpenLearn, however we believe there are lessons that are transferable to other similar projects and researching informal learning in the mobile environment. "Web2.0" (O'Reilly, 2005) had been used as a label to characterise the change in expectations on the support for interactions between web sites, increased flexibility and greater value of placed on user generated actions. Arguably, in the research area we need to change the way we research and adopt a "Research 2.0" approach. O'Reilly identified 8 distinct patterns for web developers to embrace as they worked towards Web2.0 behaviour. In Table 17.1 we offer 8 variations on those patterns to act as advice for researchers trying to work with informal learning, the table includes shortened versions of O'Reilly's list as a comparison.

"Research 2.0"	"Web 2.0"
1. Study the interesting things that happen	The Long Tail
In the long tail (Anderson, 2006) those who work with Web 2.0 can expect to find just as much value in the low volume tail as with the high volume aspects at the head. It becomes counter productive to plan too much, rather switching from filtering on the way in to filtering on the way out (Weinberger, 2007). For researchers we need to spot the interesting and unpredictable that can be found as much in the unexpected actions of individuals as the mass actions that we planned for.	
2. Look for patterns that can apply more widely	Data is the Next Intel Inside
The value of data about lies in the patterns that can be extracted and lessons drawn from use at scale. Unless we try to draw out patterns though we can miss on ways to feed this information back into our research.	
3. Encourage all to be part of the experiment	Users Add Value
That users add value is a cornerstone of taking a user-centred approach to research, passive observation can give some of that value but extending an invitation to all involved, end-users and producers, will help maximise this value and also enable routes to get extra information.	
4. Build valuable activities that give data	Network Effects by Default
If we can find a way to draw on activity by default then we will have less need to ask users to provide us with data just for our research. For example, activities that help support the user, such as reflective logs, also give the researcher access to those reflections.	
5. Recognise openness has a lot of benefits	Some Rights Reserved
The decision to release rights as far as possible has brought great benefits to OpenLearn that should extend to the research. In particular allowing transfer between systems, using early discussion, and open publication.	
6. Draw conclusions though you wish you had more data	The Perpetual Beta
No computer system is ever completely finished or perfect, rather it is always a beta release that can be refined. Similarly no research project ever has all the data and can be sure of the results, but to be of value indicative results need to be available in early forms. This challenges the peer review process and encourages the use of forms of self-publication such as internal technical reports and blogs.	
7. Be prepared for the user that arrives anywhere	Cooperate, Don't Control

	The design pattern to cooperate rather than control is a reminder to avoid imposing rigid paths, instead encouraging and cooperating with users. For research purposes this means we need to allow for users that start at any point. Data gathering that depends on users reading advice or passing through other points (e.g. logins) will not work in all circumstances.	
8.	Realise there is no way to control all access	Software Above the Level of a Single Device
	The content that enables us to build our site can also be used to build alternative sites, and indeed alternative ways to access the content from other devices. In some cases it will be feasible to track some remote usage, but at some point there will be activity that we know nothing about. As researchers we must therefore operate with incomplete data, and be happy if we find out even a little of what is happening in these remote sites.	

Table 17.1: Design patterns for Research 2.0 (Web 2.0 column based on O'Reilly (2005)).

This advice is in itself tentative but has provided a structuring framework and evidence can be found for the operation of each of these patterns within in OpenLearn. We believe such a set of patterns can help to shape the interests of those involved in the production, use and reuse of open content and encourage informal learning. Such research also challenges standard approaches to ethics; we cannot expect someone who briefly visits a web site to then read through conditions and confirm statements. For OpenLearn a strong ethical framework was established and followed but in practice occasional interesting anomalies arose. If someone has registered on the site and indicated that they do not wish to be approached for research purposes (the default option during registration) then we also do not use their postings as illustrations or in analysis for research. This at first seems reasonable as the best way to comply with their wishes. However, their postings are public and it was the clear majority view during the workshop when this paper was first presented that others looking at OpenLearn as a research resource would feel able to quote and use the same posts as they would be unaware of the user's position. In practice we feel a weaker approach to ethical treatment of user activity is needed and Internet users in general are likely to accept that public activity can be both reused, and be the subject of research without their direct agreement. In all cases users would retain their own rights, which would for example prohibit malicious use.

6. Reflections for informal and mobile learning

The definition of informal learning established by Livingstone (2001) as "any activity involving the pursuit of understanding, knowledge of skill which occurs without the presence of externally imposed curricular criteria" seems to encompass OpenLearn. Among our users there appears to be a continuum from chance arrivals who may pick up some knowledge, to those who are preparing to register for a paid-for course. Open content that has no licencing restrictions and can be transformed is also a suitable base for use on mobile devices, with sample content transferred into mobile content sites and the underlying XML format suitable for automated transformation. However it is the open availability of the content that allows general mobility through no need to belong to a group associated with an institution (e.g. be a registered student) rather than mobility in the device it is offered on. We expect advances in open learning approaches to focus on the provision of a ubiquitous social environment rather than supporting particular devices. In this view we align with Sharples, Taylor and Vavoula (2005) in seeing "the learner that is mobile, rather than the technology." We also feel that we have faced common research challenges with those who are studying the use of mobile devices, the suggestions of design patterns for Research 2.0 may at first appear to imply an acceptance of reduced rigour, however instead they are an indication of the need for research itself to evolve and become more agile, in line with the technologies it studies.

References

Anderson, C. (2006). *The Long Tail: How Endless Choice Is Creating Unlimited Demand.* Random House

Esslemont, C. (2007). Bridging the abyss: open content to meaningful learning. In OpenLearn: Researching open content in education, *Proceedings of the OpenLearn2007 Conference,* 30–31 October 2007. pp. 44–46. Available at http://kn.open.ac.uk/public/workspace.cfm?wpid=7979

Godwin, S.J. and McAndrew, P. (2008). Exploring User Types and What Users Seek in an Open Content Based Educational Resource. In *Proceeding of Ed-Media 2008*

Harley, D. and Henke, J. (2007). Toward an Effective Understanding of Website Users: Advantages and Pitfalls of Linking Transaction Log Analyses and Online Surveys. *D-Lib Magazine* 13(3/4). Available at http://www.dlib.org/dlib/march07/harley/03harley.html

Hirst, T. (2007). Feeding from open courseware: exploring the potential of open educational content delivery using RSS feeds. In OpenLearn: Researching open content in education, *Proceedings of the OpenLearn2007 Conference,* 30–31 October 2007. pp. 15–16. Available at http://kn.open.ac.uk/workspace.cfm?wpid=7979

Jones, S. (1999). Studying the Net: Intricacies and issues. In S. Jones (ed.), *Doing Internet research: Critical issues and methods for examining the Net,* pp. 1–27. Thousand Oaks, CA: Sage

Livingstone, D.W. (2001). Adults' Informal Learning: Definitions, Findings, Gaps and Future Research. *NALL Working Paper* No.21, CSEW, OISEUT, University of Toronto, Canada

O'Reilly, T. (2005). *What Is Web 2.0: Design Patterns and Business Models for the Next Generation of Software.* Available at http://www.oreillynet.com/pub/a/oreilly/tim/news/2005/09/30/what-is-web-2.0.html

Sharples, M., Taylor, J. and Vavoula, G. (2005). Towards a Theory of Mobile Learning. *Proceedings of mLearn 2005 Conference,* Cape Town. Available at http://www.mlearn.org.za/CD/papers/Sharples-%20Theory%20of%20Mobile.pdf

von Hippel, E. (2005). *Democratizing innovation*. Cambridge, MA: MIT Press. Available at http://web.mit.edu/evhippel/www/democi.htm

Weinberger, D. (2007). *Everything Is Miscellaneous: The Power of the New Digital Disorder*. Times Books

18. Newbies and Design Research: Approaches to Designing a Learning Environment using Mobile and Social Technologies

PALMYRE PIERROUX

Overview

The highly motivated engagement of young people to participate in, contribute to, and collaborate on social networks in web-based communities "anywhere, anytime" is an emerging phenomenon being explored in learning and design research. The *Gidder* (Groups in Digital Dialogues) research project similarly explores the potential of mobile and social technologies to support learning. This chapter presents methods and approaches used in the design of a wiki-based learning environment for upper secondary students interpreting art in classroom and museum contexts. Based on an understanding of new technologies as always already forming and intervening in the lives of young people, a combination of ethnographic methods and an agile programming approach is used in the design of tasks and a wiki prototype that incorporates a mobile blogging feature. Participating in the design research and the three-week pilot study described in this chapter are a curator from the Astrup Fearnley Museum of Modern Art in Oslo, upper secondary school teachers and students specializing in art, myself as learning researcher, and interaction designers, programmers, and developers at InterMedia, an interdisciplinary research center at the University of Oslo, Norway.

1. Introduction

The significance of technological developments in mobile communication devices for how, when, and where people learn has been explored during the past decade or so in the field of mobile learning (see Naismith et al., 2005). This research has highlighted a number of issues, including the need for improved methods and longitudinal studies to better conceptualize – and design for – learning in today's networked knowledge society in which mobile, social, and ubiquitous technologies figure most central.

Accordingly, the contours of current mobile learning research may be traced in interests in *tracking patterns of use* of laptops, smart phones, and handheld computers in different settings (McGreen and Arnedillo Sánchez, 2005; Wali et al., this volume), *theoretical model building* of mobile learning (Sharples et al., 2007), *design approaches* that address both the emergent character of mobile technologies and envisioned user settings (Vavoula and Sharples, 2007), and *methods* of collecting and analyzing empirical data related to learning when mobile devices are used (Taylor et al., 2006). In this chapter I focus on the latter, specifically, methods and approaches for designing tasks and a web-based learning environment that can support youths' meaning making encounters with art in museums using, among other means, personal mobile phones.

The research project and learning environment are called *Gidder* (Groups in Digital Dialogues), a Norwegian slang word that translates as "engagement" – a central aim when designing technology for museum experiences. *Gidder* may be related to initiatives in museum education departments that specifically seek ways of integrating technologies into learning activities for teens, based on knowledge that identity, social activities, and personal technologies are uniquely coupled in the multiliteracies of youth culture (Paris and Mercer, 2002; Pierroux, in press; Schwartz and Burnette, 2004). Among these learning technologies are mobile devices such as mp3 players, handheld computers, and mobile phones, which in one respect may be seen as a continuation of more than forty years of experience with audio and multimodal content delivery devices in museums (Nickerson, 2005; Proctor and Tellis, 2003).

Yet it is the content production potential of mobile phones that is particularly interesting for the *Gidder* project, as a personal technology with specific features that match young people's motivations to document, manage, and share individual and collective interests and experiences on a museum's website or social networking sites like *YouTube*, *Flickr*, *Facebook* and *MySpace*.[1] As discussed in greater detail below, this kind of highly motivated engagement on the part of young people to participate in, contribute to, and collaborate on web-based communities "anywhere, anytime" is an emerging theme in contemporary research on technology enhanced learning in formal as well as informal settings.

2. Framing the research questions

At the time of writing this chapter, *Gidder* has gone through two design iterations in a time span of about six months, involving the corresponding prototypes in pilot and case studies. Participating in the design research are a curator from the privately owned Astrup Fearnley Museum of Modern Art in Oslo, upper secondary school teachers and students specializing in art, myself as learning researcher with a background in art history and in design (architecture), and interaction designers, programmers, and developers at InterMedia, an interdisciplinary research center at the University of Oslo, Norway.

Research in the overall project has followed two distinct yet intertwined themes. The first is concerned with the design process, framed by the purposely open-ended question: how can tasks and specific features of social software and mobile phones be designed to support meaning making across school and art museum settings? The second theme is concerned with analysis of meaning making processes and asks: how are specific aspects of technologies and tasks – but also artworks, subject knowledge, exhibition

---

1   See for example http://newmedia.walkerart.org/aoc/index.wac, http://modblog. tate.org.uk/, http://www.ookl.org.uk/web/whatisthis.php.

design, and interactions with teachers, museum hosts, and other students
– made relevant in students' meaning making activity? The perspective on
meaning making is grounded in the work of Vygotsky (1978, 1986) and a
sociocultural approach to understanding the collective aspect of human
and cognitive development, mediated by cultural-historical semiotic arti-
facts and "tools" (Wertsch, 2002). The two themes are related in the sense
that (mainly) interactional data is collected and analyzed through shifts in
focus to inform an iterative design process and to understand how meaning
in art is mediated and constructed.

  This chapter will investigate the first of these two themes, that is, the
task and technology design process for the first version of a wiki-based
learning environment that incorporates a mobile blogging feature. This
focus means that the discourse and multimodal texts produced by students
during their participation in the pilot – the empirical results of meaning
making – are kept to the background and serve mainly to illustrate how
such findings are taken up in the design process.

  The chapter is organized as follows. I briefly present the theoretical
framing of the design research, which draws on sociocultural perspectives
on meaning making and design interventions. The methods of collecting
and analyzing data through different phases of the project are described,
which include ethnographic observations, a participatory design workshop, interaction analysis, and interviews. I discuss the agile programming
approach that was used to address the complexity of design issues associated with the development and implementation of the mobile blogging
and wiki prototypes, and I summarize the activities in the pilot. I conclude
with a discussion of the appropriateness of the methods and approaches
for this project and mobile learning research, and I consider designing
with social technologies in light of what Engeström (2008) calls "formative interventions."

3.   Newbies and designing with social technologies

In the learning sciences, "design research" and "design experiment" are among the many terms in interaction design, HCI, CSCW, and CSCL emerging from the work of Brown (1992) and Collins (1992) that reflect awareness of the need for designs to take into account the naturalistic and meaningful contexts in which information technologies are used. However, as Engeström (2008) points out, some of the positivist assumptions that design research initially aimed to critique remain in place, including interests in generalization, evaluating and assessing results in relation to some optimal result, and identifying gaps between a current design and ideal design goals. Despite a broad range of participatory design methods developed in recent decades, such research-driven agendas may account in part for conflicts between researchers' design aims for learning technologies and the authentic concerns of teachers, school leaders, and policymakers, making it difficult to gauge actual benefits of new technologies in formal learning settings (Jewitt, 2006).

Situating the design of learning technologies as a research practice is further compounded by recent developments in web-based software for collective knowledge building and social networking. These developments have been described by Lankshear and Knobel (2006) as bringing about a *mindset* that is fundamentally different from the individual assessment focus in schools and researcher interests in designing technologies "to do familiar things in a more technologized way" (p. 34). Instead, today's networked society embodies an *enabler* mindset (Lankshear and Knobel, 2006) of knowledge and social production, with expertise and authority that is open, collective, and distributed rather than housed in closed systems, individuals, and institutions. Therefore, as researcher *newbies* – newcomers to social networking technologies – purposely bring these two different mindsets together in designs for formal learning settings, "questions about whether and how aspects of practices like blogging, instant messaging, text messaging, and generally being in 'i-mode' can, with integrity, be taken into account in school-based learning becomes a subset of a much larger and more fundamental question" (Lankshear and Knobel, 2006, p. 194). This larger question centers on change, and the ways in which schools – but also, I argue, museums – will in their respective practices take up not only enabling technologies but the mindset as well.

Engeström (2007b, 2008) similarly notes that social networking technologies have created a new landscape for learning and present uniquely different challenges for researchers and designers. People's motivations to participate in *Facebook* and other forms of social production extend beyond self-expression and the more bounded notion of "communities of practice" proposed by Lave and Wenger (1991). Instead, Engeström argues, such extremely highly motivated activities may be likened to a "runaway object," which is "very poorly controlled and has the capability of expanding beyond any anticipated limits or boundaries, often to global scale" (Engeström, 2007b, p. 6). These uncertainties and complexities require a different involvement from researchers, where outcomes are not predictable and it may be neither possible nor desirable to know what the changes are (Engeström, 2008).

3.1   Formative technologies – formative interventions

The impact of these trends is manifest in a range of perspectives and approaches to learning technology design. At one end of the scale are participatory methods to envision future technologies and as yet unimagined use (Vavoula and Sharples, 2007). At the other end are concerns with sustainable processes of organizational change, and an approach to *design interventions* that builds on activity theory and a model of "expansive learning" (Engeström, 1987, 2007a). Design interventions are most effective when emerging from participants' articulations of actual problems in practice, Engeström (2008) proposes, as they constitute a kind of "first stimulus" in Vygotsky's (1986) theory of *double stimulation*. Thus the participants themselves, through a series of researcher-led meetings, generate the design intervention, which may take the form of new technologies, revised procedures, and organizational structures. This intervention then becomes a kind of "second stimulus" that mediates knowledge building and opens up the way for further new concepts and practices. Engeström

(2008) describes this method and design approach in terms of *formative interventions.*

Mobile learning and technology-led research often have aims and methodologies that fall somewhere in between future use scenarios and the kind of formative interventions that Engeström describes. Rather than being invited into a long-term collaborative process with expansive learning goals, where participants themselves give form to tools that can implement desired change, researchers generally initiate and lead short-term interventions in which schools, workplaces, and museums participate as "testbeds" for designs that explore the potential of emergent technological innovations to support learning. However, there are problems of added value for institutions participating in such projects in that, in contrast to Engeström's formative interventions, these technologies are seldom integrated into actual practice and "may soon become obsolete anyway" (Vavoula and Sharples, 2007, p. 396). Furthermore, concepts used to frame findings are often drawn from various traditions in the computer sciences, which may be an obstacle for teachers and curators when they attempt to apply these to their own practice in meaningful ways (Pierroux et al., 2007). These are some of the larger challenges in design research, and also frame the methods and approaches used in *Gidder.*

4. Museum learning research

Problems in bridging art encounters on museum field trips with pre and post visit school tasks are familiar from a large body of existing research into museum learning, field trips and the teaching of art theory in upper secondary schools (Falk and Dierking, 1997; Hooper-Greenhill and Moussouri, 2002; Griffin, 2004; Pierroux, 2006). Time and physical constraints, and a lack of communication between curators, teachers, and students before, during, and after a museum visit, make it difficult for concepts in art to be introduced in ways that are relevant for students' meaning making across the distinct activity contexts in museums and schools. Resources such as worksheets and guided tours, commonly used on museum field trips, may stifle interest and motivation by being too "school-like", and real meaning making often happens among students as they talk and move *between* works of art (Griffin, 2004; Pierroux, 2005). Such findings remind us that meaning making entails more than the mastery of disciplinary knowledge and is intertwined with the formation of personal identity, as an artwork's meaning is appropriated and made "one's own" (Wertsch, 2002).

This model of preparing for, engaging in, and following up on art encounters, moving from school to museum and back again, served as point of departure for the initial design idea for *Gidder*. This idea involved the design of a wiki-based learning environment to support students' pre and post visit work with classroom assignments in school, and the use of mobile phones during a museum visit to bridge this classroom work. However, before moving into a systems development phase, an ethnographic study of existing classroom and field trip activities was conducted, and a workshop was held with the participants, in order to first identify existing problems and then develop solution ideas. Permission was obtained from a teacher and thirty students majoring in art at an upper secondary school in Oslo for the following sequence of research activities:

- *Ethnographic investigation:* observe and video record existing classroom practice and conduct semi-structured interviews;

- *Participatory design workshop:* participation in a workshop prior to the pilot with the teacher, curator and six students;

- *Pilot study of prototype:* observe and video record all classroom and museum activities during the three-week pilot and conduct semi-structured interviews after the pilot.

Table 18.1 presents an overview of the type(s) of data that was collected and the analysis methods used in each research activity.

RESEARCH ACTIVITY	DATA TYPES	PURPOSE OF DATA	ANALYTIC METHODS
Ethnographic study: classroom and field trip	– 6 hours video – 1 hour audio (interviews) – field notes	Identify material ecologies and problems in existing practice Develop "solution ideas"	Interaction analysis
Participatory workshop – Scenario enactment	– 4 hours video – wiki texts – phone logs	Formative evaluation by participants of tasks and technologies	Interaction & text analysis Usability testing
Systems development and interaction design	– project wiki – user stories – JIRA©	Agile programming, bug and issue tracking	Iterative testing and analysis of pedagogical and technical features
Three week pilot in classroom and museum	– 20 hours video – 2 hours audio (interview) – field notes	Analyze design/ redesign issues Analyze meaning making issues	Usability testing Interaction & text analysis

Table 18.1: Data collected and analytic methods used in Gidder research.

5. Ethnographic investigation

As part of the research into the problems in practice to be addressed in the design, an ethnographic study was conducted to better understand the activity contexts (Pierroux et al., 2007) and material ecologies of the school setting: the nature of tasks, the role of the teacher, semiotic resources, and how the students interact, collaborate, and make meaning. This empirical research, along with the subsequent workshop described below, may thus be likened to the first part of a two-phase process in what Vavoula and Sharples

(2007) call a "socio-cognitive engineering framework," which entails "a phase of activity analysis to interpret how people work and interact with their current tools and technologies, and a phase of systems development to design, build and implement new interactive technology" (p. 394).

5.1 Methods and data collection

The participating class was observed and video recorded by the learning researcher during four hours of classroom activity and two hours of field trip activities. One video camera and two sound feeds were used, with one microphone fastened to the camera and a remote microphone worn by or placed near the students or teachers. Two sound tracks are useful when editing noise to transcribe and analyze discourse and for capturing sound off camera. Following video observations, the teacher was interviewed regarding lecture and studio practices, facilities, and the kinds of tasks, resources, and assessment criteria that are typically used. Students were also interviewed after observations regarding the use of worksheets and other resources, such as mobile phones, cameras, and laptops in their work in the classroom and on field trips. The interview data comprises notes, audio, and video recordings.

Excerpts from the video material were selected by the researcher for closer analysis in order to develop a rich description of the respective classroom and field trip activity contexts. These excerpts were presented at a data workshop at InterMedia, where researchers meet once a month to view and discuss empirical data using interaction analysis methods (Hall, 2000; Jordan and Henderson, 1995).

5.2 Findings from ethnographic study

In analyzing the ethnographic data, two main observations were useful for the pedagogical design. First, school laptops are integrated along with personal and social technologies into the students' creative work with messy art materials. It was not unusual to write assignments while searching the Internet, listening to music on iPods, trawling Facebook, uploading and formatting images from cameras, downloading assessment criteria from a learning management system (LMS), chatting on MSN, and text messaging on mobile phones (see Figure 18.1). The teacher is aware of the nearly overwhelming role that social and personal technologies play in the students' lives and work, but is primarily concerned with maintaining a focus on the curriculum.

Figure 18.1: Use of complex multimodal resources characterizes classroom activities.

Second, the video recordings show that students are practiced at discussing their respective art projects using subject knowledge and disciplinary concepts. Yet when one of the students in a group shifts into *writing* the "what I learned" summary required by the task, collective and productive discourse breaks down. Instead, still seated with other students at the table and a Word document open on her laptop, the student worked alone for over twenty minutes to finish the task, uploading the file to the LMS when done. She "thought aloud" while writing the text, both managing her ongoing social participation in the group and pointedly inviting the others to share ideas and comments. However, neither task nor technologies (Word and LMS) supported cognitive processes by the group (Stahl, 2007).

This may be explained by the strongly individual assessment culture in schools, which LMS features are generally designed to support (Kløvstad and Kristiansen, 2004; Lund and Rasmussen, in press). Assessment issues are thus a challenge for learning technology designers, teachers, and students working with wiki software in school settings, and features are often developed to track and visualize individual contributions to collectively developed texts (Pierroux et al., 2008).

In sum, interaction analysis of classroom and field trip activities were useful in developing a holistic understanding of the activity contexts that *Gidder* aimed to bridge as a design intervention. Findings from the ethnographic study suggest that students.

- master the integration of multiple personal, multimodal technologies and social network sites into classroom and field trip activities;

- master subject knowledge and appropriate disciplinary concepts through discourse with others about their respective art productions;

- use tasks on worksheets to organize their looking and discourse on field trips and to structure their work in the classroom;

- experience tensions between collective processes of meaning making and tasks and technologies that emphasize assessment texts written by individuals.

6.   Participatory design workshop

Shortly following the ethnographic study, a half-day workshop was held at InterMedia in which the participants – curator, teacher, and six students from the class – were invited to act out and discuss the activities planned for the upcoming three-week pilot. In contrast to scenario building and more open-ended participatory techniques endorsed by Vavoula and Sharples (2007) to allow direct input into designing for future technology use, the purpose of the workshop was more pragmatic, namely to obtain input from the participants regarding the researchers' solution ideas for activities, tasks, and technologies for the particular problems in practice. As mentioned above, initial ideas for the task and technology design were informed mainly by previous research. The ethnographic study corroborated these initial design ideas, provided insight into existing problems in practice, and gave form to the task activities acted out in the workshop – their sequencing, content, and collaborative aspects. I return to a discussion of this approach below.

As a participatory design technique, then, the workshop methods are more closely aligned with *formative evaluation* traditions in museum exhibition design (Borun and Korn, 1999; Taxén, 2004), in which visitors enact scenarios using mock-ups and prototypes with "best available" technologies in order to identify potential problems and inform the design process. Pedagogical interests also directed particular design attention to the description and presentation of the task and analytic attention to how it was understood and mastered by the students (Lund and Rasmussen, in press; Rasmussen et al., 2003).

6.1 Methods and data collection

A large meeting room at InterMedia served as the "classroom", with the teacher and each student bringing his or her own laptop, while the "museum", was constructed in InterMedia's studio with six artworks on loan from a local gallery. A basic wiki space was created in *Confluence©* and three different types of mobile phones were distributed among the students, each of which emphasized a different multimodal feature: 1) an extended keypad for typing text; 2) high quality video camera for moving images and sound; and 3) high quality image camera for still images.

All of the activities envisioned for the actual three-week pilot – the "solution ideas" – were acted out using best available technologies. First, working in groups of two and three in the "classroom", students researched and selected three works of contemporary Chinese art to interpret using resources in the wiki (pre-visit). They visited an exhibition of Chinese art at the "museum", which contained a minimal amount of text and label information, and they used their mobile phones to send text, images, audio, and videos that could be used in their interpretations to the wiki (visit). Back in the classroom they continued to work in groups to develop their interpretations as presentations in their "group space" in the wiki (post-visit). Feedback about the tasks and technologies was elicited through discussions with the students, teacher, and curator, which were also videotaped.

6.2   Findings from workshop

The workshop was useful in moving the project from a phase of analyzing activity in naturalistic settings and general solution ideas to focusing on practical issues and the design of specific technological features. Many of the issues that emerged from the workshop supported findings from previous studies in mobile learning research: the *usability* issue of mastering unfamiliar mobile phones, which tends to create "heads-down" behavior and disrupts social interaction (vom Lehn and Heath, 2003); the *task* issue of creating a sense of purposeful activity to avoid excessive, unreflective "collecting" and picture-taking behavior (Walker, 2007); the *appropriation* issue of users' desires to personalize new technologies (Mifsud and Mørch, 2007); and the *subject knowledge* issue of the role of disciplinary concepts and the teacher in meaning making (Krange and Ludvigsen, 2008).

Another familiar issue in design research that became apparent during this session, and which was significant for the next iteration, was the displayed reluctance on the part of the teacher to take "ownership" in the design, despite her positive interest in the project and attempts to draw her into the design process in the workshop. As mentioned above, and confirmed by interview data, this *motivation issue* is linked to problems of time constraints and the question of added value for stakeholders participating in researcher-led projects. In contrast, the curator was engaged in contributing information about the upcoming exhibition of contemporary artworks by young Chinese artists to the *Gidder* website. She also emphasized the need for designing restricted access to content into the wiki, during and after the pilot, for copyright reasons. Perhaps the most relevant findings for the design process were the students' motivation and engagement in discussing, collecting, and sending information using the mobile phones, and their ease in mastering writing and editing texts in the wiki, which was a new platform for most of the students.

7. Systems development and pedagogical/interaction design

Data collected and analyzed from the ethnographic study and the workshop, along with findings from previous research, allowed the design team to formulate a set of broadly defined *success criteria*. Similar to the *mirror method* employed by Engeström (2007a), the success criteria articulate problems in practice and inform the technical and pedagogical design work of aligning task and technology features with specific situations and activity contexts. These success criteria are:

- students work collaboratively to solve tasks
- mobile phone use does not disrupt direct encounters with art
- technology supports social interaction and discourse
- integrated use of technology across settings
- teacher presence in the wiki
- minimal demands on museum personnel
- awareness of individual and group contributions
- students produce and share interpretations using disciplinary knowledge
- collection of interaction data to analyze meaning making

7.1 Pedagogical design for wiki

The design team included the learning researcher, two programmers specializing in system infrastructures and architectures, an interaction/pedagogical designer, and a user interface developer. InterMedia has several years experience designing wiki-based learning environments using *MediaWiki*,[2]

2   http://www.mediawiki.org/wiki/MediaWiki.

XWiki,[3] and *Confluence*© (Lund and Smørdal, 2006; Pierroux et al., 2008). A wiki is a collection of web pages that enables anyone with access to contribute or edit content using a simple-to-use markup language. *Confluence*© was chosen for this project because it was crucial that the technology functioned well during the short-term pilot and it is arguably the most stable of wiki applications, with good support and a large online community of developers working on new features.

Wiki technology is interesting from a learning perspective, among other reasons, for its potential to foster group cognition (Lund et al., 2007; Stahl, 2007) through collective practices of writing and editing multimodal texts in schools. Accordingly, one of the main wiki design challenges is to develop features and tasks that build students' awareness of contributions at group and class levels. The technical features designed in *Gidder* to address this challenge are a tag cloud and a blog with posts from the entire class, both of which appear on all pages in the website. Students can either use their own tags to describe the main idea of the content they produce, or they can use keywords provided by the teacher and the curator in the wiki. In this way, tag keywords – also referred to as "labels" – were designed as a means of more closely integrating the presence of the teacher and curator in the wiki, and of making links to the resources and assessment criteria that they had developed. By clicking on labels in the tag cloud, students can view, compare, and discuss how others relate metalevel concepts, ideas, and descriptions to specific content in their respective group spaces in the wiki and in their individual blog entries. As such, blogs and tag clouds are designed and explored in *Gidder* as collectively generated resources that can support metalevel reflection and learning. From a pedagogical design perspective it is important to note that writing labels, or "tagging" content also adds a level of complexity to a task.

Another challenge for the pedagogical design centered on striking a balance between the open, flat architecture of a wiki, in which texts tend to be "misplaced", and a navigable structure with group spaces that students can easily personalize and edit. In sum, the main design features developed

3   http://www.xwiki.org/xwiki/bin/view/Main/WebHome.

for the *Gidder* wiki are 1) a tag cloud, 2) a Flash object displaying images from the exhibition, 3) group work spaces, 4) a class "mobile blog" and 5) navigation links to teacher and curator resources, including an image database and assessment criteria (see Figure 18.2).

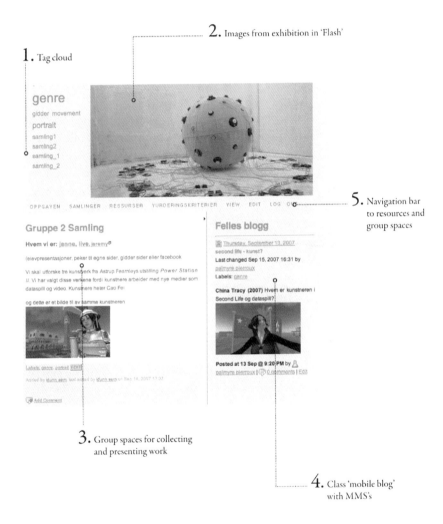

2. Images from exhibition in 'Flash'

1. Tag cloud

5. Navigation bar to resources and group spaces

3. Group spaces for collecting and presenting work

4. Class 'mobile blog' with MMS's

Figure 18.2: Main features in first Gidder prototype.

7.2   Pedagogical design for mobile phones

Mobile phone ownership among adolescents in Norway is close to one hundred percent (Ling, 2007), with good network coverage and costs that are generally considered affordable. Although some experiments have been conducted in Norwegian museums with mobile devices and phones (Olsson, 2006), the Astrup Fearnley Museum of Modern Art leads in this area through its integration of mobile phones in its educational program, where Norwegian visitors can for a small, flat fee use their own phones to call a number and listen to additional information about the museum's exhibitions (Ueland, 2006).

The design of the use of mobile phones in *Gidder* is framed by these considerations, and informed by the extensive research on mobile devices in museums (see Hawkey, 2004). In particular, the *MyArtSpace* (Vavoula et al., 2006) and *OOKL*⁴ projects were important references. Similar to these projects, the main idea is to use mobile phones to capture impressions, information, and discussions with others during encounters with art in the museum. Images, texts, audio, and video are labeled and sent as MMSs to the *Gidder* wiki, where the content appears in the form of blog entries and tags. This multimodal content is used when the groups interpret their selected works.

Although more comprehensive design solutions were explored during the design process, a simple messaging service operation was eventually employed. This decision was made, among other reasons, in order to allow students to use their own mobile phones and thus promote usability and appropriation. As illustrated below (Figure 18.3), an application was written to unpack and format media and text as blog entries in the wiki when SMS and MMSs' arrived from the messaging service. Receipt SMSs are then sent from the InterMedia "tag guy" thanking the student for the blog entry, and referring her to similar tags or prompting her to tag if no label was included in the message.

---

4   http://www.ookl.org.uk/web/index.php.

GIDDER: Technical model

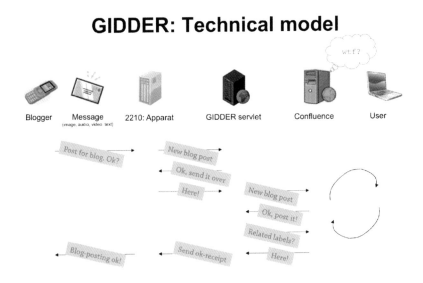

Figure 18.3: Gidder's technical model.

7.3 Methods and data collection

Design methods are grounded in an *agile programming*[5] approach, which is useful when working with existing technologies and open source software for aligning, tweaking, and developing components and features. The ethnographic investigation and the workshop provided the basis for developing *user stories*,[6] a method that serves as an alternative to detailed requirement specifications. In contrast to *epics*,[7] which are longer stories and describe an overall scenario, user stories are collaboratively written in frequent team meetings and become a "to do" list of items with prioritized deadlines.

5   http://mauriziostorani.wordpress.com/2008/07/04/agile-method-and-extreme-programming-differences-and-similarities/.

6   http://www.extremeprogramming.org/rules/userstories.html.

7   http://www.agile-software-development.com/2008/01/thats-not-user-story-thats-epic.html.

These are items that can be tested and are actively monitored using *JIRA*[8] to track development. In terms of data collection from the design process, a project wiki for *Gidder* contains meetings notes, media files, whiteboard diagrams, links, and management tools. The wiki is accessed and edited by all team members, and is important to the project both as empirical data and as a design/managerial tool.

8. Pilot methods and data collection

One month before the pilot, the learning researcher presented the project and its aims to the teachers and students in the class. Practical issues of filming and interviewing, consent forms, and mobile phone expenses were taken up. Students using their own phones to blog received one hundred Norwegian crowns (about fifteen US dollars) on the first day of the project to cover MMS expenses, and six students were selected to use mobile phones provided by InterMedia. These students agreed to familiarize themselves with the features of the new phones and to actively blog during the project. One day before the class was to begin working in *Gidder*, the learning researcher, interaction designer, and programmer from the design team met with the class for forty minutes to assist the students in registering as users of the wiki using their mobile phones and to familiarize them with the mobile blogging procedures.

Activities were observed and recorded using field notes and two video cameras on tripods. As mentioned above, the classroom is a large studio filled with art materials, laptops and personal technologies, ensuring that the physical presence of the two cameras was not intrusive (Figure 18.4a). Further, as the students had become accustomed to being filmed during the ethnographic study, it was possible by moving the camera to both follow certain groups over time, and to capture more general patterns of interaction, activity, and wiki use as they emerged at the classroom level.

8   http://www.atlassian.com/software/jira/.

The interaction designer and the programmer from the design team were also present during all sessions to assist with any technical questions, which were mainly about formatting wiki presentations and uploading large media files from mobile phones. In class the teacher introduced the tasks and answered students' questions regarding the assignment.

Figure 18.4a: Recording methods in the classroom.

Two cameras were also used at the museum (Figure 18.4b), as different groups of students alternated in wearing remote microphones and being followed by a member of the research team as they moved through the exhibition (for a discussion on similar methods see Leinhardt and Knutson, 2004). The museum visit lasted for approximately two hours, and students were able to leave when they felt they had finished. The post-visit group work, along with the groups' presentations of their interpretations to the class and curator, were similarly recorded.

Figure 18.4b: Recording methods at the museum.

9. Discussion

The design of tasks, activities, and technologies in this first *Gidder* pilot is based on analyses of data collected from existing classroom and museum field trip practices, a participatory design workshop, and on previous mobile and museum learning research. The ethnographic methods and analyses are crucial to the *learning research* track in the project. The interactional data are also central for the *design research* track in two ways.

First, analyses of ethnographic data are used to develop success criteria, which describe the "ideal" learning conditions that the technical and pedagogical designs aim to achieve. The success criteria thus frame the design work in a general way, as input to a design process focused on supporting meaning making and not as evaluation specifications for assessing results. As discussed above, this is an important distinction for learning researchers working within sociocultural perspectives.

Second, interactional data allow fine-grained descriptions that are used to develop *user stories*, an agile programming method that informs more specific decisions made by the design team about how to develop certain features and "tweak" available and existing technologies to produce, in this case, a robust prototype. Agile programming is an iterative and participatory design method in that, ideally, users collaborate to continually develope new stories, and changes in the technologies are rapidly implemented based on this ongoing feedback and observations of actual use over time. This approach is useful when working iteratively to develop and tweak features of existing and emerging technologies for specific contexts of use. Based on an understanding of new technologies as always already forming and intervening in the lives of young people, this combination of ethnographic methods and an agile programming approach is suitable for researching the potential of mobile and social software to support meaning making.

At the same time, as pointed out at the beginning of the chapter, design interventions in which researchers take the lead in articulating and addressing participants' existing problems in practice risk projects with less potential for realizing truly innovative technologies and formative change. Within the context of the ongoing *Gidder* research project, a future technology workshop approach (Vavoula and Sharples, 2007) would be appropriate for allowing participants to explore ideas for new technologies more creatively. Activity theory methods (Engeström, 2007b) to involve participants in articulating their own problems in practice and proposing their own solutions could also be employed to promote greater ownership in sustainable, ongoing change in the respective institutional settings of school and museum. Methods that allow moving between these approaches to strike a balance between participation, innovation, and realizable change is particularly important for design research exploring the potential of this new landscape for learning in which mobile and social technologies figure most prominent.

Acknowledgements

Thanks are extended to the teachers and students who contributed so actively to the first version of *Gidder*. The participation of the Curator, Director, and museum hosts at the Astrup Fearnley Museum of Modern Art, Oslo has been central to this research and their ongoing collaboration is greatly appreciated. Special thanks to Sten Ludvigsen, Ole Smørdal and Idunn Sem at InterMedia, University of Oslo, for their comments on an earlier draft.

References

Borun, M. and Korn, R. (eds). (1999). *Introduction to Museum Evaluation*. Washington, DC: American Association of Museums

Brown, A.L. (1992). Design Experiments: Theoretical and Methodological Challenges in Creating Complex Interventions in Classroom Settings. *Journal of the Learning Sciences*, 2(2), 141–178

Collins, A. (1992). Towards a Design Science of Education. In E. Scanlon and T. O'Shea (eds), *New Directions in Educational Technology*. Berlin: Springer, pp. 15–22

Engeström, Y. (1987). *Learning by Expanding: An Activity-Theoretical Approach to Developmental Research*. Helsinki: Orienta-Konsultit

Engeström, Y. (2007a). Putting Vygotsky to Work: The Change Laboratory as an Application of Double Stimulation. In H. Daniels, M. Cole and J. Wertsch (eds), *Cambridge Companion to Vygotsky*. Cambridge: Cambridge University Press, pp. 363–382

Engeström, Y. (2007b). From Communities of Practice to Mycorrhizae. In J. Hughes, N. Jewson and L. Unwin (eds), *Communities of Practice: Critical Perspectives*. London: Routledge

Engeström, Y. (2008). From Design Experiments to Formative Interventions. In *ICLS 2008 Conference Proceedings*. Utrecht

Falk, J. and Dierking, L.D. (1997). School Field Trips: Assessing Their Long-Term Impact. *Curator*, 40(3), 2111–2217

Griffin, J. (2004). Research on Students and Museums: Looking More Closely at the Students in School Groups. *Science Education*, 88 (Suppl. 1), 59–70

Hall, R. (2000). Video Recording as Theory. In D. Lesh and A. Kelley (eds), *Handbook of Research Design in Mathematics and Science Education*. Mahweh: Lawrence Erlbaum, pp. 647–664

Hawkey, R. (2004). *Report 9: Learning with Digital Technologies in Museums, Science Centres and Galleries.* FutureLab

Hooper-Greenhill, E. and Moussouri, T. (2002). *Researching Learning in Museums and Galleries: A Bibliographic Review.* Leicester: University of Leicester

Jewitt, C. (2006). *Technology, Literacy and Learning. A Multimodal Approach.* London: Routledge

Jordan, B. and Henderson, A. (1995). Interaction Analysis. *The Journal of the Learning Sciences*, 4(1), 39–103

Kløvstad, V. and Kristiansen, T. (2004). *Report on the Status of Digital Technologies in Schools.* Oslo: ITU

Krange, I. and Ludvigsen, S. (2008). What Does It Mean? Students' Procedural and Conceptual Problem Solving in a CSCL Environment Designed within the Field of Science Education. *Journal of Computer Assisted Learning*, 3, 25–52

Lankshear, C. and Knobel, M. (2006). *New Literacies. Everyday Practices and Classroom Learning.* Maidenhead: Open University Press

Lave, J. and Wenger, E. (1991). *Situated Learning. Legitimate Peripheral Participation.* Cambridge: Cambridge University Press

Leinhardt, G. and Knutson, K. (2004). *Listening in on Museum Conversations.* Walnut Creek: Altamira Press

Ling, R. (2007). Mobile Communication and the Emancipation of Teens. *Mobile Media Conference 2007.* Sydney

Lund, A., Pierroux, P., Rasmussen, I. and Smørdal, O. (2007). Emerging Issues in Wiki Research: Knowledge Advancement and Design. In *CSCL 2007 Conference Proceedings.* New Brunswick, NJ

Lund, A. and Rasmussen, I. (in press). The Right Tool for the Wrong Task? Match and mismatch between first and second stimulus in double stimulation. *International Journal of Computer-Supported Collaborative Learning*

Lund, A. and Smørdal, O. (2006). Is There a Space for the Teacher in a WIKI? *The 2006 International Symposium on Wikis.* Odense

McGreen, N. and Arnedillo Sánchez, I. (2005). Mapping Challenge: A Case Study in the Use of Mobile Phones in Collaborative, Contextual Learning. *IADIS International Conference Mobile Learning.* Lisbon

Mifsud, L. and Mørch, A. (2007). "That's my PDA!" The Role of Personalization for Handhelds in the Classroom. *IEEE Workshop of PervasivE Learning*. New York

Naismith, L., Lonsdale, P., Vavoula, G. and Sharples, M. (2005). *Report 11: Literature Review in Mobile Technologies and Learning*. FutureLab

Nickerson, M. (2005). 1–800–FOR–TOUR: Delivering Automated Audio Information through Patron's Cell Phones. In J. Trant and D. Bearman (eds), *Museums on the Web 2005: Proceedings*. Toronto: Archives and Museum Informatics

Olsson, A. (2006). *Nordic Handscape Norge*. Oslo: ABM-utvikling

Paris, S. and Mercer, M. (2002). Finding Self in Objects: Identity Exploration in Museums. In G. Leinhardt, K. Crowley and K. Knutson (eds), *Learning Conversations in Museums*. Mahwah: Lawrence Erlbaum, pp. 410–423

Pierroux, P. (2005). Dispensing with Formalities in Art Education Research. *Nordisk Museologi 2*, 76–88

Pierroux, P. (2006). *Meaning, Learning, and Art in Museums: A Situated Perspective*. Oslo: Unipub

Pierroux, P. (in press). Real Life Meaning in Second Life Art. In B. Gentikow, E.G. Skogseth and S. Østerud (eds), *Literacy – Technology – Cultural Techniques: How does Communication Technology Mediate Culture?* Creskill, NJ: Hampton Press

Pierroux, P., Bannon, L., Kaptelinin, V., Walker, K., Hall, T. and Stuedahl, D. (2007). MUSTEL: Framing the Design of Technology-Enhanced Learning Activities for Museum Visitors. In J. Trant and D. Bearman (eds), *Proceedings: International Cultural Heritage Informatics Meeting (ICHIM)*. Toronto: Archives and Museum Informatics

Pierroux, P., Rasmussen, I., Lund, A., Smørdal, O., Stahl, G., Larusson, J.A., et al. (2008). Supporting and Tracking Collective Cognition in Wikis. *ICLS 2008 Conference Proceedings*. Utrecht

Proctor, N. and Tellis, C. (2003). The State of the Art in Museum Handhelds in 2003. In J. Trant and D. Bearman (eds), *Museums on the Web 2003: Proceedings*. Toronto: Archives and Museum Informatics

Rasmussen, I., Krange, I. and Ludvigsen, S. (2003). The Process of Understanding the Task: How is Agency Distributed Between Students,

Teachers, and Representations in Technology-Rich Learning Environments? *International Journal of Educational Research*, 39, 839–849

Schwartz, D. and Burnette, A. (2004). Making Web Sites for Young Audiences. In J. Trant and D. Bearman (eds), *Museums on the Web 2004: Proceedings*. Toronto: Archives and Museum Informatics

Sharples, M., Taylor, J. and Vavoula, G. (2007). A Theory of Learning for the Mobile Age. In R. Anrews and C. Haythornthwaite (eds), *The Handbook of E-learning Research*. London: Sage, pp. 221–247

Stahl, G. (2007). Meaning Making in CSCL: Conditions and Preconditions for Cognitive Processes by Groups. *CSCL 2007 Conference Proceedings*. New Brunswick, NJ

Taxén, G. (2004). Introducing Participatory Design in Museums. *Proceedings of the 8th Biennal Participatory Design Conference* (PDC 2004). Toronto, pp. 204–213

Taylor, J., Sharples, M., O'Malley, C., Vavoula, G. and Waycott, J. (2006). Towards a Task Model for Mobile Learning: A Dialectical Approach. *International Journal of Learning Technology*, 2(2/3), 138–158

Ueland, H.B. (2006). How to Use Mobile Telephones in an Art Museum. *Nodem 2006 Conference*. Oslo, Norway

Vavoula, G., Meek, J., Sharples, M., Lonsdale, P. and Rudman, P. (2006). A Lifecycle Approach to Evaluating MyArtSpace. In S. Hsi, T.C. Kinshuk and D. Sampson (eds), *Proceedings of the 4th International Workshop of Wireless, Mobile and Ubiquitous Technologies in Education (WMUTE 2006)*. Athens: IEEE Computer Society

Vavoula, G. and Sharples, M. (2007). Future Technology Workshop: A Collaborative Method for the Design of New Learning Technologies and Activities. *International Journal of Computer-Supported Collaborative Learning*, 2, 393–419

vom Lehn, D. and Heath, C. (2003). Displacing the Object: Mobile Technologies and Interpretive Resources. In J. Trant and D. Bearman (eds), *Proceedings: International Cultural Heritage Informatics Meeting (ICHIM 2003)*. Toronto: Archives and Museum Informatics

Vygotsky, L.S. (1978). *Mind in Society. The Development of Higher Psychological Processes*. Cambridge: Harvard University Press

Vygotsky, L.S. (1986). *Thought and Language*. Cambridge: MIT Press

Walker, K. (2007). Visitor-Constructed Personalized Learning Trails. In J. Trant and D. Bearman (eds), *Museums and the Web 2007: Proceedings*. Toronto: Archives and Informatics

Wertsch, J. (2002). *Voices of Collective Remembering*. Cambridge: Cambridge University Press

19. Are They Doing What They Think They're Doing? Tracking and Triangulating Students' Learning Activities and Self Reports

ESRA WALI, MARTIN OLIVER, NIALL WINTERS

Overview

Researching mobile learning requires studying learners' activities that take place across multiple contexts (formal and informal). However, collecting data on learners' activities in these contexts is difficult. In addition, learners' self reports may not be consistent with their mobile learning practices and so should not be the sole basis for claims about practice. This chapter discusses a study that investigates mobile learning using research methods that (a) enable the study of learners' activities that take place in and across multiple contexts, (b) provide information about the context of learning activities and (c) ensure the accuracy and validity of learners' self reports. The chapter sets a methodological benchmark for studying mobile learning and elaborates on the challenges and concerns that arise when applying this approach.

1. Background

Numerous studies have explored mobile learning through investigating learners' utilisation of portable devices to accomplish activities in multiple contexts (e.g. Hennessy, 2000; Waycott, 2002; Corlett et al., 2005). In these studies, students were supplied with portable devices to accomplish their (or researcher determined) learning tasks. Data was mainly collected through self report methods such as questionnaires and interviews. However, using self report methods as the main source of data is insufficient (see Robson, 2002 for details on questionnaires) for studying mobile learning for three reasons. First, the collected data lacks detailed description of students' activities that take place in different contexts. Second, the methods do not provide researchers with sufficient information about the context where learning activities take place. Third, differences can be found between what learners say they have done and what actually they did. On the other hand, using self report methods to collect data has the advantage of enabling respondents to reflect on their experiences and realise that they have actually learnt something which otherwise may not be recognised, revealing issues that may not be visible during observations.

An example that illustrates the typical methodology used to investigate mobile learning is a study conducted by Waycott (2002). She investigated the change in the activity of reading course material when introducing PDAs as learning tools. Data on participants' use was then collected via telephone interviews and questionnaires. Waycott (2004) stated that relying on self report methods to collect the data was limiting, especially in terms of determining the accuracy of the data. In addition, she acknowledged that it would have been beneficial if she could have conducted in-depth observations of the activities under analysis to resolve this limitation.

Not all researchers rely solely upon self report methods. Others use multiple techniques to triangulate and add a valuable secondary perspective to the interpretation of self report data. For example, Crook and Barrowcliff (2001) studied how campus-resident students make use of a network and the versatile infrastructure of desktop computers. Although this study is not from the field of mobile learning, arguably, it is relevant because it is concerned with students' educational practices in different contexts. The researchers selected a random sample of campus-resident students and used two methods to collect data: interviews and students' computer log files. Students agreed to install system-monitoring software on their computers to keep track of their computer use. The software continuously identified and time stamped background system activities and changes in input focus between application windows. The resulting information was appended to a database file on the students' hard disk. These files were then collated for analysis. The researchers also interviewed the participants before conducting the study and used the gathered data from the system logs to adjust and validate the data gathered through interviews. For example, when the researchers wanted to measure students' work-play ratio, they compared the data given by students in the interviews and an estimated ratio based on the categorisation (based on their relevance to the curriculum) of visited web sites from the students' computers log files. Only a slight difference was found between the two ratios, which meant that in this case the log files were validating students' self-reports.

Other researchers used multiple research methods to get in-depth data about the utilisation of portable devices in different settings. For example, Sharples et al. (2007) conducted a study to evaluate the MyArtSpace project which used mobile phones and web-based services to support learning between schools and museums. In the study, prior to the museum visit, students were introduced to the topic of the visit and provided with worksheets that included questions that students were to investigate in the museum. During the museum visit, students were supplied with mobile phones to help them explore the museum in groups and collect items relevant to the topic in the worksheets, such as pictures, audio commentaries and notes. The researchers collected data through combining self report methods, questionnaires and interviews, with observations of students during their engagement with the mobile phones in the museum and using computers to develop a gallery about the museum visit at school. However, although these methods helped with investigating learners' activities in the museum and in pre- and post- visit sessions, they were not designed to support the broader study of learners' activities outside the school or museum that might also have been aimed at achieving these same objectives.

Similarly, Papadimitriou et al. (2007) conducted a study to investigate a collaborative learning activity created for a historical museum. The main aim of the study was to introduce students to a new form of interaction with the exhibits in the museum, focusing on the tools used and the interaction between participants. In the study, groups of 4–5 students were provided with PDAs and were asked to use these during a museum visit to collect, manipulate, and combine data that is extracted from the exhibits in order to identify the exhibit that is described by the learning scenario. The researchers collected data through recording the dialogue among the participants, video recording the participants in one museum room, and screen capturing of the PDA. The researchers then used a tool (Collaborative Analysis Tool – ColAT) to synchronise the different sources of data and look at the low-level operations and actions of students' activities. The methods and the tool used to conduct the study helped with organising the data and providing detailed description of students' learning activities. However, their study was focused on the learning activities that took place in the museum room and did not look at cross-contextual issues such as students' learning activities that took place in different museum rooms or outside the museum.

The discussion above illustrates that researching mobile learning, which involves people using devices to carry out learning activities in multiple contexts, requires three things. First, it requires using research methods that can provide detailed descriptions of learners' practices and enable studying the longitudinal pattern of these activities in and across multiple contexts (formal and informal). Second, it must generate data about the context of learning activities to understand the relationship between context and learning activities. Context is considered here to involve both the *physical* (location including any available devices) and the *social* (roles and rules within the community engaged in the learning activity) features of learning activities, as both are essential to understand learning activities that take place in multiple contexts (Wali et al., 2008). Third, multiple methods should be used to collect data that triangulate and add valuable additional perspectives to the interpretation of self reports data. The next section provides a discussion of three studies that investigate mobile learning and implement a methodology that addresses these points.

2. The Study

2.1 The study context

Three studies were conducted at two Institutes of Higher Education to (a) investigate the concept of mobile learning, (b) explore how students utilise portable devices to accomplish their routine learning activities in and across formal and informal settings and (c) investigate the relation between context and learning activities. The studies not only aimed to investigate the utilisation of portable technologies for learning, but also how students use other devices such as handouts to accomplish their tasks. Access to the universities was obtained to study students' utilisation of portables in both formal (e.g. classroom, laboratory and tutorial rooms) and informal (e.g. university library and canteen) settings. In the studies, formal settings were considered to be locations where students' learning is directed by an instructor; other settings, where instructors are not present and which were not determined by the set timetable were considered informal. Data was collected through questionnaires, observations, system-monitoring software and interviews. The methodology implemented in the studies is discussed further below.

The first study was undertaken in October 2005 in a university where instructors mainly use traditional technologies such as OHPs (over head projector) during lectures; others use laptops to present lecture slides. Students are usually supplied with handouts to be used during lectures and lab sessions to write down notes and solve exercises. The study investigated students' utilisation of handouts, mobile phones and laptops in two traditional higher education courses (computer science and physics). Students were approached during a lecture, provided with information about the study and asked to take part. Students' participation included completing a questionnaire, being observed during lectures, installing system-monitoring software on their laptops (if available) and being interviewed. Students in both classes agreed to be observed as a whole group, with the researcher being seated at the back of the class. A total of 109 (60 in the computer class, 49 in the physics class) students were observed. The computer class students were observed over four weeks, two hours a week. The physics class students were observed over three weeks, one hour a week. Only 5 students from both classes returned the questionnaires. The study also investigated students' utilisation of portable devices in informal settings. A total of 5 students were observed in the library each for 30 minutes, 2 of whom retuned the questionnaire. Only one student from the computer class agreed to install system-monitoring software on his laptop. A number of informal interviews were also held with that student to clarify some issues that were observed in the classroom and found in the log files collected from his laptop. The interviews were held either face-to-face during the log files collection meetings (5 instances) or chatting online (3 instances). The participant was interviewed after log files and observations analysis to help with clarifying some issues and findings. For example, the interviews clarified how often the student used his laptop, where, when and why.

The second study was conducted in December 2006 in a university that implements a campus wide laptop program. The university provided all students and academic staff with laptops to be used to accomplish their routine tasks. Students had access to resources that enabled utilising their laptops in different contexts (formal and informal) such as power sockets, wireless Internet and electronic learning resources especially through a VLE (Virtual Learning Environment). In this study, students were mainly studied in formal settings, through observations, as studying students in informal settings was not possible because of restrictions placed by the university as a condition of access. This also prevented the interviewing of students to provide more information about some issues that were observed. However, one of the participating students agreed to be contacted (during the third study discussed bellow) through an instant messaging application to provide more information about some issues that were observed in a tutorial session. In addition, getting the institute's agreement to install the system-monitoring software on students' laptops proved impractical. In the study, the same group of students, 50 in total, were observed in Anatomy, Pharmacology, and Chemistry classes. The Anatomy class students were observed in three sessions. Each of the Pharmacology and Chemistry classes were observed in only one session. Students were also asked to complete the questionnaire at the end of one of the classes and return them before they left; 31 of the students completed the questionnaire.

The third study was conducted in February – March 2007 in the same university as the second study However, this time students were observed in both formal and informal settings. In this study, the sample comprised a small number of students from each group that was studied. The aim was to focus on a number of case studies that provide more focused information about students' utilisation of portables for learning in formal and informal settings. This also helped to provide details about the longitudinal pattern of students' learning practices in different contexts and the context of learning activities. A total of 11 students from three groups (2 first, 5 second and 4 third year students) agreed for system-monitoring software to be installed in their laptops and were observed and interviewed. The university's agreement on observing students in informal settings and installing the system-monitoring software on their laptops was granted after personnel changes in the ethical committee in the university. Nine of them also answered the questionnaire. Students were observed for 4–5 hours a day in multiple formal and informal settings. Second year students were observed and their laptops were logged for 4–5 weeks, and both first and third year students were studied for 1–2 weeks. The third year students were studied in a different environment as they were in hospital placement where they were engaged in both theoretical and practical sessions in a hospital.

3. Methodology

In these studies, first, all students in the cohort were asked to participate and complete a questionnaire which aimed to provide a general idea about their utilisation of portable devices in formal and informal settings. Then, the participants were observed in multiple contexts (formal and informal) to collect more data on their utilisation of devices in these contexts. However, in the third study, the observations were focused on a small number of participants. The observations also covered the rest of the students in different contexts (e.g. classes or library) as some interesting activities were carried out by these students. Cases were first observed and then students were approached and asked for their permission to use the collected data for the study. (The ethical complexities of these studies are considered in detail later in the chapter.) All observations were carried out by one researcher who observed a group of students and concentrated on certain students at a certain time. The observations focused on students and their portables usage such as the applications used, when, where and why they were used and the relation to the features of the context.

At the same time, system-monitoring software (Activity Logger[1]) was installed on the participants' laptops (a total of 12 students in all studies) to provide information about their activities in different contexts, especially in locations where they could not be observed. The observational notes and log files, which consisted of a set of screenshots captured from students' laptops and showed the applications that students ran, helped with (a) providing detailed descriptions of students' learning activities in different contexts and (b) triangulating the validity and improving the accuracy of the data gathered through questionnaires. The screen shots were examined visually by inspecting each and filling in a form that includes: date, time, application, purpose and notes. The log files also included screenshots, around 30%, that indicated no change in activity (e.g. screensaver). Students were also interviewed during and at the end of the three studies to clarify issues raised by the observations and the log files. For example, during the observations in the first study, the participant that agreed to install system-monitoring software on his laptop rarely used the device during lectures, although he had it with him. The student clarified that he does not use his laptop during lectures to take notes because it is easier for him to write down his notes and draw diagrams which is time consuming when using a technology. He also clarified that he usually uses his laptop outside lecture theatres as a result of the lack of space and power supply inside lecture theatres. The interviews were structured based on the observational notes and log files and thus the questions varied according to what the interviewees had done

1   www.softactivity.com/spy-software.asp.

with their technology. Figure 19.1 shows the sequence and purpose of data collection methods used in the studies.

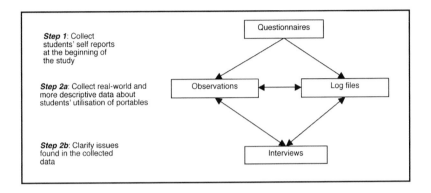

Figure 19.1: Research methods order.

The methods, especially observations and system-monitoring software, used in the studies helped with gathering information about the context of learning activities. Determining the context of learning activities through observations was less complicated than using the log files. The physical context where learning activities took place in the log files was determined by comparing the time recorded on the screenshot with the students' timetable, and supporting that with observational data when this was available. However, in some cases, the physical context had to be inferred by studying the applications that students used, shown in log files, and the activities that they engaged in. This provided an idea of the location where learning activities took place in relation to where they are supposed to be in the timetable. For example, in one case in the third study, even though observational data was unavailable, the log files from a student's laptop showed that he was viewing lecture slides and taking notes for an hour; this was consistent with what happened during lectures. In some cases the physical context was determined by referring to students' online conversations through instant messaging software with friends and family where they mentioned where they were.

The social context of learning activities was determined through the observations, which clarified the rules and roles within the community in the different formal and informal settings. In addition, determining the location where learning activities took place through log files helped clarify the social context. This reflects the interplay between the physical and social setting of learning activities.

4. Discussion of the Methodology

The methodology used in the studies allowed learners' longitudinal patterns of use, collected through observations and log files, to be explored in depth. This enabled the study of mobile learning. The methodology also enabled self reports, collected through questionnaires and interviews, to be triangulated by data collected through other methods (observations and log files). This was data on students' utilisation of portable devices to accomplish their routine learning activities in and across formal and informal settings. Moreover, the methodology generated data about the context of learning activities which helped with understanding learning activities and their relationship with context (physical and social).

The methodology can thus be helpful for research investigating students' utilisation of portable devices in multiple contexts. The methodology is also useful for research studying the development of students' practices using portable devices over time. Moreover, it is helpful for research that investigates the relationship between context (physical and social) and learners' activities.

An example (derived from the third study) that illustrates how the methodology used helped with understanding the issues above (specifically mobile learning) is as follows: Observations of a student, backed up with log files collected from her laptop, showed that the student's questionnaire responses regarding using her laptop in formal and informal settings were accurate. The student reported that she uses her laptop to engage in learning activities and discussions with colleagues through instant messaging software in formal and informal settings. The log files showed that the student used her laptop to view lecture slides in the classroom, revise these at home and used them to facilitate group discussion during a group meeting. The spaces the student was in were determined by using the observational notes and log files which showed the conversations that took place through instant messaging software (in which she mentioned where she was) and comparing the time logged in the log files with the student's timetable to determine whether the student was in a formal or informal setting. The student was also interviewed to provide more information about the purpose of the group meeting and how portable devices were used. Learning in this case was clarified as mobile as the student pursued learning activities that are directed towards the same learning objective in different contexts such as the classroom and home. The methodology also helped with studying students' learning activities in relation to the context (physical and social) where these are situated. For instance the observations and interviews clarified that the student limited using instant messaging software during lectures because instructors discouraged this.

However, although this approach was useful, some challenges and concerns also arose. These are discussed below. Table 19.1 provides a comparison of the strengths, weaknesses and triangulation of each of the research methods used in the methodology discussed in this chapter.

4.1 Kind of data collected

Students' self reports collected through questionnaires and interviews provided data about their utilisation of portable devices to accomplish routine learning activities in different contexts. However, the collected data was limited in terms of providing detailed descriptions of these activities in and across contexts, especially longitudinal data. Moreover, the data lacked descriptions of the context of learning activities, especially the social context, which helps with understanding learning activities. The interviews provided more descriptive data, compared to the questionnaires, about the activities that students pursue in different contexts. The lack of detail was mainly due to the nature of self report methods which did not provide the level of detail needed for studying mobile learning.

RESEARCH METHOD	STRENGTH	WEAKNESSES	TRIANGULATION
Questionnaire	• Collect introspective data	• Data might not be accurate or honest • Collect subjective data • Limited details of learners' activities and context (physical and social)	Observations, log files and interviews
Observation	• Collect real-world practices • Collect in-depth data about learners' practices and context (social and physical)	• Misinterpret situation • Learner's practices affected by observer's presence	Log files
Log files	• Collect real-word practices • Collect detail descriptions of learning activities • Provide information about learning activities in informal contexts	• Do not provide information about the context (physical and social) • Learner's practices affected by logging awareness	Observations
Interviews	• Collect introspective data • Provides the opportunity of reflection and expression • Collect some data about the context (physical and social)	• Data might not be accurate or honest • Collect subjective data	Observations and log files

Table 19.1: Comparison of the research methods.

The observations and log files were more useful in terms of getting in depth data about students' utilisation of portables to aid learning activities in different contexts. They also enabled collecting longitudinal data about learners' activities in and across contexts which could not be collected through the self report research methods. The example discussed above illustrates the depth of data that observations and log files could collect.

Combining observations and log files was also useful for providing a more detailed and somewhat deeper description of the context of learning activities (both physical and social) which the self report methods lacked. Observations were especially helpful as the context was more readily apparent than in log files. In addition, observations enabled the researcher to understand the changes in context and the effect these had on students' learning activities. Observations were also useful in providing data about the change of context, especially social context represented in the rules and roles of the community engaged in the learning activity, as a result of the change in learning activities. For example, during a lecture observation in the first study, students were viewing lecture slides and taking notes while the instructor illustrated a topic. The instructor then asked students to work in groups of 3 to solve an exercise. The change in the activity caused a change in the context which originally included the student and the instructor with a different set of rules (set, view lecture slides and write notes) and roles (student/instructor). The new context created included the student and the other two students who were engaged in solving an exercise, which changed the rules (discussing the exercise, proposing solutions, writing down the solution) and roles (students) of that community.

However, adding log file data to the observational records provides in-depth detail about students' learning activities, and how these relate to their context. Importantly, these detailed interactions with tools may not be noticed during observations but yet can be particularly important in making sense of students' use of technology for learning.

An example of this was provided by observations and log files involving a student who used her laptop to communicate with others through instant messaging software during lectures. (The discussion was about the topic illustrated during the lecture.) In these cases, the student achieved the aim of the activity (communicating with others), but in doing so, she created a different social context than the conventional lecture format. Changes included the rules (view lecture slides and write notes), roles (student/instructor) and community (students/instructor). The social context created included the student and the other person engaged in the online discussion as the community, which changed the rules (write a message and read response) and roles (reader/writer) of that community.

Thus, studying learners' activities through observations enables the context of learning activities to be analysed, and at the same time supports inferences about the new context that may be created by these activities. Nevertheless, supporting the observational data with data from log files enables this picture to be developed further, by providing more detail about how the activities were pursued and whether the use of technology led to further changes to the context.

4.2 Degree of accuracy and validity

Students' self reports in the studies were, in general, consistent with other sources of data. Most of students' responses were validated through observations and log files. This was also found in Crook and Barrowcliff's (2001) study, discussed earlier. This suggests that self report methods can be used as a reliable data collection method, but we believe that it remains prudent to compare this with data collected through other research methods. For example, in these studies, there were some instances where students' responses reported in their questionnaires contradicted what they actually did. In one case in the third study, a participant reported in his questionnaire that he never uses his laptop in formal settings to communicate with others through instant messaging software. Nevertheless, when the student was observed, and also as shown in the log files collected from his laptop, the student frequently did exactly this, and some of the communication helped with problem solving. This highlights the possibility that what participants tell interviewers may involve inaccurate recollections, or else may reflect their desire to present themselves in a particular way.

Log files and observations can help assess the accuracy and validity of students' self reports, provided that these investigate a wide variety of students' activities that take place in different contexts. At the same time, however, using observations as a method to collect research data does have some limitations. Students might behave differently and may not engage in the activities they usually accomplish when they are not observed (Robson, 2002). In addition, the observer may misinterpret what students are doing or might be affected by past experiences. Moreover, the researcher may not notice some detailed changes because of observing students for a long time. However, observations over time can help assess the reliability of the data collected as it can show that observed instances are not unique but happen regularly. The same applies to the data collected through system-monitoring software as students' practices may have been altered by their awareness of the software running on their laptops.

4.3 Practical difficulties

A major difficulty that was encountered related to installing the system monitoring software on laptops. Students were mainly concerned about their privacy and anonymity. In addition, getting the universities' agreement to observe students in formal and informal settings and install the system monitoring software was challenging as the universities were also concerned about student privacy and confidentiality. Moreover, some technical problems were encountered with the system-monitoring software. This was due to conflicts between the security software installed on students' laptops and the system-monitoring software. In addition, during the first week of installing the software in the third study, the monitoring software stopped logging students' activities because the log files exceeded the limit that was specified by the software. This problem was resolved by changing the folder's size option in the software to reflect students' estimated usage of their portables.

Using questionnaires to collect data in the studies was also difficult. The questionnaire response rate in the first study was low. Students were handed the questionnaires and were asked to complete and return them in future lectures, but most did not. The questionnaire response rate increased when the questionnaire was administered in the second study. Students were given the time to complete the questionnaire before leaving the class. In addition, the questionnaire included some open-ended questions. Students' responses to these questions, as discussed earlier, lacked detail and in some cases were left incomplete.

4.4 Ethical issues

The methods used to collect the research data raised a variety of ethical concerns. However, we do not have the space to discuss the ethical issues in depth here; rather, we highlight a selection of notable ethical concerns and challenges that were raised by the studies. First, students' (12 participants in total) informed consent to install system-monitoring software in their laptops to gather data about their laptops' usage had to be obtained. Students were also notified of the reason for such recording and the usage of the data. Second, students' informed consent to be observed in formal and informal settings was obtained. In some cases, students were first observed and then approached to ask for their permission to use the collected data. This was because it was impossible to sample students' unplanned and unscheduled learning in advance; relevant data had to be identified by relating observations to the theoretical concerns that were being explored as they happened. Consequently it was only after observational episodes were complete that it was possible to approach students to discuss whether they were willing to take part in the work or not. (In all cases where they were not, the observational notes were immediately destroyed.) Third, students' anonymity and privacy was considered by keeping students' identities and the gathered data confidential. This was done by removing students' identification from the data, especially log files. It also involved ensuring that the collected data is not accessible to anyone other than the researcher.

A couple of students in the third study asked to have access to the folder that contains the screenshots that were captured by the system-monitoring software as a condition for their participation. The students required access to delete the screenshots that include personal material such as conversations with other students and friends through instant messaging software. This access was granted as part of the ethical considerations that framed the work. Such data could contain information that these students judged to be private, sensitive or irrelevant to the study; this permission gave them a way of managing their involvement in the project without feeling the need to opt out entirely in order to secure their privacy. This represented around 1% of the collected screenshots.

4.5 Issues of data analysis

As studying mobile learning requires understanding the learning activities that students carry out in multiple formal and informal contexts, determining these activities through students' questionnaires and interviews was straight forward because students explicitly listed them (e.g. reading course materials, chatting with friends and family, working on course assignments). However, students' responses were not sufficient to study mobile learning as they lacked longitudinal data that reflects on the continuity of these activities in multiple contexts. In addition, the collected data needed comparing them with data that reflects on students' enacted practices in formal and informal settings. This was collected through other research methods such as observations and log files.

Determining learners' activities through log files was more challenging in comparison to questionnaires and interviews because these could not be easily decided through studying the applications that a student used in multiple contexts. And so was determining the location where learning activities took place and thus helping to understand the context (physical and social) of learning activities because the files do not provide any information about the location. This problem was resolved through other techniques, discussed earlier, which helped with determining the location where learning activities took place. The uncertainty of the location influences the understanding of the context of learning activities and thus the relationship between contexts and learning activities. In addition, determining the context that is created by learning activities through log files alone was challenging especially in cases where observational data was not available to clarify the context of learning activities. As discussed earlier, combining observations and log files provide more details on the students' activities and the context that might be created, thus understanding learning activities.

5. Conclusion

The analysis and reflection of this chapter demonstrated that studying mobile learning, which involves people using devices to carry out learning activities in multiple contexts, requires using research methods that provide descriptive and longitudinal data about students' learning activities in and across multiple contexts. In addition, different sources of data need to be used to triangulate students' self reports to ensure the validity and accuracy of the data collected. It is also important to collect data about the context of learning activities (physical and social) since these activities take place in ever changing contexts. However, even taking these considerations into account, the situation remains complex. Logistical, interpretative and ethical issues still require attention, and researchers will need to take these into account for future work in this area.

Future research can aim for large amounts of longitudinal data that reflects on students' learning activities in multiple contexts. This helps with better understanding of students' learning activities in multiple contexts, the context of learning activities, and thus a more in depth insight into mobile learning.

References

Corlett, D., Sharples, M., Bull, S. and Chan, T. (2005). Evaluation of a Mobile Learning Organiser for University Students. In *Journal of Computer Assisted Learning*, 21, 162–170

Crook, C. and Barrowcliff, D. (2001). Ubiquitous Computing on Campus: Patterns of Engagement by University Students. In *International Journal of Human-Computer Interaction*, 13(2), 245–256

Hennessy, S. (2000). Graphing investigations using portable (palmtop) technology. *Journal of Computer Assisted Learning*, 16, 243–258

Papadimitriou, I., Tselios, N. and Komis, V. (2007). Analysis of an informal mobile learning activity based on activity theory. Paper presented at the WLE Workshop on "Research Methods in Informal and Mobile Learning: How to get the data we really want" WLE Centre of Excellence, Institute of Education, London, UK

Robson, C. (2002). *Real World Research*. Oxford: Blackwell

Sharples, M., Lonsdale, P., Meek, J., Rudman, P.D. and Vavoula, G.N. (2007). An Evaluation of MyArtSpace: a Mobile Learning Service for School Museum Trips. Paper presented at the mLearn 2007 conference, Melbourne, Australia

Wali, E., Winters, N. and Oliver, M. (2008). Maintaining, Changing and Crossing Contexts: an Activity Theoretic Reinterpretation of Mobile Learning. *Association for Learning Technology Journal*, 16(1), 41–57

Waycott, J. (2002). Reading with new tools: an evaluation of Personal Digital Assistants as tools for reading course materials. *Association for Learning Technology Journal*, 10(2), 38–50

Waycott, J. (2004). The appropriation of PDAs as learning and workplace tools: an activity theory perspective. Unpublished PhD Thesis. Milton Keynes: Open University

PART V

Way Forward

20. Issues and Requirements for Mobile Learning Research

GIASEMI VAVOULA

Overview

In December 2007 the editors of this volume organised a one-day workshop at the Centre for Work-based Learning for Education Professionals (WLE) at the Institute of Education, London, UK, to explore the issues and requirements for mobile learning research (Vavoula, Kukulska-Hulme and Pachler, 2007). The workshop included a series of keynote talks, presentations, and group and plenary discussions, structured into three strands. Each strand explored one of three workshop themes: theoretical frameworks, methods, and designs for mobile learning research. The presentations in each strand were intended as stimuli for subsequent group discussions, which aimed to identify issues pertinent to the strand's theme and to elicit requirements for future developments. This chapter summarises the main issues that emerged during the workshop.

1. Introduction

With the first mobile learning research projects having appeared in the second half of the 1990s and the first international research conferences on the topic having started less than a decade ago, it should not come as a surprise that research practice in the field has not been standardised yet, in terms of research frameworks, methods and tools. Thankfully, mobile learning has a lot of common ground with other fields, including Technology-Enhanced Learning and Mobile Human-Computer Interaction (other chapters in this volume have identified these affinities, see for example Chapter 11). "Borrowing" frameworks and techniques from these areas has been common practice for early mobile learning research, and has indeed provided researchers with useful starting points.

As our conceptions and understanding of mobile learning deepen, these borrowed frameworks and tools are no longer sufficient. We now appreciate mobile learning not just as learning that is facilitated by mobile technology, but also as the processes of coming to know through conversations and explorations across multiple contexts amongst people and interactive technologies (Sharples, Taylor and Vavoula, 2007). We increasingly admit that "mobile learning is not about 'mobile' as previously understood, or about 'learning' as previously understood, but part of a new mobile conception of society" (Traxler, 2007; also Traxler, this volume). Such evolving conceptions introduce numerous challenges to all aspects of mobile learning research. As the field matures, our frameworks and tools need to respond to these challenges.

2. The need for longitudinal studies – on the shifting sands of mobile learning (research) contexts

Learning does not result from single, individual experiences but is cumulative, "emerging over time through myriad human experiences [which] dynamically interact to influence the ways individuals construct scientific knowledge, attitudes, behaviours, and understanding" (Dierking et al., 2003, p. 109). Even in a single experience, the interactions that relate to learning may not be continuous; rather, their emergence may reflect Mercer's dolphin effect (1994, cited in Scanlon, Isroff and Murphy, 1999), resurfacing periodically during the experience. Thus, isolating a distinct time-bound event as the site of the learning and the research is difficult at best, especially when it comes to informal, mobile learning. Rather, learning needs to be viewed as an ongoing, lifelong process of personal transformation, requiring longitudinal, historical assessment across learning experiences and contexts. Such studies pose significant challenges to researchers who need to cross contexts and cultures as their mobile learners cross formal-informal, private-public, home-school, and participant-researcher boundaries. There are inherent difficulties in shadowing mobile learners as they move between places, settings, learning tasks and technologies. Interactions critical to the learning may be inaccessible, obscure, or overlooked by researchers and learners alike, as learning objectives develop and evolve on-the-fly as a response to interactions with the environment. Learning may not be recognised as such even after it has taken place: "Few people actually call their learning projects by that name; many do not even apply the term learning to their efforts. They simply regard the series of learning episodes as an interest or hobby, or as part of some responsibility. During the first few minutes of an interview, helping a person to identify his learning projects is often a challenging task" (Tough, 1971, p. 14).

Recent research efforts have focused on devising tools and methods appropriate for capturing and analysing mobile learning in context. Some efforts concentrate on implementing technology-based solutions for data collection, such as mobile eye tracking (Mayr et al., this volume) or wearable interaction capture kits (Roto, Oulasvirta, Haikarainen, Kuorelahti, Lehmuskallio and Nyyssonen, 2004). Such technical solutions have the advantage of capturing accurate data in context; but have also limitations, including the obtrusiveness of the apparatus used, and a focus on behaviour which is not straightforward to translate into cognitive activity. Other efforts opt for approach-based solutions, such as using learners' accounts of the experience through retrospective interviews, diaries, or attitude surveys (Clough and Jones, 2006; Vavoula, 2005). Hsi (2007) labels these as "cooperative inquiry" approaches to research. These come with their own shortcomings such as the questionable accuracy of recall, the degree to which post-rationalisation skews data, and the effect of the participants' concern over the image they project. Increasingly, mobile evaluation designs include mixed data collection methods and approaches responding to the need not only to validate data, but also to capture different perspectives of the learning experience (see for example Wali et al., this volume). Thus, collected data might include recorded video, audio transcripts, observation notes, artefacts produced by the learners, application screenshots, and learner accounts. Interpreting such rich collections of data is equally challenging, in terms of assembling it into a meaningful, accurate and elaborate account of the learning experience. Related research addresses the design of tools and methods to support the sequencing, inter-relation and visualisation of evaluation data (Papadimitriou, Tselios and Komis, 2007; Smith, Heldt, Fitzpatrick, Hui Ng, Benford, Wyeth et al., 2007).

Equally challenging to the method for capturing context is the design of the capturing procedure. Each context a mobile learner finds themselves in has its own "local culture", be it a classroom, a museum, home, or a hobby club. Research procedures need to adjust to this culture accordingly, taking into account not only the requirements for accurate and unbiased data, but also the requirement for seamless integration of the research activity into the social, physical and technical context of the learning.

Personal mobile technologies are a significant element of mobile learning. But personal mobile technologies date quickly. For example, most mobile phone service providers in the UK offer their contract customers the option to upgrade their phones every 18 months. This means that the "lifespan" of a phone (in terms of desirability) is somewhat less than this 18 month contract period, possibly even less than a year. The implications of such short-lived appeal may affect the relationship between learner satisfaction and learner motivation, and can be substantial in terms of upgrade costs. In addition, as Pachler (this volume) notes, this has consequences for the research design in terms of replicating studies with the same technology and adjusting research instruments to changing technology.

With varying and changing learning settings, technologies and objectives, mobile learning research contexts resemble shifting sands; research methodologies need to address these uncertainties with flexible, layered designs that allow research practice to adapt on-the-fly.

3. Evidence of mobile learning

As discussed in the previous section, mobile, informal learning can be both personal and elusive. The learning may be personally initiated and structured, such that it is not possible to determine in advance where the learning may occur, nor how it progresses or what outcomes it has. It may also be difficult to track the progress of learning if it occurs across multiple settings and technologies. Identifying and quantifying mobile learning is not straightforward.

Instead, suggestions have been put forward to examine the experience for evidence which might suggest that productive learning is taking place. For example, in the context of museum learning, Griffin and Symington (1998) suggest to watch for instances where learners show responsibility for, and initiate, their own learning (e.g. by writing, drawing, or taking photos by choice; deciding where and when to move), are actively involved in learning (e.g. by absorbed, close examination of resources; or persevering with a task), make links and transfer ideas and skills (e.g. by comparing evidence), and share learning with experts and peers (e.g. by talking and gesturing; or asking each other questions). One method to do this is critical incident analysis, described by Sharples in this volume. It involves videotaping the activities of learners who wear radio microphones and are observed by a video-camera at a discrete distance. The evaluators then watch the videotapes to identify observable critical incidents that appear to be breakthroughs (indicating productive new forms of learning or important conceptual change) or breakdowns (where a learner is struggling with the technology, is asking for help, or appears to be labouring under a clear misunderstanding). These incidents can be assembled into a compilation tape and reviewed with the learners.

Of particular interest in mobile learning and technology-enhanced learning in general are the artefacts produced by the learners including the online quizzes and media they create, their personal reflective accounts such as blogs and e-portfolios, and logs of their interactions with and through the technology. Mobile learning research will benefit from methods for assessing the quality of such artefacts.

Besides the process and products of mobile learning, many studies focus on learner attitudes towards the mobile technology and enjoyment of mobile learning experiences. Although these may evidence learner satisfaction, in most cases the question remains to what extent can enjoyment be equated with learning: are we assessing whether learning is fun or are we qualifying fun as learning? Research in science learning has a good exemplar to offer here, as research on learners' attitudes to science is based on validated attitude measurement scales (Gogolin and Swartz, 1992; Moore and Sutman, 1970; Simpson and Troost, 1982). Similar instruments are needed in mobile learning research.

Identifying and quantifying learning is a concern for all educational and learning research. Take for example a traditional learning setting such as the classroom, where there are well-established and accepted methods for the assessment of learning activities including essay writing, multiple choice tests, open-book exams, and unseen examinations. Such summative assessment is often used as a measure of success of the teaching as well as a measure of effectiveness of the learning (Boud, 1995), but with many (often unresolved) issues regarding the reliability and validity of summative assessment methods (see Knight (2001) for a discussion of these issues). Mobile learning research can inform and be informed by learning assessment practice in other areas.

4. Learner as co-researcher

To overcome some of the obstacles discussed in the previous sections regarding capturing learning across contexts, mobile learning studies increasingly engage participants as co-researchers. The degree of engagement ranges from participants simply agreeing to log their interactions with technology, through carrying or wearing interaction capturing equipment, to actively recording their learning experiences manually. The benefits of involving learners in the research in this way are obvious: they are always at the site of learning, they have access to and are possibly familiar with the context, and they are arguably more likely to know whether and what they have learned than anyone else.

Establishing and sustaining research partnerships with participants, however, can be challenging (see for example Trinder et al., this volume; Vavoula, 2005). One way to keep participants onboard as researchers is by offering them something back for their assistance. For example, suitably designed diary-based or blog-based studies might offer participants their personal diaries/blogs as reflective records of their learning; the artefacts produced by learners may be offered to them to keep; or the research findings may be put at the participants' disposal. Central to a productive partnership is also the training of participants as researchers, to ensure good quantity and quality of participant-collected data.

5. Ethics

Mobile learning typically involves the use of personal mobile technology. Tapping into a person's mobile phone to find out how they have been using it to learn might mean invading that person's privacy. Although research ethics frameworks are implemented by most research institutions and organisations, mobile learning research raises profound ethical issues that are not straightforward to address.

The extent to which learners are willing to be monitored and the extent to which they will be ready to let the evaluators into their private lives is one particular concern. Obtaining informed consent can be problematic: the previous sections discussed the instability of mobile learning context and the elusiveness of mobile learning outcomes. When evaluators are uncertain of what will constitute the mobile learning experience, how accurately can they inform the participants of what data is sought and why? Assuming that a vague description of the requirements for participations is acceptable, how can learners consent to disclosing information about events they currently do not know when, where and under what circumstances will take place? Finally, the right to withdraw remains with participants throughout the research; how should researchers deal with withdrawals during the late stages of the research?

There are also important issues relating to the degree to which participants themselves will respect ethical guidelines in using their mobile technologies for learning. For example, in the process of reporting their learning, participants might disclose information (including photographic material) about others who have not consented to such indirect participation to the research. In fact, improper use of personal mobile technology might take place outside the remit of mobile learning research in the course of everyday use. Thus, in the context of involving participants as co-researchers, but also more generally, mobile learners themselves need to be aware of the rules and laws and to be educated in ethical practices.

Mobile learning research ethics require researchers and participants to be sensitive to issues of privacy, data ownership, and informed consent. Ethical policies are needed to sensitise researchers to related issues and to guide them to design ethical research. Access to a community of researchers with similar concerns can be beneficial and can help disseminate and share best practice.

6. Conclusions

As this book testifies, a range of appropriate tools, methods and approaches are emerging, which aim to advance mobile learning research. This chapter signals the issues that research practice needs to acknowledge in deploying these instruments.

In an ideal world, researchers will be allowed and enabled to know everything of relevance to the research topic, participants will comply with research protocols, and technology will work wonders in both supporting and capturing learning. However, the previous sections outline a rather different reality for research practice, and point to requirements for researchers, participants, and research technology.

In the course of designing research, researchers need to plan for the unexpected: for missing data and for the piece of data that should not have been captured. They need to establish ethical guidelines for conducting their research, and also for their mobile learners' use of mobile technology. And they need to be trained and train their participants / co-researchers into adhering to these guidelines.

To be effective co-researchers, participants need to understand the basics of research practice, including the complex world of research ethics. They need to be motivated to participate and co-research, and this motivation needs to be sustained throughout with clear, tangible benefits – be it the ownership of their learning products, or research tools that double as personal reflection tools.

Technology is often used to facilitate mobile learning research. This may be the participants' mobile learning technology, owned or loaned, which is also employed to log learning interactions with the technology; wearable or portable technology carried by participants to record learning interactions in context; or research tools for data visualisation and analysis. A core requirement is that such tools are non-invasive and can easily integrate with the learning practice. This does not necessarily translate to invisible tools, but rather transparent tools the use of which is of benefit to both the learning and the research processes.

References

Boud, D. (1995). Assessment and learning: contradictory or complementary? *Assessment for Learning in Higher Education*. Knight, P. London: Kogan Page, 35–48

Clough, G. and Jones, A. (2006). The Uses of PDAs and Smartphones in Informal learning. MLearn 2006, Banff, Canada

Dierking, L.D., Falk, J.H., Rennie, L., Anderson, D. and Ellenbogen, K. (2003). Policy Statement of the "Informal Science Education" Ad Hoc Committee. *Journal of research in science teaching*, 40(2), pp. 108–111

Gogolin, L. and Swartz, F. (1992). A quantitative and qualitative inquiry into the attitudes toward science of nonscience college majors. *Journal of Research in Science Teaching*, 29, 487–504

Griffin, J. and Symington, D. (1998). Finding Evidence of Learning in Museum Settings. Evaluation and Visitor Research Special Interest Group Conference "Visitors Centre Stage: Action for the Future", Canberra

Hsi, S. (2007). Conceptualizing Learning from the Everyday Activities of Digital Kids. *International Journal of Science Education* 29(12), 1509–1529

Knight, P. (2001). A Briefing on Key Concepts: Formative and summative, criterion and norm-referenced assessment. Assessment Series, LTSN Generic Centre

Moore, R.W. and Sutman, F.X. (1970). The development, field test and validation of an inventory of scientific attitudes. *Journal of Research in Science Teaching*, 7, 85–94

Papadimitriou, I., Tselios, N. and Komis, V. (2007). Analysis of an informal mobile learning activity based on activity theory. Workshop Research Methods in Informal and Mobile Learning, WLE Centre, Institute of Education, London, UK

Roto, V., Oulasvirta, A., Haikarainen, T., Kuorelahti, J., Lehmuskallio, H. and Nyyssonen, T. (2004). Examining mobile phone use in the wild with quasi-experimentation. HIIT Technical Report 2004-1. Available online at www.hiit.fi/publications

Scanlon, E., Isroff, K. and Murphy, P. (1999). Collaboration in a primary classroom. In Littleton, K. and Light, P. *Learning with computers: analysing productive interaction*. London: Routledge, 62–78

Sharples, M., Taylor, J. and Vavoula, G. (2007). A Theory of Learning for the Mobile Age. In Littleton, K. and Light, P. *The Sage Handbook of E-learning Research*. London: Sage, 221–247

Simpson, R.D. and Troost, K.M. (1982). Influences of commitment to and learning of science among adolescent students. *Science Education* 69, 19–24

Smith, H., Heldt, S., Fitzpatrick, G., Hui Ng, K., Benford, S., Wyeth, P., Walker, K., Underwood, J., Luckin, R. and Good, J. (2007).

Reconstructing an informal mobile learning experience with multiple data streams. In Vavoula, G., Kukulska-Hulme, A., and Pachler, N. *Proceedings of Workshop Research Methods in Informal and Mobile Learning*, WLE Centre, Institute of Education, London, UK

Tough, A. (1971). *The Adult's Learning Projects: A Fresh Approach to Theory and Practice in Adult Learning*. Toronto, Ontario Institute for Studies in Education

Traxler, J. (2007). Defining, Discussing, and Evaluating Mobile Learning: The moving finger writes and having writ.... *International Review of Research in Open and Distance Learning* 8(2)

Vavoula, G.N. (2005). A Study of Mobile Learning Practices, MOBIlearn deliverable D4.4. Available online: http://www.mobilearn.org/download/results/public_deliverables/MOBIlearn_D4.4_Final.pdf

Vavoula, G.N., Kukulska-Hulme, A. and Pachler, N. (eds). (2007). *Proceedings of the Workshop Research Methods in Informal and Mobile Learning*. London, WLE Centre, Institute of Education

21. Conclusions: Future Directions in Researching Mobile Learning

AGNES KUKULSKA-HULME

Overview

The purpose of this chapter is to summarise important points raised and conclusions reached by the volume's contributing authors. Their key messages converge in four areas, suggesting four generic principles that might guide future mobile learning research. The chapter also points to new directions in mobile learning research within the broader research agenda of technology enhanced learning. These indicative directions should be helpful to all involved in setting future agendas for mobile learning research and development.

1. Introduction

As mobile learning matures and becomes integrated into formal education and informal learning, it is also in the process of developing its identity as a distinct field of research with particular concerns and challenges. As researchers, we have been reflecting on the extent to which we will continue with existing research approaches and what could be changed or developed. What can we learn from neighbouring disciplines and how can we harness new techniques and technologies, to smooth the way for our research efforts?

Most contributors to this book have remarked on the complexities and difficulties involved in researching mobile learning, based on their experience. This echoes Naismith and Corlett's observation, that "The mLearn literature is rich with complaints about the challenges facing mobile learning" (2006, p. 17). To help understand the complexities and overcome the difficulties, our contributors have shared some insights on what they have found to be the most important aspects to focus on, what worked well or not so well, and possible reasons. Suggestions are put forward for future modifications, combinations and extensions of current methods and designs. This chapter attempts to draw together the conclusions and discussion points from research reported in the book. It then briefly considers future directions in researching mobile learning, within the broader agenda of the overarching field of technology enhanced learning. It should assist with thinking about the next stage of a current project, when planning a new piece of research, or when reviewing research undertaken or proposed by others. We aim to raise issues for ongoing discussion amongst all who have an interest in researching mobile learning, and point to directions that should be considered for future agendas in mobile learning research and development.

2. Conclusions from research reported in the book

This section brings out some key messages from the book's contributors, covering both general reflections on mobile learning research and more specific conclusions and recommendations. Good frameworks and methods exist for well-defined evaluations, for analysing mobile device appropriation and for studying informal learning, as discussed in the chapter by Sharples. The considerable success of current methods is evidenced by work such as that on learner activity tracking undertaken by Mayr et al., Trinder et al., and Wali et al., reported in this book. Here, we concentrate on researchers' reflections on their experience, especially where these reflections point to new directions with regard to emphasis, method, or who should be involved in research.

Overall, the authors' key messages converge in four areas, suggesting four generic principles that could guide future mobile learning research, which are elaborated below. Please note that since the remainder of this section constitutes a summary, the wording used here is not always exactly that of the authors even though authors' names are attached to particular statements. Readers are advised to read the relevant chapters to ensure a full understanding of an author's position.

2.1 *Research should be in tune with new thinking about learning*

Mobile learning is a different way of learning that changes the nature of what is learnt, where and how, chiefly by its capacities to take advantage of a learner's specific location and moments of heightened motivation. It frequently foregrounds the social nature of learning and societal implications. As mobile learning researchers we investigate this, but we also have a role in making the learning explicit and ensuring that our designs and methods are not at odds with the essential ethos of mobile learning. The following authors advocate aligning research with aspects of new thinking about learning:

- What is the implicit ethos of mobile learning, and how does it match up to the philosophy of its research and evaluation methods? Few evaluations use techniques and tools indigenous to mobile learning (Traxler)

- Informal activities place different demands on evaluating learning outcomes and require different approaches to designing learning: e.g. mobile communities, expertise on demand (Spikol)

- We should not reify learning by identifying it with frequent use of computers or other tools. Reflective learning is central to our lives. Measures of learning via tools or tests are inevitably limited (Livingstone)

- In museum learning, the learning agenda is set by the user reflecting their motivations and interests and not by an institution. Sometimes there are unexpected learning outcomes (Dodd)

- Take a closer look at process rather than product of learning (Van 't Hooft)

- Today's networked society embodies a mindset based on expertise and authority that is open, collective and distributed, rather than housed in closed systems, individuals and institutions (Pierroux)

- Shift attention from technology as a tool to seeing it as a site that shapes social practices and identities (Ros i Solé)

- Both human factors and social-cultural perspectives are important elements to consider when evaluating mobile learning (Mwanza-Simwami)

- Research should be personalized yet collaborative (Van 't Hooft)

- Research needs to become more agile; Research 2.0 can mirror Web 2.0 (McAndrew, Godwin and Santos)

What is different about teaching and learning, when mobile technology is used? What can be discovered about learning, and will it change perspectives in the discipline? Several authors recommend a focus on change:

- *History*: How does teaching and learning of history change when learning while mobile? (Van 't Hooft)

- *Mathematics*: Probe into the nature of mathematical thinking and learning in context; boundary objects increase visibility of what learners do and do not understand, help learners to externalize it (Kent)

- *Astronomy*: personal meaning mapping can capture knowledge acquired during a museum visit, which might not have been identified by traditional tests (Lelliott)

- *Language learning:* Challenge current conceptions of language learning: focus on social habits and the sense of the language learning self; change perspective on what counts as communication (Ros i Solé)

2.2 *Research should consider the impact of context*

Mobile learning research involves studying activities that take place across multiple formal and informal settings. Authors' general reflections on context and specific recommendations on context and method include the following:

- Context is not fixed, activity can span formal and informal settings, it can spread over long periods of time; therefore methods need to be sensitive to time and context (Sharples)

- There is a need to communicate use genres that cross boundaries of public and private spaces, bound up with learners' life worlds which are inconspicuous (Pachler, Cook and Bradley)

- It is challenging to gather data from real-world learning (Kramer); activity-oriented design methods characterise the messiness of real world practices in a way that is valuable to others (Mwanza-Simwami)

- Large amounts of longitudinal data are needed to reflect on continuity of activities in multiple contexts (Wali, Oliver and Winters)

- Collect data about physical and social context (Wali, Oliver and Winters)

- Look at continuous engagement with linguistic activity in a variety of contexts [for language learning] (Ros i Solé)

- Where different social worlds intersect, boundary objects can mediate negotiation (Kent)

2.3 Research should consider different types of data and analysis

As implied by the variety of contexts involved in mobile learning, and to ensure validity, mobile learning research needs to make use of several sources and types of data and adopt appropriate methods of analysis. Authors have mentioned that multiple technologies already make it difficult to capture evidence of learning. Being aware of the totality of a learner's environment and range of learning tools will become ever more important:

- There is a need to look at different types of data – spatial, temporal, learner, etc. – and analyse it for patterns (Van 't Hooft)

- Traditional qualitative data collection can be supplemented with an electronic mobile diary system (Dearnley and Walker)

- Different sources of data are needed to triangulate self reports: learners' self reports may not be consistent with their mobile learning practices (Wali, Oliver and Winters)

- Automatic logging may be influenced by group dynamics; multiple sources of information are needed for analysis (Trinder, Roy and Magill)

- Narrative approaches to data collection and analysis may help to draw out meaning from different sources (Pachler, Cook and Bradley)

- Researching informal learning could mean using a mixture of tracking, simplified surveys and gathering interesting stories (McAndrew, Godwin and Santos)

- Take note of personal meaning, e.g. in informal learning in museums (Lelliott)

- Mobile eye tracking gives insights into cognitive processing; combine eye tracking with other methods, to increase validity. Could combine eye tracking with Personal Meaning Mapping (Mayr, Knipfer and Wessel)

- For an immediate record of experience, Personal Meaning Mapping could be made available on mobile devices (Lelliott)

- Automated analysis of video data is needed (Mayr, Knipfer and Wessel)

- Ethnographic methods and analyses are valuable for learning research, whilst interactional data is valuable for design research (Pierroux)

2.4 Research should involve learners as co-designers or co-researchers

Learners will be a key source of data in mobile learning research, but it is also becoming more common to involve them more closely in the design of learning, and the design and execution of research, as endorsed by several authors:

- Place learners at the centre of research and design, using scenarios. Other emerging methods include simulations and enactments (Kramer)

- Engage learners in discussions about possible uses and attendant barriers (Pachler, Cook and Bradley)

- Gather rich data from learner's perspective (Mayr, Knipfer and Wessel)

- Collaborative co-designing and co-teaching can encourage an organization to take control of what begins as researcher-led intervention (Kent)

- Participatory research design can shift locus of control in data collection processes (Dearnley and Walker)

- Co-design practices have been used for mobile games to support learning. Involving children in the design process may give us new perspectives on the nature of their learning practices and address new literacies (Spikol)

- Encourage all to be part of the experiment. Extending an invitation to all involved, end-users and producers, will help maximise value and enable routes to get extra information (McAndrew, Godwin and Santos)

- Personal meaning mapping could be successful because it requires no prior experience on the part of learners (Lelliott)

- A future technology workshop approach (Vavoula and Sharples, 2007) would be appropriate for allowing participants to explore ideas for new technologies more creatively (Pierroux)

Involving learners is not necessarily easy, as noted by Trinder, Roy and Magill with regard to activity logging. Van 't Hooft suggests that data collection should go unnoticed by the learner; otherwise there is a risk of interfering with the learning experience. Ethical concerns are raised by several authors, e.g. the issues raised by installing system-monitoring software on students' laptops (Wali, Oliver and Winters). An ethical procedure is suggested by Mayr, Knipfer and Wessel.

The remaining part of this chapter addresses new directions in researching mobile learning within the broader research agenda of technology enhanced learning. These will be relevant to future agendas in mobile learning research and development.

3.   The future of technology enhanced learning

Mobile learning shares many of the concerns of the broader field of Technology Enhanced Learning (TEL) and its focus on defining the role of technology in learning, for example in relation to the social networking ethos of Web 2.0. Conole (2008) argues that there appears to be "an irresolvable tension between current educational practice which is essentially individualistic and objective, and the philosophies inherent in Web 2.0 – namely social and subjective" (¶9); however she goes on to say that in actual fact "there has never been a closer alignment between the current practices of Web 2.0 technologies and what is put forward as good pedagogy – what we need are means to realise and harness this match" (¶10). This implies thinking about pedagogical theories (e.g. social constructivism, situated learning) and how they map to technologies, as well as identifying practices that educators may wish to promote (e.g. reflection, interaction).

The field of technology enhanced learning is currently characterized by attempts to reconcile teacher-led learning with the opportunities created by technology to hand over more control to learners. Writing about new horizons in learning design, Ravenscroft and Crook (2007) recommend starting from "the learner's own devices, preferences and behaviours", to design "meaningful and relevant interactions for a generation of technology-enabled learners" (p. 213).

Researchers who contributed to a Kaleidoscope Network of Excellence collective working paper on the future of TEL (Balacheff, 2006) declared the need for a research programme combining collaborative, mobile and inquiry learning, with a view to questioning underlying concepts and theoretical frameworks. This programme should develop a new ecology of learning, with models accounting for learning as an emergent process and models of "context-as-construct". They note that organizational, economic and socio-institutional issues play a vital role in the research agenda and conclude that "the complex process of adoption of TEL in the different learning contexts is at the centre of where we should concentrate research efforts in the future" (p. 6). This can be taken as a helpful reminder that even an apparently successful mobile learning implementation will need to concern itself will researching issues of adoption.

The standard textbook by Cohen et al. (2005) gives a helpful general framework for planning research in education, starting with strategic decisions such as "Who wants the research?", "Who owns it?", through to decisions about research design and methodology, to data analysis and the presentation and reporting of results. As is typical of research in the social sciences, many questions and decisions revolve around human participants and stakeholders. As soon as information technology is used in education, the focus shifts to the intersection of human learning and the use of technology, generating new questions around interrelationships between the two. A strong focus on technology can mean that the human dimension gets relegated to second place. To bring learners' views to the fore, Conole et al. (2006) have used audio blogs successfully in the LearnerXP project, for in-situ, emotive diaries giving a real flavour of learner experience with technology. The human dimension should always remain at the centre of research in learning, and this continues to be true for mobile learning (Kukulska-Hulme, 2008).

4. Future research in mobile learning

As is evident from all contributions to this book, mobile technology has intensified the need to cultivate awareness of the social and cultural dimensions of learning and it has put a spotlight on "context". Laurillard (2007) reaffirms the importance of context, combined with motivation, when she writes that mobile technologies "offer digitally-facilitated site-specific learning, which is motivating because of the degree of ownership and control" (p. 157). From her perspective, important research questions for mobile learning concern pedagogic forms that fully support the learning process and exploit the richness of a remote environment, and best ways for teachers to construct such remote environments for learning.

Giving due attention to learners, teachers, technologies and contexts, in all their complexities, will never be easy. This is set to increase as learning technology becomes ubiquitous. Naismith and Corlett's (2006) retrospective on the mLearn conference series (2002–5) lists several positive outcomes of successful projects, and points to a number of critical success factors for mobile learning, namely: availability of technology, institutional support, connectivity, integration and ownership. These outcomes and factors should be considered in mobile learning evaluation, but they will need to be reviewed and updated as the field develops.

As noted by Huang et al. (2008) who have developed a system for synchronous mobile learning with context-awareness, in a fully ubiquitous learning environment there will be additional challenges, since the context includes "ambient objects, such as available services, locations, peers, resources, states of learners, and so on" (Huang et al., 2008, p. 1221). Human-computer interaction researchers are developing tools and methodologies that use elements of context, for example Intille et al. (2003) developed a PocketPC tool for context-aware "experience sampling" that uses sensors to detect a person's location and combines it with other data to trigger appropriate questions about the user's experience. To understand situated social interactions, Paay and Kjeldskov (2007) have carried out a study of social experience of a physical space in a city centre, using "rapid ethnography" as a method. This will inform development of mobile services for fostering social connections in public places. Again from the field of human-computer (or computer-human) interaction, Hagen et al. (2005) consider that "more technologically sophisticated and contextually appropriate ways for participants to provide their own field data is an emerging area in mobile research methods" (p. 8), along with "mediated data collection" methods where access to data about actual use practices is mediated by both participants and technology. The probable convergence of mobile learning and research on informal mobile-supported social interactions in public spaces will require even closer collaboration between experts in mobile learning and in human-computer interaction research.

As mobile learning is fast becoming a global phenomenon, it is also necessary to bear in mind that "western" research approaches and methods are not always relevant and appropriate when studying mobile learning in other parts of the world. Papoutsaki (2006) has argued for the "de-westernisation" of research methodologies for education research in developing countries, to take account of alternative ways of learning and distinctive understandings of local knowledge. Such alternative perspectives can enrich our conceptions of context and may eventually lead to improved ways of researching mobile learning.

References

Balacheff, N. (2006). 10 issues to think about the future of research on TEL. A collective working paper, Kaleidoscope Network of Excellence. Available at http://www-didactique.imag.fr/Balacheff/TextesDivers/Future%20of%20TEL.pdf

Cohen, L., Manion, L. and Morrison, K. (2005). *Research Methods in Education*, 5th edn. London: Routledge

Conole, G. (2008). New Schemas for Mapping Pedagogies and Technologies. *Ariadne* (56). July 2008. Available at http://www.ariadne.ac.uk/issue56/conole/

Conole, G., de Laat, M., Dillon, T. and Darby, J. (2006). JISC LXP: Student experiences of technologies. Final Report. Available at http://www.jisc.ac.uk/media/documents/programmes/elearningpedagogy/lxp_project_final_report_nov_06.pdf

Hagen, P., Robertson, T., Kan, M. and Sadler, K. (2005). Emerging Research Methods for Understanding Mobile Technology Use. *Proceedings of OZCHI 2005*, Canberra, Australia

Huang, Y.-M., Kuo, Y.-H., Lin, Y.-T. and Cheng, S-C. (2008). Toward interactive mobile synchronous learning environment with context-awareness service. *Computers & Education*, 51(3), November 2008, 1205–1226

Intille, S., Rondoni, J., Kukla, C., Iacono, I. and Bao, L. (2003). A context-aware experience sampling tool. *Proceedings of the Conference on Human Factors and Computing Systems*. Available at http://web.media.mit.edu/~intille/papers-files/IntilleETAL03.pdf

Kukulska-Hulme, A. (2008). Human Factors and Innovation with Mobile Devices. In Hansson, T. (ed.), *Handbook of Research on Digital Information Technologies: Innovations, Methods and Ethical Issues*. IGI Global. Available at http://oro.open.ac.uk/10670/

Laurillard, D. (2007). Pedagogical forms of mobile learning: framing research questions. In *Mobile Learning: Towards a research agenda*, ed. N. Pachler. WLE Centre Occasional Papers in Work-based Learning 1

Naismith, L. and Corlett, D. (2006). Reflections on success: A retrospective of the mLearn conference series 2002–5. Paper presented at mLearn 2006 conference, Banff, Canada

Paay, J. and Kjeldskov, J. (2007). Understanding Situated Social Interactions: A Case study of Public Places in the City. *Computer Supported Cooperative Work*, 17, 275–290

Papoutsaki, E. (2006). De-westernising Research Methodologies: Alternative Approaches to Research for Higher Education Curricula in Developing Countries. Global Colloquium of the UNESO Forum on Higher Education, Research and Knowledge, 29 Nov – 1 Dec 2006, Paris. Available at http://ahero.uwc.ac.za/index.php?module=cshe &action=viewtitle&id=cshe_95

Ravenscroft, A. and Crook, J. (2007). New Horizons in Learning Design. In *Rethinking Pedagogy for a Digital Age*. Ed. H. Beetham and R. Sharpe. London: Routledge, 207–218

Vavoula, G. and Sharples, M. (2007). Future Technology workshop: A Collaborative Method for the Design of New Learning Technologies and Activities. *International Journal of Computer-Supported Collaborative Learning*, 2, 393–419

Index